A Man's Town

Dr Ken Dempsey is Reader in Sociology at La Trobe University and author of *Conflict and Decline: Ministers and Laymen in an Australian Country Town* and of *Smalltown: a Study of Social Inequality, Cohesion and Belonging.*

For Rae and Rowan

A Man's Town

Inequality Between Women and Men in Rural Australia

KEN DEMPSEY

Melbourne
OXFORD UNIVERSITY PRESS
Oxford Auckland New York

OXFORD UNIVERSITY PRESS AUSTRALIA

Oxford New York Toronto
Delhi Bombay Calcutta Madras Karachi
Kuala Lumpur Singapore Hong Kong Tokyo
Nairobi Dar es Salaam Cape Town
Melbourne Auckland
and associated companies in
Berlin Ibadan

OXFORD is a trade mark of Oxford University Press

First published 1992

National Library of Australia
Cataloguing-in-Publication data:

Dempsey, Kenneth.
A man's town: inequality between women and men in rural Australia.

Includes index.
ISBN 0 19 554997 X.

1. Sex discrimination against women—Australia. 2. Rural women—Social conditions—Australia. I. Title.

305.420994

Edited by Nan McNab
Designed by Peter Shaw
Typeset by Solo Typesetting, South Australia
Printed by Impact Printing Victoria Pty Ltd
Published by Oxford University Press,
253 Normanby Road, South Melbourne, Australia

Contents

Acknowledgements

I wish to thank Lois Bryson, Janice Chesters, Julie Dempsey, David de Vaus, Sue Harvey, Beryl Langer, Katy Richmond, Bruce Rollins, and Lisa Woods for their help and constant encouragement.

I am indebted to Anne-Maree Sawyer for her many hours of excellent research assistance and for urging me to write a book about gender relations in Smalltown. Bruce Bickerdike, David Hamilton, John Lawrence, John McDonald, Helen Oliver, and Margaret Purvis gave indispensable assistance with interviewing and observation.

David de Vaus, Freya Headlam, Eleanor Hodges, Brian Graetz, David Hamilton, Frank Jones, Helen Nichol, Bob Powell, Peter Schmidt, Yoshio Sugimoto, and Bev Tannock have all helped selflessly with the analysis of quantitative and qualitative data.

I am particularly grateful to Rowan Ireland for, yet again, providing ideas and numerous suggestions for improving the text, and for spending many hours discussing and carefully critiqueing the draft of this manuscript. I am also indebted to the Oxford University Press reviewers who offered numerous helpful comments.

Nan McNab's careful editing and useful suggestions have made it a better book than it would otherwise have been. Alan Fettling deserves my thanks for the great interest he has taken in the project. I am especially grateful to Louise Sweetland for being helpful, supportive and extraordinarily enthusiastic.

Rae Ball's help and support have been indispensable. She has spent innumerable hours observing, interviewing, and editing. Her enthusiasm for the project has never waned, nor has her willingness and ability to discuss the many problems of content and interpretation. She has been, once again, a constant source of encouragement during a long period of writing.

There are others who, in different ways, have contributed to the production of the book, and whom I wish to thank: Judy Carr, Marlene Ferguson, Jill Gooch, Glenis Massey, Beth Robertson, Noelle Vallance, and Elaine Young. I am particularly grateful to Therese Lennox and Barbara Matthews for their cheerful and professional typing of the manuscript.

I am indebted to the members of the Commission on Strategic Ministries of the former Methodist Church of Australasia (now a part of the Uniting Church in Australia) who suggested the project be conducted and who in the early years provided financial assistance and helped organize accommodation and transport for interviewers. I am grateful to the J. E. Ross Trust; the Australian Research Council; and the Research Committee of the School of Social Sciences, La Trobe University, for providing essential funding for field-work, and assistance with the coding and analysis of data.

I would like to thank the hundreds of Smalltown people who helped with the work for this study. Many were interviewed on at least a dozen occasions. Smalltown people gave selflessly of their knowledge, time, and hospitality for a project that was of no tangible benefit to them or their community and which they, at best, only partially understood. My greatest debt is to them.

CHAPTER 1

Introduction

A Man's Town is the story of gender relations in the 1970s and 1980s in 'Smalltown', an agricultural community in the Australian state of Victoria.[1] It shows that continuity rather than change characterizes relationships which subordinate women. Smalltown is called a man's town because men exercise a disproportionate control of capital—especially in the form of land—and they dominate most of the activities of daily life: paid work, town politics, organized sport, the pubs, service-club activity, organized religion, formal education, and friendships. It is also called a man's town because men play a key role in transmitting an ideology which helps subordinate women; and because they have more control over the choices that women make about paid and unpaid work, leisure, social relations, and their public identities than vice versa.

Men's domination is never unqualified, and it is more decisive in some institutional spheres and activities than in others. Furthermore, since the study began in 1973, there have been some signs of its diminution. For example, in the 1990s there are a few women occupying positions on several of the more influential community committees whereas in 1973 there were none. Notwithstanding these changes, men's subordination of women is sufficiently widespread, and the use of their superior power to exploit women sufficiently common, to justify calling Smalltown a man's town.

A Man's Town is the latest in a long line of locally-based community studies carried out in Australia and overseas that have examined structured inequality.[2] As Frankenberg (1976), Delamont (1980), and Bryson and Wearing (1985) have observed, with few exceptions such studies have *not* focused on gender inequality but on class and status stratification.[3] Most of the community researchers who have given any attention to either women or their relationships to men have concentrated on family and domestic life.[4] Fewer have considered women's status-enhancing activities on behalf of their husband and family,[5] or women's leadership activities, especially among members of their own sex.[6]

This book attempts a more comprehensive approach to the study of gender inequality in a locally-based community. It is in large measure a response to the observation made repeatedly by feminists that what is required is research that looks at women in their totality and uses what is sometimes called a holistic approach.[7] Some of those who are calling for such an approach have themselves conducted studies in which they have sought to examine women's leisure or lack of it 'in relation to their lives as a whole' (Green *et al.*, 1987a:76). They have shown how the nature, location and quality of women's sporting and other recreational activities are affected by the disadvantaged position of women in the domestic division of labour, child care and paid work.[8] These studies have, however, relied mainly on surveying rather than on observation. Deem has recently argued that we now require contextual studies of inequality (1988). It is not possible, she points out, to grasp the nature and implications of gender inequality in any specific area of women's lives without examining the structure and culture of the community in which women live.

Ideally, adopting this approach means delineating the

nature of women's relationships to men in as many of their day-to-day activities as possible—domestic, child-care, sport, voluntary organizational, friendship, community decision-making, and paid-work—and articulating the interconnections between these activities. This is essential because, as Connell *et al.* assert, any particular set of gender relations is part of a system:

> It is not a question of one gender pattern in a school, and another in a family, and another in a workplace, all independent of each other. They are related: they mesh with each other to make an overall pattern, one of the most general and powerful structures in our society (1982:72).

Here it will be shown that the gender system is one of the most powerful structures of the Smalltown community and one which draws much of its power from the hierarchical character of gender relations in the wider society. It is a system of male superordination and female subordination and, at times, exploitation. It is a system in which men often exclude women of all ages and classes from valued activities in many areas of daily life and in which men are the major recipients of its material, social and psychological rewards.[9] When men do admit women it is usually as supporters and facilitators of their activities. Men individually and collectively frequently appropriate the time and skills of women without reciprocity. They, on occasions, use women to purchase their own leisure or help enhance their public status at the expense of the leisure and autonomy of the women.

Throughout the book I wrestle with these issues. Why are these inequities occurring? Why do men repeatedly achieve their ends and preserve their advantage even in the face of the resentment and resistance of some women? Why are men able to exclude, subordinate, and exploit women? As earlier writers have shown, there are no really satisfactory answers to such questions.[10] Nevertheless, it is important to attempt to answer them.

I show in subsequent chapters that there are two major axes to men's dominance and control in a wide range of domestic and community activities in Smalltown. The first axis is men's superior power, especially material power, and the economic dependence of women that results.[11] The second axis is an ideology of gender which defines men and their activities as superior and women and their activities as inferior. This ideology legitimates men making paid work a central life interest and women treating home-making and child-rearing as central life interests (Finch, 1983).[12] Bryson points out that the maintenance of men's domination of women, which is called patriarchy, depends in large measure on men using their ideological hegemony to define their own roles as economic and women's as non economic (1984:114–15). Much of men's success in this direction derives from their long-standing ability to gain acceptance of their typifications of themselves as *the* providers and of women as *the* home-makers and child-rearers; the latter are, of course, defined as non-economic activities.

Bryson argues that the ideological processes that are invoked to support hierarchical arrangements between men and women have a dialectical character. Each 'cultural message' about the superiority of a man's activity conveys simultaneously a second message about the inferiority of women's activities (1990:173). Bryson adopts and modifies Baker Miller's (1976) term 'inferiorization' to refer to the effect that this dialectical process has on women.[13] The concept is very useful in this context for delineating the way in which men's ideological hegemony is maintained. Men do not always implement or control these processes but they are their major beneficiaries (Barrett, 1980: Imray and Middleton, 1983; Bryson, 1984; 1990; Collins, 1985; Connell, 1985).

The study confirms Barrett's observation that women's

economic dependency, the material organization of the household, and ideology of gender reinforce each other (1980:179). Consequently, a good deal of this book is given over to showing just how stable is the cultural support in Smalltown for men making work a central life interest, and for women making wifehood and motherhood so central that paid work can only be considered if it is in the interests of husband and children.

Marriage is a crucial organizational mechanism for subordinating and exploiting women not only in the family but in community political, religious, service, and sporting activities. We shall see that the patriarchal system is also maintained by some women dominating other women as well as by men dominating women. For example, many Smalltown women will apply pressure to other women and girls to conform to mores based on the premise that women ought to play a supportive and subordinate role to their menfolk.

A major aim of the study is to offer at least a partial answer to the question that is often posed by students and colleagues: 'Why do these women put up with it?'. It often proves to be a rhetorical question, for the inquirer quickly answers her or his own question: 'I never would! or 'My girlfriend wouldn't stand for that!'. While men's power is superior to women's and women do develop identities that help maintain men's dominance, it would be a mistake to view Smalltown women as powerless or helpless victims. Neither they nor men are passive recipients of the social forces that impact on them; they are active participants in the organization of gender relations (Connell *et al.*, 1982). So, in counterpoint to the analysis of a system of gender inequality in Smalltown, I will examine the likelihood of change occurring in women's deprivation and in men's oppression of women in marriage, paid work, community leadership and recreational activities.

To summarize, I will list the things I propose to do to

establish that Smalltown is a patriarchal system and explore the possibility of changes in the system.

1 Delineate those patterns of segregation, superordination, exclusion and exploitation that occur in the relationships between men and women in the domestic division of labour, child care, decision-making, community leadership, paid work, friendship, sporting activities, pub life, organized religion and charitable and service club activities.
2 Articulate the interconnections between dominance and oppression in one sphere, say domestic labour, and exclusion or subordination in others, such as paid work and recreational activities.
3 Demonstrate that men's action is far more likely to restrict the choices and autonomy of women than women's action is to affect men in such ways. This occurs to such a degree that I am justified in describing some relationships between men and women as exploitative.
4 Show that men's superior material power produces economic dependency of wives on husbands, and women's organizations on men's organizations, and contributes to the social dependency of women individually and collectively. These forms of dependency are reinforced by a gendered culture which justifies this asymmetry by conferring superior value on the provider activities of men, stereotyping women as men's supporters, and typifying men and their good works as superior to women and their good works.
5 Demonstrate, especially in processes of socialization, some of the ways in which the messages about the superiority of men and their activities simultaneously inferiorize women.
6 Delineate the ways in which socialization encourages women and men to internalize attitudes, skills, and values, and develop an understanding of themselves

which is congruent with the present division of labour, distribution of power, and evaluations of superiority and inferiority; and influences men to perceive their bread-winning as the central life interest and a major component of their masculinity, and for women to view themselves primarily as wives and mothers, nurturers and carers.

7 Show that many, but far from all, women serve as men's accomplices in maintaining dominance of a range of community activities and marriage relationships.

8 Demonstrate how the social and demographic features of this community, such as close-knit social networks and high visibility, facilitate the use of gossip and criticism to control women and maintain men's social solidarity.

9 Show that marriage serves as a mechanism for the incorporation of wives in husbands' paid work, leisure, and status-enhancing activities, and in the leisure activities of his friends, mates, and his organizations.

10 Investigate to what extent gender influences the job aspirations of adolescents and of parents for children and the subsequent occupational achievements of both females and males.

11 Consider the likelihood of either women successfully challenging men's dominance and control in at least some areas of domestic community life, or of men themselves initiating more equitable relationships with women.

Research methods

Research work for this study spanned seventeen years. Participant observation, interviews and numerous conversations were the major methods for gathering data. These are described in some detail in Appendix 1. I catalogue the fourteen major surveys that were conducted in Smalltown between 1973 and 1987 in the same appendix. The multimethod approach allowed me and several research assistants to see, in the lives of Smalltowners and in actual social events, how inequities between men and women arise in both the private and public spheres. It helped us to see men and women acquiring and having reinforced the beliefs and attitudes that maintain the gender system. The combination of methods meant that we could not only note in individual cases how being known, accepted, and feeling a sense of belonging attached people to the gender system, but also generalize about the importance of these motivations.

Several of Smalltown's key geographical, social and demographic characteristics make it ideal for realizing such research aims. First, it is geographically isolated—40 kilometres from any other urban centre and 110 kilometres from a centre larger than itself. Consequently, within Smalltown's boundaries are all the institutions in which women and men participate in the course of their daily lives. This means they work, shop, play, socialize, politicize, perform their good works and worship (those that do)[14] where they live, or, at most, a few minutes from their homes. The children of most residents are educated in neighbourhood schools. This geographical concentration of activities allows a wider range of forms of gender inequality to be studied directly than is usually feasible in larger settlements of the kind Deem (1986) and Green *et al.* (1987a) have been studying. It also allows us to examine the interconnections between these institutions rather than treat them 'as closed units that can be understood in isolation [from each other]' (Ferree, 1990:866).

Second, the small size of the community's population helps such a study. There are fewer than 4000 residents. As a result, much of the social interaction is highly visible and therefore easier to research. Fellow researchers and I have been able to observe women and men in a wide range of formal and informal situations, including many sporting activities, a variety of voluntary organizations, church organizations, private parties, in the home, and in some paid employment.

Third, delineating various forms of gender inequality and articulating some of the causal connections among them is facilitated by the density and redundancy of social ties. This last point requires explanation. In part because of the isolation of the community, in part because the population is small and stable—76 per cent have been resident for at least ten years—and in part because of the geographical coincidence of all the institutions in which people participate, close-knit networks have developed among residents and among their organizations and groups, and what Frankenberg (1966) calls 'role redundancy' has occurred.

A close-knit network is one in which there are multistranded rather than single-stranded ties between actors and groups (Barnes, 1954; Bell and Newby, 1976b). In this instance this means, for example, that several people who belong to the local branch of the Red Cross also belong to the Country Women's Association (hereafter called the CWA), some members of the CWA also belong to the Anglican Church Guild and to the Ladies Bowling Club, while some of the bowlers are also members of the Red Cross but not necessarily of the CWA, and so on. Furthermore a number of the women participating in several of the same organizations nominate each other as close friends. This example could be repeated many times. Interconnections of these kinds produce a complex close-knit network of overlapping social ties linking many of the community's organizations and residents, and facilitate the investigation of processes of inclusion, exclusion, and subordination, etc.

Role redundancy is conceptually similar to the notion of a close-knit network, focusing attention on social positions and the actors occupying them. It is produced in a community by there being very few players and many parts to play. As a result the same people relate to each other in a variety of social settings and roles. In Smalltown a woman's neighbour may also belong to the same tennis club, be a fellow member of the Red Cross, serve in the same school tuck-shop, belong to the same church, and work for the same boss. They may also be cousins.[15]

In a community in which close-knit networks and role redundancy are commonplace, not only is it much easier than in settlements lacking these characteristics[16] for one set of actors to control another set, but the study of the processes of control and of any rebellion against them are also made easier. I found in Smalltown that once I had access to a group or friendship network through gaining the confidence of one of its members, it usually led to me having access to several others as well. In the early days of field-work I discovered that at whatever social function I attended I would meet people I had already met at previous social activities. For example, on one field-work trip, a man I met at a public meeting was serving in a shop I entered next day. He greeted me at the door of the Presbyterian Church on the following Sunday. Through him I met his wife who, in turn, introduced me to several women who belonged to a number of town organizations. These women provided me with information about their organizations and I arranged for a woman researcher to attend meetings of some of these organizations. This led to further invitations to attend social activities, introductions to people belonging to other organizations and more interviews. By such processes I expanded my knowledge of women and of their relationships to men in most spheres of their daily lives: in other words I was able to adopt relatively painlessly a holistic approach which is difficult for researchers to use if they work in socially fragmented settings.

Of course all methods of social investigation have their

limitations as well as their strengths. The extensive use of quantitative data and the attempt to be as comparative as possible—especially with studies from a tradition that makes heavy use of numerical data—have precluded my incorporating more event analysis and making much more use of case-study data collected during interviews and periods of observation. My inability to learn as much about the domestic lives of men and women as I would have liked was another limitation. I and a number of other researchers did live for two or three weeks at a time with Smalltown families, conducted what were often lengthy interviews in hundreds of homes, and made numerous social calls on families with whom we became friendly. However, our observations on these occasions only yielded impressionistic data on such matters as authority and power relationships, the occurrence of deference, and harmonious and conflictual relationships. It is worth emphasizing that what we witnessed usually corroborated rather than challenged the data collected during formal surveys. These data show that men are much more likely than women to make important decisions unilaterally, or have the final say on such decisions, especially those entailing the expenditure of money, and to leave women with the responsibility for more demanding domestic tasks. Our observations also uncovered far more instances of wives deferring to husbands on routine issues than of their resisting or taking charge of the situation.[17] These were only impressions, and it is possible that, when out of sight of researchers, Smalltown women exercised much more influence over decisions, protested vigorously over the repeated absence of a husband engaged in sporting activities rather than deferring, refused to co-operate with him in some enterprise, and so forth. Our research of the politics of domestic life was also limited by our acceptance of the etiquette of the outside investigator, which is to keep clear of the bedroom door. There may be considerable power being exercised by wives that has eluded us, and rebellions underway in Smalltown that have escaped our gaze.

Disguising the identity of actors

A further important reason for not incorporating more case material in this volume is the need to protect the identities of local people when reporting issues, events, and attitudes that the actors and informants themselves often do not want traced back to them. Some have gone so far as to say they do not wish to recognize themselves as individuals in what is written. It can be difficult to comply with this request at times because so much of what is said by a particular individual has been said by many others as well. In order to offer the maximum protection possible, I often bring together in one quotation segments from different interviews. This can be accomplished without invalidating the account where people have expressed similar sentiments but in somewhat different ways. I almost always change details of the speaker's identity, which can also be done without introducing significant distortion. For example, where the same kind of response has been given as frequently by women as men I sometimes change the gender of the speaker, or where it is as likely to have been made by a businessman as a farmer I put the farmer's words into the mouth of the businessman. The only occasion on which I deviate from this practice is when I am quoting someone who has spoken publicly on a formal occasion or has been previously cited in the local newspaper. They are not named but the occupation and gender given is usually accurate unless the particular quotation is likely to embarrass the speaker.

The representativeness and relevance of the study

The responses of many students and some colleagues to oral and written accounts of parts of this material indicate that there is little chance of readers viewing the findings as typical of their experiences of the relationships between men and women. Rather, many readers will distance themselves from the findings by declaring that the community is idiosyncratic and the patterns of dominance and subordination are totally foreign to their social worlds. The oppressive actions and social arrangements that are portrayed will be dismissed as examples of rural conservatism and male chauvinism that could not possibly occur, say, among educated urbane city dwellers: 'I never dream of living in a place where men behave as badly as this.'

However, I believe that many readers who respond in such ways will be deluding themselves about the egalitarian quality of their own gender relations. Any social situation has its unique qualities and Smalltown is no exception. It is also true that as this is a study of gender relationships in a particular community over a limited period of time I cannot claim that the findings on gender inequality are representative of other communities or of society generally. Nevertheless, a growing body of research carried out in urban as well as rural contexts shows that patterns of gender subordination similar to many of those delineated in this study occur in a range of settings. In order to demonstrate that this is so I have made the study as comparative as possible by relating the Smalltown findings to those of earlier community studies. Most community studies, however, are conducted in small centres and do not focus on gender relationships, so I will also refer to findings from specialist literature in the fields of the domestic division of labour, child care, marital power and decision-making, paid work, and leisure activities. This comparative literature demonstrates that the urbane educated city-dwelling male can be as dominating and oppressive in his dealings with women as his rural counterparts.

CHAPTER 2

Place and people

Smalltown is situated in north-west Victoria, and, as the name implies, is a small township of 2700 people; a further 1050 people live in the surrounding farming district. In the town, no inhabitant is more than a five-minute drive from any other inhabitant. Although the farming hinterland covers an area of approximately 2300 square kilometres, any inhabitant can reach Smalltown in less than half an hour on one of the many asphalt roads that converge on the township itself.

The town exists primarily to service its own and the farming population, and this is manifested in the main street. For most of its length it is flanked by private houses, but for three short blocks these give way to an assortment of shops, banks, stock and station agencies, garages, a post office, a court house, local government offices, and six hotels. There has not been any increase in the number of businesses during the seventeen years of this study.

Smalltown, as a service centre, has been adversely affected in recent years by the government and its satellites adopting a policy of regional centralization. Staff that were once spread over several townships are now concentrated in one township in an effort to improve management and produce more cost-effective services (O'Conner, 1981). However, Smalltown is losing out as other towns are chosen as mail centres for Australia Post, for the establishment of a Telecom phone exchange, for regional offices for the State Road Construction Authority, the State Electricity Commission and the Department of Community Services. The Clerk of Court of Petty Sessions has been moved to another town and the services provided by the clerk reduced. The offices for the Department of Crown Lands and Conservation have been amalgamated and their staff reduced.

Although, as we shall see, Smalltowners believe their community offers a superior life-style to that available to city dwellers, in reality Smalltown is something of a poor relative to Australia's capital cities. There is a state primary school and secondary college, and a Catholic primary school and secondary college, but there is no tertiary educational institution in the district. Smalltown does have a district hospital employing about 100 people but state government authorities are likely to close this hospital in the next few years. There are two general medical practitioners and a dentist working in Smalltown now (1992) but there are no medical or dental specialists within 100 kilometres.

A newcomer from the city would find an abundance of sporting amenities and pubs, but few other recreational facilities. Smalltown has neither a cinema nor a theatre, and only three restaurants. Much of the informal social life of the town is situated in and around its seven pubs, where men and women go for a night out—a counter tea or a leisurely drink with friends in the pub's lounge. The town's most prestigious organizations—the Rotary, Lions, and Jaycees clubs—meet there, and some male sporting organizations use pubs for their 'business' meetings.

Smalltown is located 40 kilometres from any other town and 110 kilometres from a town that is substantially larger than itself, so local people have little alternative but to work, do much of their shopping, and pursue their leisure activities within the community's geographical boundaries.

Unless they are very prosperous they must also send their children to a local school.

One of Smalltown's most striking features is the ethnic homogeneity of its population. Less than 5 per cent of Smalltowners were born outside Australia (most of these are of British descent) whereas 25 per cent of Victoria's population were born in other countries. At present there are only four Asians, four Greeks, four Italians, twelve Germans and about a dozen other Europeans living in either the township or the surrounding district. There are fewer than a dozen Aborigines living locally.

The vast majority of Smalltowners have always been Anglo-Celtic, so it is not surprising that over 90 per cent describe themselves as Christians and claim that they belong to a particular Christian denomination. In practice, most of them ignore their church most of the time: less than 20 per cent of them are in church on any given Sunday. There are five churches: Anglican, Catholic, Church of Christ, Salvation Army, and Uniting. Support for all churches, but especially the larger Protestant churches, is steadily declining, and, either individually or collectively, they are not serving as focal points of vigorous community activity for either men or women (Dempsey, 1991).

Population decline and economic stagnation

Smalltown is declining numerically and its economy is stagnating. At the turn of the century the population of the township itself stood at about 4000, but now there are only 2700 residents. In 1901 there were more than 4500 people living in the Smalltown farming district, but by 1986 the population of the farming community had fallen to about 1050 people. Decline of this order is a long-term trend and is the rule rather than the exception in rural Australia. It is due, in large measure, to dramatic changes in farm technology but, in Smalltown, it is also due to a decline in manufacture and in tertiary economic activities.

In the 1990s the proportion of people engaged in retailing, education, and the provision of services to community members is only about two-thirds of that for Victoria as a whole.

Manufacturing has never been a dominating force in the Smalltown economy, but small-scale manufacture, building, and road construction were, until very recently, stable and significant components of that economy. However, in the late 1970s a cordial factory, a brick works, and the largest manufacturing concern, the flour mill, closed. The stock feed company, which was an off-shoot of the defunct flour mill, has markedly reduced its work-force in recent years.[1] During the financial year to June 1991 the town's two steel-fabricating plants which, at the height of annual production, had a combined work-force of approximately ninety people, went into receivership and the biggest employer of female labour, the knitting mill, was closed. One of the steel-fabricating plants has reopened under new ownership but with a markedly depleted work-force. Now, the major manufacturing concerns are a turkey-processing plant, several piggeries, the stock feed company, an offal-processing plant and a chemical-spray equipment plant. The combined work-force of these industries would probably not exceed 100 persons.

Despite the town council's continuing attempts to attract new entrepreneurs to the district with offers of low-interest loans and factories at low rentals, manufacturing will remain a relatively minor part of this economy. The recent decline in industry has increased the rate of unemployment and will force families with a long connection to the district to leave in the hope of obtaining employment elsewhere.

Farming is the single most important economic activity in this community and has been for more than 120 years. About one-third of the community's work-force is employed as farmers or farm labourers. Yet the mechanization of farming has led to a dramatic reduction in the number of farming units and the size of the rural population. A little over a century ago a farm worker probably produced enough food for four additional people. Today he or she produces enough for over seventy people. The size of holdings has increased as the size of the farming population has decreased: whereas a century ago the typical farm was little over 300 acres, today it is over 2000 acres. This trend will continue. Local leaders of the farming industry are projecting that within a few years farming will not be viable on less than 3000 acres.

Since 1921 the number of people engaged in agriculture has fallen from over 1000 to about 500 people and the proportion of the work-force they constitute has declined from roughly one-half to one-third. This decline is not only due to a fall in the number of farm owners but to the almost complete disappearance of farm labourers as a class of employees. This change has occurred throughout Australia. Between the two censuses of 1933 and 1971 the number of farm employees throughout Australia was halved (Nalson, 1977:305). Mechanization, increased costs of equipment, and seasonal fluctuations, have reduced the demand for farm labour dramatically in Smalltown. As Powell and Jensen (1981) observe, the movement away from the employment of non-family labour in farming is a long-term trend in the industry induced by the growth in farm mechanization accompanied by a decline in farm profitability. Farmers are increasingly responding to a declining economic situation by using family labour. Sons are used for the 'farm work' and wives for providing 'back-up services' such as going to town to obtain a spare part so that the men can continue with farm work.

The family unit plays a key role both in farming and in the town's business activities. All of the 250 or so farms in the community and more than 80 per cent of the town's retailing, manufacturing, building and transport firms are family concerns. Many operators of town businesses, like their farming counterparts, rely on unpaid or partially paid family labour. The family, particularly the entrepreneur's wife, is likely to be involved in all aspects of the business: management, selling, and even cleaning.[2] As the economists Powell and Jensen show, these patterns are typical of economic activity in small towns across Australia (1981). In sum, what Smalltown possesses today is a petit-bourgeois economy servicing a petit-bourgeois farming industry.

An ageing population

Smalltown's population is not only declining but ageing rapidly. Whereas people aged sixty-five and older constitute approximately 10 per cent of Australia's population, they constitute more than 15 per cent of the combined population of Smalltown and the surrounding farming district. The proportion of the town's population that is elderly is higher—approximately 18 per cent compared to 7 per cent for the population of the surrounding farming district. This dramatic contrast in the age composition of the population of the town and of the farming district is due principally to the town functioning as a retirement centre for farmers and their wives, and retirees from Melbourne who are attracted by cheap housing, the mild climate, and what residents describe as the easy-going and friendly life-style.[3]

Smalltown's population is also ageing because approximately 60 per cent of Smalltown's young people move away permanently. They go because Smalltown is a no-career town. For most locally born young men and women it offers only unskilled, semi-skilled or, in a few cases, skilled employment. Those who wish to 'better themselves' must move to Melbourne or a nearby provincial city. Smalltown lacks the bureaucratic structures to provide career paths, and it lacks the post-secondary educational institutions to provide the diplomas and degrees that are standard prerequisites for a middle-class career. As a result, fewer Smalltowners than average possess tertiary qualifications: under 2 per cent compared to more than 4 per cent for the state of Victoria. This lack of educational opportunity affects women more adversely than it does men because many Smalltown men can obtain middle-class jobs without any educational qualifications, whereas women are dependent on such qualifications to gain entry to any middle-class occupation (see Chs 5, 9, and 10). A few women circumvent the local structural impediments to upward mobility by moving to Melbourne and obtaining tertiary qualifications, after which they return to Smalltown to teach or nurse.[4]

The out-migration of about 60 per cent of school leavers is, to some extent, offset by the in-migration of semi-professionals, professionals, technicians and management personnel: that is, of people who possess qualifications that cannot be obtained in Smalltown. Most people with tertiary qualifications living locally are, in fact, transients who are pursuing professional or administrative careers in Smalltown, or they are women married to men following such careers. Most of these will move on eventually. The husbands will initiate career moves and their wives will accompany them to a new centre. The men are able to advance their careers as they move. These options are not available to most locally-born Smalltowners, whose inferior educational qualifications and work skills bind them to Smalltown or similar rural settlements. Those who lack such qualifications will probably occupy a disadvantaged position in the local economic class structure.

Structured inequality

The economic inequality that characterizes Australian society generally is found in Smalltown, however the range is more limited. There are no individuals or families with capital commensurate to that held by the upper class described by Encel (1970), Playford (1972), and Connell

(1977). It is not even particularly useful to speak of a propertied class as distinct from a petit-bourgeois class because most people engaged in farming or business are self-employed. The biggest private employer living locally has fewer than forty people working for him and most other employers have no more than five people working for them. Farming land is the most common source of capital to generate market power in this community, but no farmer has holdings comparable to those of say some of the more prominent graziers of Victoria's Western District or of the New South Wales New England Tablelands, and only one or two have diversified their economic activity into manufacture and finance, unlike many of Australia's leading graziers. Smalltown farms range in size from less than 1000 acres to 5000 or more acres, and the modal size is between 1500 and 2000 acres.

Members of this community with the most economic strength, consumable income, and social standing, are the farmers with extensive holdings, the members of the traditional professions who 'work for themselves', and the executives of the larger public and private enterprises—including the town clerk, shire secretary, hospital manager, school principals, managers of some manufacturing concerns, and the owners of the larger town businesses. The most disadvantaged are the unemployed, the unskilled and semi-skilled workers, those elderly whose only source of income is the pension, and women, particularly those such as widows and the wives of manual workers who have no income of their own.

The class structure

Community sociologists have favoured analyses of social stratification based on status rather than class (Wild, 1974; Oxley, 1974), however I have shown in *Smalltown* (Chs 7 and 8) that an analysis of structured inequality based on economic class helps make more sense of social relationships in Smalltown than one based on status. Classes are understood here to consist of aggregates of people occupying a similar position in the economic and work system, together with those who are economically dependent upon them. Occupation and employment status (e.g. self-employed, employee) are used as the major criteria for determining an individual's class position. In Appendix 2, Smalltown's class structure and the criteria used to delineate it are discussed, as well as the problems associated with allocating women to a position in a class system and the solutions that have been adopted in this study. There is also an account of how people who do not participate in paid work, such as children and many of the elderly, are allocated a class position.

There are three class categories in Smalltown: the middle class, the lower middle class, and the working class. The middle class is divided into four segments or subclasses:

class 1—the higher level professional and executive class (principally professionals such as doctors, lawyers, and senior managers of both the private and public sectors);
class 2—the farmer class (owners and employees);[5]
class 3—the business class (mainly owners of main-street businesses and other enterprises based on male skilled and semi-skilled jobs);
class 4—the lower level professional and executive class (principally teachers, nurses, and middle managers).

Classes 2 and 3 (the farming and business classes) together comprise Smalltown's petit-bourgeois class.

The lower middle class consists of one subclass:

class 5—the ordinary white-collar class (mainly typists, clerks, and sales-persons).

The working class consists of two subclasses:

class 6—the upper working class (skilled employees, heavy equipment operators and supervisors[6]);
class 7—the lower working class (semi-skilled and

unskilled workers, including labourers, drivers, and domestics).

Smalltown is aptly described as a predominantly middle-class community because two-thirds of the work-force are employed in a middle-class, or lower middle-class occupation. Yet one of the first things visitors to Smalltown remark is the striking similarity in the material culture of the community. There are no distinct working-class or middle-class residential areas, apart from two small Housing Commission areas on the periphery of the town. There are a couple of streets that have a 'better end' but even these are not class homogeneous. Smalltown lacks a nob's hill. There are no mansions and only a handful of houses valued at about $150 000. There are less than a dozen European cars in the district. Prosperous business people, farmers with large enterprises, and town professionals drive Australian-made family cars, especially Holden Commodores and Ford Falcons. There are no exclusive clothing boutiques and no 'upmarket' restaurants. Workers, farmers, businessmen and their wives interested in dining out eat a counter tea at adjoining tables or sometimes at the same table in one of the town's pubs. Working-class and middle-class golfers belong to the same club and members of these classes drink in the same pubs.

These inter-class similarities in life-style are linked to the fact that the core membership of Smalltown's middle-class consists of the descendants of nineteenth-century selectors of small holdings. In the 1990s the descendants and their families, who probably comprise more than half the farmers, enjoy what, by national standards, is a modest level of prosperity. It is true that a majority of the farmers, towns' business people, and professionals are wealthy by comparison with workers. However, in the case of the petit-bourgeois class this wealth is in the form of equipment, land, and commercial buildings rather than investments providing an income for consumption. Their wealth offers a certain level of economic security and could be put to producing income if necessary. The owners of this wealth, however, are reluctant to spend the income it does generate on consumer goods. Their reluctance is due in large measure to the uncertainty of agricultural prosperity on which all petit-bourgeois families are directly or indirectly dependent.

Notwithstanding the similarities between the members of Smalltown's middle and working classes in domestic material culture, it is important not to lose sight of the real differences that exist in their economic power. Generally speaking, material resources of the four higher classes are far superior to those of the other classes. Currently they have greater incomes and their income advantages over classes 5, 6, and 7 (the lower middle and working classes) are likely to increase in the future (see Ch. 6). There are also significant differences in consumption among the classes even if they are not as marked or as highly visible as class differences found in Australia's largest cities. Although members of Smalltown's four higher classes rarely own European cars, they are much more likely than members of the lower middle class or the working classes to be driving late-model Australian or Japanese cars. More middle class people are living in large and well-furnished homes than working-class people. Some members of the middle class own accommodation in holiday resorts. The extremely expensive practice of sending children away to private school reveals, more than any other form of consumption, the much greater economic power of the higher segments of the middle class. Many middle-class children go to schools in provincial cities, but the wealthiest families send their children to exclusive schools in Melbourne or Geelong. The ultimate strength of the financial resources of this segment of the middle class is reflected in the fact that they continue to send their children to such schools even during a period when farming incomes are falling substantially. By contrast, the lower middle and working classes have no option but to educate their children in one of Smalltown's state or Catholic schools.

In conversation and interviews, however, working-class members of the community do not focus on the differences in life-style between themselves and the higher classes. Rather, they draw attention to their shared activities: belonging to the same football team and bowling club, and drinking together. In Smalltown, pub drinking is a highly visible activity which often gives rise to some inter-class mixing at the bar. Indeed, there is sufficient mixing to confirm members of all classes in their belief in the essential egalitarianism of their community.

More visible than any social distinctions between the classes are divisions between the activities of men and women. We shall see in the next chapter that pub life is but one of many spheres of social activity in Smalltown where men keep women at a distance. While observers might dispute whether a particular pub is more middle class or working class, there could be no dispute that all pubs are men's territories.

Smalltown's image of itself

Smalltown's men and women of all classes and ages never tire of singing the praises of the community, of its life-style, and its people. Despite the community's chronic economic and employment problems residents perceive life in Smalltown as superior physically, socially and emotionally to life in many other places, and especially to life in the city. Participants in the Community, School, and Gender Surveys were systematically questioned about their views of the relative merits of living in the city and living in the country. In all three surveys more than 90 per cent of the respondents offered favourable comments on the experience of country-town life. By contrast, more than 90 per cent of adults and adolescents said they disliked the idea of living in the city. In the Community Survey there were only twenty-three favourable comments about the city but 618 unfavourable ones. Roughly one-third of the answers given stressed the physical shortcomings of the city and the physical peril of living there. A further one-third drew attention to the pressure of city life, and about one-fifth of the responses drew attention to the anonymous, impersonal, uncaring character of city life: 'Everybody is out for themselves, no one cares about anybody else. It is a terrible place to send children, let alone raise them. City people keep to themselves, they don't want to get involved. It is so different to here.'

Smalltown residents praise the physical characteristics of Smalltown: fresh air, nearby open spaces, lack of congestion, and peacefulness; the security it offers from violent crimes; and the availability and cheapness of a wide range of sporting and recreational activities. Adults praise Smalltown as a place to raise children, and they also stress the value of living close to each other and close to work. Smalltown men and women say that the community is better for women principally because it is better for children, but also because it provides plenty of female companionship (these were the two advantages most frequently cited during the Gender Survey). Wives, Smalltown men believe, are saved from boredom and loneliness because of the close physical proximity of friends. The wives themselves say that access to women friends is one of Smalltown's more attractive features. Smalltown is perceived as marvellous for the men because of the proximity of work, cheap housing, and transport, plenty of sport, the prevalence of pubs, and the opportunities for 'spending times with mates'.

What members of both sexes find particularly appealing about Smalltown is the special quality of relationships, the experience of being known and of having a sense of attachment to the community and to its inhabitants.[7] In every major survey conducted in the community in both the 1970s and 1980s, respondents talked about the friendly and supportive nature of local relationships. For example, in the mid-1980s, when members of the Status Survey were asked to evaluate the contribution that each of a set of sixteen factors made to an individual's standing in the community, the factor perceived as the most important was friendliness. Friendliness was nominated by three-quarters of the respondents. More male and female respondents gave it a higher rating than they gave to any of the following: an individual's occupation (66 per cent said it had an important bearing on social status); the amount of money an individual possesses (63 per cent); the quality of his or her house (40 per cent), or car (33 per cent).

Relationships are perceived as personal, enduring, and intimate, with a kin-like quality: 'We're like one big happy family here, that's what makes Smalltown so different' (town councillor). They regard themselves as loyal not only to friends and relatives but to the community and its members. They are concerned about presenting a united front and preserving the unity and harmony of the community. Nothing must be said that places the community in a bad light. Consequently, many Smalltowners wince when the word class is introduced during the course of an interview or reference is made to men's practice of excluding women from many of their activities. They wince because such observations imply something negative about the community, something potentially divisive, even disruptive. It is not surprising therefore that few community members believe men exploit women, or that the great majority either believe that there are no classes in Smalltown or that classes have little bearing on the character of social relationships. For example, in the Community Survey about one-third of the respondents insisted that Smalltown lacked classes, and about 80 per cent of those who acknowledged the existence of classes claimed that they were, at most, of marginal importance in Smalltown. Such statements were as likely to be offered by members of the working class as by farmers, businesmen and professionals. These people were not denying the presence of classes in Australia nor of economic distinctions in Smalltown but of social distinctions of any significance. They were affirming the community's social egalitarianism. Those who during an interview were offended, angered, or unsettled by talk of class, sometimes responded in ways such as: 'I don't like the word class . . . I've got nothing to say about that!' (a typist married to a labourer).

Despite local beliefs to the contrary, inequitable relationships do occur in Smalltown. They occur between the young and the old, the working class and the middle class, and between men and women. As Bell and Newby (1976a) stress, inequitable relationships are inherently unstable. It is important to emphasize that the positive feelings of Smalltowners of all classes and both sexes about their community is one of several factors that help prevent conflict developing around the hierachies of inequality in this community. They hide the inequalities from the eyes of many of the disadvantaged and subordinated while encouraging others to take the view that the benefits of accommodating present inequitable social and political arrangements outweigh the costs of challenging them, or of leaving the community.

Among the cultural, experiential and emotional factors that help bond superordinates and subordinates are their common conviction about the superiority of their way of life, shared enmity towards the city and towards the centralized government authorities that are steadily reducing their services and threatening their futures, and a sense of a common fate. Smalltown is a community under siege economically and bureaucratically and nothing is more likely to bond people with disparate interests than a common enemy.[8] The demographic and structural factors facilitating bonding include the community's small and stable population, its geographical isolation, the prevalence of multiplex organizational, economic, kinship, and friendship ties, and the relatively low degree of economic differentiation between community members (see Ch. 6). Together these factors ensure that people who in larger settlements would not have any social contact at least know one another and that many of them co-operate in a variety of activities. They also encourage the development of a common culture and a sense of shared destiny (see Dempsey, 1990a, especially Chs 3, 5, and 6).

In the Community Survey 86 per cent of participants said they felt, to a considerable extent, a part of Smalltown. Nearly half of the participants in the Status Survey uttered one or more statements of the following kind when they were asked to explain why they found Smalltown a good place to live:

This is where I belong and will always belong.
I am known here and I know everybody else.
It's the greatest place I have ever lived!
I love the place and I love the people.

Here is evidence of strong sentiments of attachment to place and people, of communal feelings grounded in locality. Smalltown women were as likely as men to express strong feelings of belonging. This research suggests that the need to belong can be so strong that when that need is met it often softens or hides the inequities many are experiencing or compensates them enough to discourage rebellion (see Ch. 11).

Individual achievement and community attachment

The need to belong and the experience of belonging are valid and important phenomena in the lives of Smalltown people. There is a high degree of loyalty to Smalltown and a sense of counting for something in a world somewhat larger than one's family and circle of close friends. But there are other needs and motivations operating in Smalltown: one of these is the need for individual advancement, particularly through occupational mobility and economic success. Most of Smalltown's younger people give priority to individual advancement when they have to choose between 'getting on and getting their just desserts' and, enjoying the secure, personalized and supportive life-style of Smalltown. More than 90 per cent of the students attending Smalltown's secondary schools said they disliked the idea of living in the city and, like their parents, they were more articulate about the disadvantages of city life and the relative advantages of country-town life than they were about any other topic discussed with them. Yet when we asked about their job future approximately two-thirds of the girls and more than half the boys expressed a desire for an occupation which could only be pursued if they moved to the city, either to engage in the job itself or to obtain the qualifications to do so. Most of them were aspiring to a professional job of one kind or another.

Belief that 'Smalltown is a great place to live' is very strong, but even stronger is the commitment to 'moving up in the world', if it is at all possible. These girls and boys probably mirror the views of their parents because an even larger number of parents (about three-quarters) expressed job aspirations for their children that, if pursued, would mean those children would have to leave Smalltown for the city. At the same time the Community Survey showed that most parents are resentful of the fact that the children must go. For this they partially blame governments for not providing a stronger rural economy which would produce the jobs they want for the young people. When asked about the shortcomings of living in Smalltown they are most likely to mention the lack of suitable employment for young people. Eighty-three per cent of respondents in the

Community Survey criticized Smalltown for offering insufficient jobs for young people, but, at the same time, 70 per cent of respondents said that Smalltown was in general a satisfactory community for young people to live in.

Flaws in the 'one big happy family'

The reality is that Smalltown is not one big happy family for all its residents. Those young people who feel compelled to leave Smalltown do so because the community does not offer them the same opportunities to 'get on' as it offers some privileged males, especially many of the sons of farming and business families. It is as necessary for females from higher-class families as for males from working-class families to leave Smalltown in order to obtain a position that is more rewarding than an ordinary white-collar job (see Chs 9 and 10). Those who are economically privileged are also more likely to be the recipients of friendliness and neighbourliness and to be at the centre rather than on the margins of community activities and decision-making processes. Males engaged in petit-bourgeois and professional occupations are the major beneficiaries. There are at the other end of the spectrum those who experience much less acceptance and may even be socially and psychologically marginalized. They include some transients, many of the elderly, and certain categories of women.

Almost half the participants in the Elderly Survey reported that they felt less a part of the community than when they were younger, and about the same proportion said that younger members of the community treated them differently because they were older. The elderly said that feeling a part of things depended on being able to 'get out and about'. In Smalltown you go to the community; the community does not come to you. Avoiding marginalization demands good health and an adequate income, and it is also facilitated by having a partner. Most married participants in the Elderly Survey cited a spouse as their most regular source of companionship and advice.[9] Men were much more likely to have the support of a spouse because of their shorter life expectancy and the practice of marrying women younger than themselves: 72 per cent of the men in our sample were married compared with only 29 per cent of the women.

The elderly most likely to experience social isolation are widowed women living alone, especially those with a low income and a significant chronic health problem.[10] The elderly least likely to be marginalized are men still engaged in higher-class occupations or men who, although retired, have managed to carry into retirement the stereotype of successful farmer, businessman, lawyer, school principal, etc., and who possess sufficient income and good health to mix with younger community members as equals. With few exceptions those elderly who are prominent in community affairs (as opposed to organizations consisting largely of the elderly) display these characteristics. This is one of the reasons for describing Smalltown as a man's town.[11]

Among the women of all ages likely to be marginalized were those married to men who were categorized by most community members as 'no-hopers' and women who breached the mores of respectability. 'No-hopers' are so called because they have a reputation for being in trouble with the police, failing to work, drinking excessively, neglecting their properties, being dirty and unkempt, and neglecting the appearance and physical well-being of their children. By their behaviour they threaten the collective view of the great majority of community members that this is a wholesome, caring, healthy place to live, so they are despised, ridiculed and ignored.[12] Smalltown's 'no-hopers' are painfully aware of their reputation. There is no escaping the knowledge of their stigmatized status because they have to cope with being ignored or with overhearing judgemental comments about themselves in a community where convention demands that people who pass each other in the street acknowledge the presence of the other with a warm and positive greeting. 'No-hopers' told of how some community members pretended not to see them as they passed and of others making lewd comments within their hearing. The children of 'no-hoper' families are often ridiculed. Some of the women of 'no-hoper' families have spoken at length of the pain of living in Smalltown. They believe that the faults of their families are exaggerated, that innocent members are unjustly blamed and socially punished for the failings of the families' black sheep, usually their menfolk. They also said they are misjudged. If, for example, a teenage girl of a 'no-hoper' family leaves town for a period of time the rumour may circulate that she is having an abortion. The absence of a girl from a leading family is not interpreted in this way, they claimed. Some of the wives and many of the adolescent children of 'no-hopers' were anxious to leave Smalltown in the hope of finding anonymity elsewhere. Usually wives cannot leave: they lack the economic resources to move, especially with dependent children, and the job skills to gain work if they do.

Smalltowners also place beyond the symbolic boundaries of the community both locally-born and transient women who breach the mores of respectability. In this community women are primarily judged by their performances as mothers and wives (see Ch. 8). A good mother is a respectable woman, and a respectable woman is not available sexually. If she is believed to be available sexually she will be stigmatized as a woman after some other woman's husband: 'See that woman sitting over there, she's the town bike. She's sleeping at the moment with Mark Lawson' (a prominent married businessman). Such a woman will be gossiped about, criticized to her face, and possibly shunned, especially by other women. All women who are perceived to breach the mores of respectability will be gossiped about and criticized, but non-local women who are believed to be sexually deviant are the most likely to be shunned. One transient married woman was strenuously criticized for drinking regularly in the public bar and for an alleged affair with a transient man. On at least two occasions I witnessed her being snubbed by other middle-class men and women. By contrast, I have observed on a number of occasions a locally-born married woman with a reputation for having affairs with 'other women's husbands' interacting with other locals. Although she was being strongly criticized behind her back, she was always greeted in a friendly manner. 'After all,' one of my informants said, 'we're stuck with her for life'. This woman was married to a man with a middle-class job and she and her husband had many kinship as well as long-term friendship links with other members of this class.

Men may also be marginalized but they are much less likely to be than women. They are far less likely to be ostracized for breaching the mores of respectability because the standards applying to men are far more tolerant than those applying to women. For example, there was far less criticism of Mark Lawson than of the woman he was supposedly involved with sexually, and no indications that he risked social ostracism. Men are much more likely to be better off economically, occupy more powerful and prestigious positions, and enjoy more autonomy. They are also far more able to use women to help them achieve wealth, status and leisure than are women to use them for such purposes. As the next chapter shows, Smalltown is a man's town.

CHAPTER 3

A man's town

Many women are fond of describing Smalltown as a man's town. 'If there was ever a man's town this is it: what with all their pubs, service clubs and sporting activities. Plenty of chances to spend time with their mates. Men have got it made. They're on clover' (40-year-old farmer's wife). Any woman who refers to Smalltown as a man's town makes reference to sport and pubs. Some call it a man's town because, as they say, 'We raise the money and the men spend it'.[1] There are those women who have in mind men's practice of ostensibly getting together to perform 'good works' but in reality to drink and enjoy other mateship activity.

Most women offering such observations do so in a semi-serious and partly jesting manner. However, when we say to men that women see Smalltown as a man's town, they usually become defensive and respond by saying something like, 'I don't know why they'd say that. What do they mean by it?' If they are told that one thing women are referring to is their perception that men have greater opportunities than women for sport and leisure, the men deny this and claim that women have more free time because of their labour-saving gadgets while they (that is the men) have to work all day to make a living.

Some women describe Smalltown as a man's town because 'men are usually in control of things'. A few men attempt to laugh this observation off and say that the women run them, not vice versa. Most point out that each sex controls its own organizations: 'We have our organizations and they have theirs.' Some men acknowledge that men exercise greater control in community life; they usually justify this situation by saying that men are better suited temperamentally or by experience—especially in paid work—to 'running things'.

This chapter supports women's assessment that Smalltown is a town more dedicated to the interests of men than of women. Men do control most major decision-making processes that affect the lives of both women and men in this community. They have a disproportionate share of facilities and resources that are given over to recreational activity. Many men prefer one another's company to the company of women, and they are able to keep women out of many of their activities. The following chapter describes how, when men do admit women, it is usually as subordinates and supporters rather than as equals.

Dominating town affairs

Throughout the century or more of Smalltown's history men have controlled the three local decision-making bodies that have the most bearing on the daily life of community members: the Town Council, the Shire Council and the Board of Management of the District Hospital.[2] The executive officers of these organizations—the town clerk, the shire secretary and the hospital manager—have always been men, and so have the majority of elected members. There has never been a woman elected to the Shire Council, only three to the Town Council and five to the Hospital Board of Management. No woman has ever been chosen by her male colleagues as a chairperson of the Hospital Board. In the second half of the 1980s a woman was elected for the first time as mayor of the Town Council. This was a significant advance for women, but in 1992 men still outnumbered women by two to one on the council, and as council decisions are based on a majority vote of councillors this has meant that men have remained in charge of this organization. The decisions of the Town Council, the Shire Council, and the Hospital Board of Management are implemented by male full-time administrators assisted in their work principally by women.

The woman who was elected as mayor of Smalltown saw her election as proof that sexism was disappearing in Smalltown. When she had been defeated for re-election to an alderman's position a few years earlier, she was angry that after many years of conscientious service she had lost her seat to a man who lacked her administrative experience. She believed that her defeat was proof of sexism and that her subsequent re-election some years later occurred because those who would have opposed her were unaware that she was standing for the council. She said she deliberately kept her candidature secret and submitted her nomination just before the closing time for re-nominations. She was told subsequently by several men that if they had known she was standing they would have opposed her successfully. She agreed that if she had been forced to compete with men for the position she would probably have lost. She said, 'In this community it is generally believed by both men and women that men are better fitted by temperament and experience to take the big decisions.' Her assessment was supported at the time by the experience of a second well-known woman leader who twice stood for the Town Council and was defeated on both occasions by male candidates. On the first of the two occasions she had an experienced campaign manager and was opposed by a man less well-known than she was. Nevertheless, she was decisively defeated. She said, 'They don't want a woman on the council!'

When, in 1989, I reminded the woman who became mayor of what she had said earlier she changed her position, saying:

Things are different now, councillors are chosen on their merits and not their sex. My election as mayor marks a turning point: men and women are becoming more equal in this community. This change is but one significant indicator of greater equality between men and women in Smalltown community life generally.

It is true that there are now three women on the Town Council whereas for most of the town's history there were none. This is an important sign of a lessening of women's inequality in one of the more influential organizations in this community. Yet I am sceptical about the observation that women are becoming equal in a general sense for, as this book shows, there are numerous other indicators that patriarchal control often prevails in relationships between women and men. Women still constitute a minority of the Town Council. The mayoral office reverted to a man—a leading businessman—after the first woman mayor served for two years. The Shire Council is still to receive its first woman member. This and several succeeding chapters demonstrate that the marginal position of women in town politics is replicated in virtually all institutional contexts.

I doubt that even in the 1990s Smalltown is very different from the Australian communities that were studied in the 1960s and 1970s. After conducting an extensive review of these studies, Bryson and Wearing concluded that they showed that women were pushed into organizations of secondary importance and inferior status such as church committees, charities and cultural organizations (1985:355). Certainly in Smalltown most organizational activity is segregated on the basis of sex and men dominate in the more prestigious organizations. Seventy-three per cent of the 130 organizations to which participants in the Community Survey said they belonged were sex specific: they were comprised entirely of members of one sex or at least 70 per cent of the membership was of the same sex. Furthermore, the great majority of the non-sporting organizations in which women participated fitted the description offered by Bryson and Wearing. Many of them were auxiliaries attached to men's organizations that existed to further the material and often social success of their superordinate organizations (see Ch. 4).

Maintaining the boundaries: the men's service clubs

The anthropologist Gregory Bateson found that among the Iatmul the men conducted the business of their society in the Men's House while women attended to domestic chores and child care in and around the dwelling house. 'Women are never allowed into the Men's House but they are expected to listen outside when the men are preparing for the most important rituals. For women to be found inside the Men's House would be symbolic of the disintegration of the community' (cited by Imray and Middleton, 1983:18).[3]

Since their inception approximately two decades ago three of the most prestigious and influential organizations in Smalltown—the Rotary, Lions and Jaycees Clubs—have functioned like men's houses.[4] No woman has ever been admitted to membership of the Rotary and Lions Clubs of Smalltown. They usually comprise between one-quarter and one-third of the members of the Jaycees, although the Jaycees women have never formed a majority of the executive of the club and no woman has ever been elected president. When, in the 1980s, I asked an incumbent president why this was so he said that the women would not be able or prepared to devote the time to the job that the presidency demanded. What he could have added is that, without 'a wife', it would have been structurally and culturally extremely difficult, and perhaps impossible, for a woman to function as president. A president requires a wife to accompany him to a large number of community functions and to visit other Jaycees Clubs in the district.

He also needs her to play a leading role in fund raising for the club, and take an inordinate share of domestic tasks and child care so that he is freed for the many nights and weekends he is busy with the duties of a Jaycees president (see Ch. 4). Similar requirements are built into executive positions in the Rotary and Lions Clubs. During the 1980s about two-thirds of the women who became members of Jaycees were single women. At any one time there was usually only one wife of a male member holding membership in her own right and she was likely to be a woman whose participation in club activities was *not* restricted by having young children to care for.

All of these clubs are, to borrow an expression from Clare Burton, saturated with masculine values (1986:292). Their meetings are held during the normal evening mealtime or occupy the whole evening, which makes it difficult for mothers to attend. They are comprised mainly of farmers, businessmen and professionals. They are deliberately and explicitly occupationally based. Recruitment depends principally on being engaged in some form of middle-class occupation. Rotarians are supposed to be leaders in their particular occupational field. In this community, with only a handful of exceptions, all of the occupational leaders are men (see Ch. 6).

The full title of the Jaycees Club is Junior Chamber of Commerce. It is a club for business people and aims to develop members to their full potential professionally and personally. Members are expected to display community and corporate responsibility. These characteristics and goals provide much of the 'maleness' of the club because throughout Australian society the business community is still dominated by men. In Smalltown men are much more likely to be the sole breadwinners than they are in the wider society and a majority of the men belonging to this club in the 1980s were members of the most gender-exclusive business activity in this community: farming.

All three clubs are also perceived by their male members

and many of their wives as contexts in which men get together to have a good time with their mates. These are not their only functions, but the chance to put in time with other men, especially 'good mates', is acknowledged by many members (and their wives) as one of their chief appeals. All three clubs conducted their meetings in one of the town's hotels, and dinner meetings are preceded and followed by drinking in the public bar of the hotel where the meeting is held. As Caplow pointed out more than a quarter of a century ago, in Western society intimate groups—except those based on kinship or sexual ties—should be comprised of people of the same gender. This, says Caplow, is one of the major cultural themes of our society (cited by Burton, 1986:293). Smalltown men did not express this cultural value so explicitly, but we can infer it from their behaviour, the statements they made to justify it ('it just isn't the same if the women are present'), and their response when women intruded on their all-male social space.[5] The men's service clubs are contexts for male intimacy.

Women only gained membership of the Smalltown Jaycees following a decision taken in 1976 by the ruling body of all Jaycees Clubs in Australia—the National Convention—to admit women as members. All chapters (that is local branches) were requested to invite women to join their branch. In Smalltown, as in a number of other Jaycees clubs,[6] the admission of women was fiercely resisted by several members. It was pointed out to club members that once the National Convention had voted in favour of admitting women, no local club had a legal right to refuse membership to any woman who requested it. Several members left in protest at the decision of the Smalltown chapter to admit women and some of the remaining members were still claiming ten years after the event that 'it was a terrible mistake to sacrifice these good men in order to let some women into the club.[7]

Similar arguments were advanced by men opposed to

playing sport with women or admitting them to the public bars of the town's hotels.

We cannot be ourselves if women are here.
It spoils the night for the men.

As Imray and Middleton (1983) observe, it seems that women are perceived as a 'threat to the purity and integrity of the men's space and activity'. They have been allowed to occupy only a small fraction of the social and political space in the Jaycees organization. Men have maintained the boundaries structurally and symbolically. We shall see in the next chapter that when they admit women in any numbers it has been to watch, admire, and facilitate but not to stand beside men as their equals.

The threat that women are seen to pose to the integrity of men's territory and, at the same time, men's ability to maintain the sphere as their own, was demonstrated by the manner in which one woman was forced to surrender her membership of the Jaycees Club. The woman was believed to be having affairs with at least two male members. However, the men who were believed to be sexually involved with the woman were apparently not confronted with the suspicion nor was any attempt made to encourage them to leave the organization. One of the members who instigated the exclusion of the offending woman acknowledged the inconsistency in standard but explained it in this way:

It is rough justice to freeze her out. But she has not been in the club for long while Tom and Harry have been giving good service to the club for many years and will continue to do so in the future. We cannot afford to lose them.

The person whose job it was to implement the exclusion of the woman was a man—the president of the club at the time—but the pressure for the exclusion came from at least one woman member. It was the woman who had to go because the club remained men's territory to which a few women had been admitted more on sufferance than as men's equals.

The handling of this matter demonstrated the superior power of men and the patriarchal quality of club activities. It reaffirmed some of the values on which the superordination of men and subordination of women are based. The contribution of men is viewed as superior to that of women so their membership could not be sacrificed (see Ch. 8). Women are more responsible for protecting the sanctity of marriage and protecting the nuclear family than men. They are judged primarily on their effectiveness as home-makers, wives and mothers (see Ch. 8). Good women abide by the code of respectability. Nor do they threaten marriages by playing around with other women's husbands. The two men believed to be sexually involved with this woman were married. One of the key participants in the move to rid the club of the woman said, 'The two men we think are having an affair with X are married with young families. If we moved against them in any way it could put the happiness of two families at risk and that is not justified.'[8]

It is presumed that a woman is more able to exercise control over her sexual impulses than a man and it is her task to discourage any sexual advances. Whereas a woman will be sanctioned for breaching the code of respectability—an intrinsic element of the culture of femininity—men will be treated more leniently. They may escape punishment because their behaviour is not a marked deviation from the culture of masculinity. After all, they are doing what comes naturally.

Patriarchy in the churches

It is commonplace for church leaders to reiterate the claim of St Paul that in Christ there is neither a male nor female (Galatians 3:28). The reality is that throughout their history the Smalltown churches, like secular organizations, have decided on the basis of gender who associates with whom in organizations, who occupies positions of leadership, whose participation is always or usually restricted to subordinate activities, and so forth.

Smalltown possesses five churches, but the primary focus in this account is on the two major Protestant churches: the Anglican and the Uniting. The Roman Catholic Church receives less attention because of my much more limited exposure to this denomination's activities and the parish priest's reluctance to participate in the research.[9]

Single-sex organizations have always been more plentiful than mixed-sex ones in the churches and women's organizations usually more plentiful than men's. During the 1980s there were three women's organizations in the Uniting Church and one in the Anglican, all of which played a supporting role in church life. Neither church had a men's group during either the 1970s and 1980s, although in the mid-1980s an Anglican priest tried unsuccessfully to establish one. Only very occasionally has there been a social group for both sexes. Men have been more reluctant than women to participate in mixed activities associated with the churches. At any Sunday service far more women attend church without husbands than with them and very few men attend without their wives.

There is a patriarchal quality to much of the life of the churches. For instance, the two leading Protestant churches use marriage ties to incorporate women into the religious oganization itself, although in principle membership of each of these churches is viewed as an individual matter based on baptism, confession of faith, and confirmation. In reality, there is a strong tendency to view it as a family matter. So, instead of a woman's name apppearing on the roll by itself, it is bracketed with that of her husband: Mr John and Mrs Mary Smith. In some instances during the period of our field-work, the person responsible for keeping the roll in these churches added the name of a woman who had just married a male member, even though the woman had not previously been a member of that denomination and without her necessarily going through a service of confirmation. In other words, her marriage ensured her formal incorporation in the church as a matter of course because her primary status in the eyes of the local church and its officers and members, as well as of community members generally, was that of the wife of Mr Brown or Smith. In conversation she is more likely to be referred to as Mrs John Brown than as Mrs Mary Brown.

The patriarchal quality of church life is also reflected in the fact that in Smalltown as elsewhere men usually dominate the leadership of the churches. First, throughout the century or more that the major Christian denominations have operated in this community only one woman has served in the clergy of any one of the three largest churches: Roman Catholic, Anglican and Uniting. The woman was well received by her congregation, however she reported that her gender prevented her emulating her male clerical colleagues who achieved a high community profile by playing a leadership role in several prestigious secular organizations comprised mainly or exclusively of men. There were no women's organizations with comparable status or influence.

Second, men have maintained their control of the churches in the face of a steady decline in the numbers of men attending worship. When we began our observations in Smalltown in 1973, men comprised about one-third of regular worshippers in the Anglican Church. By the second half of the 1980s they comprised about one-eighth. The decline in men's support for the Uniting Church has not been as great but it has still been considerable: in 1974 men comprised 40 to 45 per cent of the worshippers in the congregations of the two churches that came together to form the Uniting Church in 1977. By 1985 male membership of the Uniting Church was down to between 30 and 35 per cent. Yet, although by that time the great majority of Protestant churchgoers were women, they comprised only one-third of the membership of the Uniting Parish Council (its board of management) and about one-quarter of the members of the Anglican Vestry (its board of management). Two of the four women's organizations referred to earlier existed primarily to raise money to hand over to these committees to dispense.

The church's rituals are also used at times to reaffirm the partriarchal boundaries prevailing in Smalltown. On one occasion this was evident at a service held in the Anglican Church in the first half of the 1980s. The purpose of the service—called 'The Blessing of the Plough'—was to ask for God's support for the community's farming activity. Wives support their husbands in the running of their farms and they provide male heirs who will eventually succeed husbands as farmers. However, farmers are men and farming land is transmitted from father to son rather than to daughters (see Ch. 7). Yet only two or three retired or semi-retired farmers and one middle-aged farmer were present at this religious service, no young farmer attended, and most of the congregation were middle-aged and elderly women. All of them knew many farmers and a number were the wives of retired farmers or the widows of farmers. Although the women were at the time (and still are) excluded by men from the economic activity that more than any other serves as the material basis of patriarchy in this community it was they who participated in the ritual activities. Their menfolk were busy elsewhere: some were farming, some were participating in their regular Sunday game of bowls, golf, or tennis, and some were possibly having a quiet drink with a few mates. As is so often the case women see to the family duties, including attending church, while the men engage in the activities that set them apart and justify describing Smalltown as a man's town. Knowingly or not, in this instance, the women were helping legitimate an economic activity and a way of life that is so inequitable to members of their gender. In so doing they were inferiorizing members of their own gender.

Maintaining the boundaries in leisure activities

When we asked participants in the Gender Survey which men would feel at home in Smalltown the responses most frequently offered made reference to sport or drinking, especially in the pubs, or both.

Interviewer: What kind of men are going to feel at home in Smalltown?

Respondents: The men into bowls and beer!
Men who love sport.
The sports-minded man.
Men like my husband who love fishing and shooting.

Respondents were four times more likely to say that a man who was interested in sport would feel at home in this community than to make such a statement about a woman. More than one-third of respondents mentioned sport or drink in the answers they gave to the open-ended question aimed at eliciting the characteristics of the man who is likely to feel at home in Smalltown.[10] Not one respondent said that a woman who drank would feel at home. Rather, a number offered the observation that a woman who was fond of drink would feel out of it in this community. Only 6 per cent of the respondents said that an interest in sport would help a woman feel at home in Smalltown.

The prevalence of the view that this was a town for the sports-loving and drinking man was also reflected in answers offered to the question: 'What kind of man is *not* going to feel at home?'

Respondents: The man who isn't into sport and doesn't like mixing.
Those who appreciate culture a bit more.
The non-drinker.

Drinking

Of course this is a man's town: have you ever seen so many pubs in such a small place? They've got their mates to drink with . . . any man will always find someone in the bar he knows to drink with even if he goes to the pub by himself. Men have got it made (65-year-old wife of retired tradesman).

The critical role that drinking plays in the segregation of the sexes and in affirming men's superior status and rights was highlighted at a public farewell in 1984 for the town clerk of Smalltown. It took the form of a dance in the town hall followed by supper and speeches. For most of the night there were only a dozen or so couples on the floor, but there were about eighty women, most of whom were married or widowed, and about ten or so men sitting on chairs placed around the walls. The dance band was on the stage. Where were the rest of the men? Just off the dance hall there was an ante-room which was furnished with a bar. Behind the bar stood two council employees who continually served beer throughout the night to about fifty men. Most of these men did not venture into the hall except for the speeches and the presentation. Few of the women in the hall went into the ante-room. At any time during the night there were no more than two or three women near the bar. There was no wine provided; beer was the only alcoholic beverage and it was served by men. The supper—which was for men and women—was served by women.

Whatever the occasion, beer is provided for the men, and usually the men separate from the women to drink it. Attend a shower tea in one of the community's halls and almost certainly there will be a barrel of beer installed in a small room at the back of the hall or, if there is no ante-room, in a 'ute' parked outside. The men will spend most of the time gathered around the keg while the women participate in the official function.

When men retreat to the space allocated for drinking, customs regulating the behaviour of women make it extremely difficult for them to take the initiative and pass through the door into what has been defined for the night as men's territory. As Imray and Middleton (1983) have shown, it is men's privilege to mark the boundaries and keep women outside, and women must accept it, however grudgingly.

In the mid-1980s a ball was held to commemorate the establishment of local government in the rural section of the community. The organizers refused to provide beer on the grounds that it had not been available on the occasion they were commemorating. Many of the husbands were upset by the decision, resisted their wives' urgings to participate in the dancing, and adjourned to the bar of one of the nearby pubs for much of the evening. Only two or three wives summoned the courage to cross the threshold of the bar to plead with their husbands to return to the dance. As well as being daunted from going into the bar by the 'men only' character of the space, the wives were discouraged by the community's standard of respectability which has traditionally affirmed that good wives and mothers do not visit a hotel bar.[11]

Men are not impeded by any norm of respectability. As in numerous other social contexts in Australia there are those men in Smalltown who drink to get drunk, and many drink excessively. This behaviour is tolerated in a male. In some circles a younger male enhances his social esteem in the eyes of his peers by boasting about the number of drinks he has 'downed' and the number of times he 'threw up' (vomited) during a heavy bout of drinking. Pub drinking is a favourite activity for men of all classes and ages. 'There's seven of 'em in a town of this size!' This is a common expression of both men and women, although men are likely to say it with a certain amount of pride whereas women state it with a note of dismayed astonishment. Men are also prone to point out that there is more beer consumed per head of population in Smalltown than in any other centre in the state. Whether or not this is true there is no doubt about the popularity of pub drinking among men of both the working and the middle classes. It is one of the main cultural activities maintaining a male solidarity that transcends class distinctions.

Until the mid-1980s local women, single or married, did not enter the public bar of any of the town's seven hotels. The only women residing in the town—as opposed to those passing through—who up till that time challenged this community norm were transient professional women, or the wives of men in professional or managerial positions. All challenges were, sooner or later, unsuccessful. For example, when in the second half of the 1970s four women schoolteachers entered a public bar, they were ordered by the hotelier to leave. The opposition to women going into public bars is, in part, an extension of a community norm permitting women to drink only in strict moderation. Any woman who drinks to excess will be stigmatized as a drunk—even if she only does so very occasionally—and, as was pointed out in the previous chapter, possibly as a sexually available woman.

In the 1990s it is becoming more common for single women to drink in the public bar. But in the 1980s a common practice was for young women to drink quietly in the lounge while their boyfriends drank and talked in the nearby bar as long as they chose to. When the young men had finished drinking they departed via the lounge where the young women were waiting. As the men passed they motioned to the women to follow.

The popularity of hotels as a gathering place for young people is understandable because, as everyone acknowledges, there is little for adolescents to do in Smalltown. There are no cinemas and no youth club rooms; the coffee shops are shut in the evenings; there are several milk bars but they offer no seating. There is often a disco held on a Saturday night, but it is patronized almost exclusively by the younger teenagers and pre-adolescents, and it is strictly supervised: once inside you are not allowed out. The pubs are the only regular public venue where people can gather in reasonable comfort to talk. As we have seen, these are mainly male domains and even in the 1990s, when more single women are venturing into the pubs, more often than not drinking is segregated.

A few married women may be seen in two or three public bars on a Friday or a Saturday night but almost invariably they are accompanied by their husbands. Women who come without a male escort, especially if they are married, run the risk of being described as 'women on the make', that is, women after someone else's man (see Whitehead, 1976). They may be severely sanctioned for their behaviour. For example, the wife of a professional man who adopted the practice of drinking every Friday afternoon in the public bar of one of the town's hotels with some working-class men received so much criticism from men and women of her own class that she eventually stopped and, partly for this reason, left the town.

Husbands stated that, if necessary, they would forbid their wives to go to the pub (see also Green *et al.*, 1987a: 85–6), partly to protect the family reputation. But there is rarely any need for husbands to control their wives because, as our interviewing indicates, the great majority of Smalltown women 'would not be seen dead in a hotel bar'. Women are, in fact, prisoners of a code of respectability they have been socialized to live by and which the community continues to impose on them. As Green *et al.* point out: 'Once identified as primarily wives, mothers and daughters, women's sexual identities and social behaviour must conform to an acceptable norm' (1987a:80–1). This makes it easy for men to control women (Hey, 1986:35) and, in this instance, to restrict their invasion of what men perceive to be one of the few remaining all-male havens. As Stanley (1981, cited by Deem, 1987b) notes, it is not uncommon for women who visit such facilities to be made to feel very uncomfortable, which ensures that most are too intimidated to use them at all. Despite the presence on a couple of nights a week of a few married women (accompanied by their husbands) and some single women, most pub drinking in the 1990s is still segregated on the basis of gender. The vast majority of Smalltown wives still never enter a public bar.

As well as functioning as men's social space the public bars remain significant symbols of a masculinity which pervades all institutional areas of Smalltown life. Here there are obvious parallels with English pubs which are important, says Smith, 'in continuing to construct a separate male and female culture' (Smith, 1987 cited by Deem, 1987a:4).

Sport

Smalltown is definitely a man's town: look at all the sporting activities it offers. If they don't want to play there's plenty to watch and talk about over a few drinks (43-year-old schoolteacher).

For men, drinking and sport usually go hand in hand. Much of the Smalltown sporting activity segregates the sexes and also helps sustain separate male and female cultures, often in a manner that inferiorizes women. Females as well as males play sport in what many locals acknowledge is a sports-mad town. In the winter the competitive sports include football, netball, table tennis, hockey, badminton, squash, indoor cricket, and golf, and in the summer cricket, swimming, bowls, tennis, and basketball.

A study we made of the leisure activities of secondary-school pupils showed that males were much more likely to be playing sport, especially competitive sport, than females.[12] Nevertheless, before marriage, many girls play sport. Just over one-quarter of the girls in our survey stated they played competitive sport on a Saturday. Many girls indicated they played two or more sports. For instance, one girl reported that in the summer she swam and played tennis competitively each weekend and played competitive basketball during the week. In the winter she would train twice a week for netball and play the game on the weekend. Badminton occupied her on two other nights and about every second Sunday. Her rate of participation was high but not unique. Her brother's participation in competitive sport was just as high, but not exceptional for a male. During the winter season he trained two to three nights a week for football and played in the Saturday competition. He also played competitive badminton one night and every second weekend, and occasionally indoor cricket. In summer he attended cricket practice three times a week, played junior cricket on Saturday mornings and perhaps 'filled in' in the afternoon for senior cricket. Because he also participated in competitive swimming he would train with the swimming club every night and swim in a carnival in another town once or twice a month following his Saturday morning game of cricket.

The gender difference in rates of participation widens with marriage and especially with the arrival of children (Deem, 1982). Women have to schedule their leisure to fit in with child care and domestic responsibilities. Often these are incompatible with participation in organized sport. Men as a rule do not have to curtail drastically their sporting activities when they become fathers. Many males go on competing as though there had been no change in their domestic circumstances: it is their prerogative as the family breadwinners. Hence women's references to sport as one of the qualities that distinguishes Smalltown as a man's town.

Smalltown is a community which has no cinema or theatre, only two coffee shops and three restaurants, a couple of clothing shops, and (only recently) a municipal library. Yet, as well as the seven pubs, it posesses a thoroughbred club and race track, a pacing track and club, a football field, a hockey ground, netball and basketball courts, sixteen lawn tennis courts and several hardcourts, squash, badminton, table tennis, indoor cricket and indoor bowls facilities, a large stadium, three lawn bowls clubs, a croquet club, a golf club, a clay pigeon shooting range, angling club, pony club, etc. It is surrounded by bush where men ferret, shoot, and fish.

Bryson points out that in Australia men control virtually all sport (1990). The pattern prevails in Smalltown where men control or have first call on probably more than three-quarters of the facilities available for recreation. They control racing, pacing, football, cricket, tennis, and golf: these are all expensive sports grounds to install and maintain and those that demand the most territory dedicated to recreation in this community.[13] Men predominate in the town's sports stadium where women and men play table tennis, basketball, badminton, squash, and indoor cricket. The ability of males to control Smalltown's sporting activities and facilities is reflected in the information presented in Table 3.1. It shows the gender composition of the community's leading sporting bodies and the gender of the president in 1991.[14] There are many mixed-gender sporting

Table 3.1 Committee composition of the community's leading sporting clubs

Committee	Males N	Females N	President
Cricket club	8	2	Male
Football club	20	4	Male
Golf club	9	2	Male
Pacing club	14	0	Male
Racing club	15	4	Male
Stadium committee	7	4	Male

clubs in Smalltown but I do not know of any instance where a woman is a president of a sporting club to which men belong. This is not surprising given the partriarchal character of the organization of this community.

The mixed sporting activities of Smalltown include badminton, squash, tennis, competitive swimming, golf, and bowling. Yet in many of these activities segregated rather than integrated sport predominates (see Deem, 1987b: 425–6). Both sexes play golf on weekends but most competitive golf is played with members of one's own sex. As a rule, in tennis and badminton competitions, two out of three matches are with partners of the same sex against opponents of the same sex. In the township mixed social bowls are played one evening a week in summer, but there are separate bowling clubs for women and men, and single-sex competition bowls predominates.

The arrangements whereby men and women play most of their sport separately are long-standing; the origins are forgotten. The most common response when we ask why things are done this way is something of this nature: 'That's the way it has always been done'. Also common, however, are responses which indicate that the arrangement is more often an expression of men's will than of women's. For example, women report that they are eager to increase the number of golf and bowling events they play with the men but the men resisted.[15] Men golfers and bowlers claim that the women's inferior play reduces the quality of their play and the women's presence interferes with them fully enjoying themselves.

Women's subordination: a case study of football

By far the biggest sporting attraction is football: a man's game. I intend therefore to use it to show how men's recreational interests take centre stage, how women are in part excluded, and in part admitted, but only as supporters. In a later section I will show that they are often expected to facilitate men's activities by placing their domestic skills at men's disposal.

An analysis of diaries, of a week's activities, provided by all 156 secondary-school pupils aged fourteen and older attending the town's two secondary schools on a particular day provides evidence of how early male dominance in and through football is established. The diaries of these adolescents, whose average age was fifteen-and-a-half showed that 92 per cent of boys played football and 80 per cent of girls watched it on a Saturday. Only 28 per cent of the girls reported playing any sport on a Saturday. The sports most likely to be played by girls were hockey and netball. Not one boy reported watching a girl's sport. In the 1990s girls said that very few boys watch or comment on their sporting activities. 'There's all sorts of resistance if you attempt to get a boyfriend along to a game of hockey or basketball but he's really hurt if you don't watch him play football. It's just assumed you will and we *all* do!' (18-year-old). During the winter months football dominates Saturday and it is the topic of conversation for much of the week. The under-16-year-olds play in the morning watched by parents, sisters and girlfriends and then frequently the whole family attends the senior game on a Saturday afternoon. Of course, only men or boys play football and only they fully understand it. So men stand at the fence yelling advice and abuse at players while most of the girls and women sit apart. They are there to cheer their heroes on: praise them after a victory and console them after a defeat. Only male spectators participate in the 'huddle' at the end of each quarter when the coach berates or coaxes his team, and only males accompany the team into the dressing shed at half-time and after the game is over.

The Smalltown football teams participate in a district competition; so do the women netballers and hockey players. The women play netball and hockey in the same towns on the same days as the men's teams play football.

The women's games finish early enough to allow girlfriends and wives of the footballers to watch the second half of the senior team's match.

Saturday night is a big drinking night for many of the football players, usually in the public bar of one of the Smalltown hotels. Now (that is in the 1990s) some of the wives and girlfriends may be present but it has traditionally been a male affair. On Sunday morning only men—players, committee members, and some stalwart supporters—gather at the club to drink and talk football.

Football is *the* topic of conversation at school or work or wherever people meet casually throughout the coming week. During the 'footy season' the boys kick a football around the playground at school while the girls sit and talk. The club holds a mid-week practice which some of the staunchest male supporters may watch. Interest and preoccupation increases as Saturday approaches: this is the highlight of the week.

An analysis of the reported conversations of more than 200 Smalltown couples with their friends shows that men's sport—particularly football— and work are the common topics of conversation when men and women are together. Displaying an intense interest in the game of football facilitates acceptance for a male newcomer to Smalltown but playing it well assures that he will be an instant celebrity.

A working-class football star will gain entry to social circles and friendships normally closed to members of his class. Local people acknowledge this. Footballers are the only people paid to play a sport in this community. To attract the right player or coach (a part-time position) the football club will organize a job for him in the town. Participants in the Status Survey most frequently mentioned three qualities facilitating the acceptance of newcomers to Smalltown: being friendly, being prepared to join in town activities, and an ability to play sport, especially football.

'They might say about a woman who comes to Smalltown that she's a good hockey player, *but* if a man who moves here is a good footballer that is really something' (45-year-old tradesman). There was no mention in this survey of a woman's status being affected by her excelling at handicrafts, acting, playing a musical instrument, and so forth.

Other recreational activities

Sport is what it is all about here. Saturday is given over totally to it. It seems as though the whole town plays. So if you are not into sport—and I'm not at all interested—you are out in the cold and you feel it (35-year-old wife of a transient professional).

For those wanting something other than sport the Arts Council organizes one or two classical concerts each year and performs a play most years. There are several book-reading groups operating in the town, but the women complain that men will not attend. A man who is 'heavily' into serious literature and music, especially if it is at the expense of masculine activities—drinking, fishing, football, etc.—may be viewed as 'a bit of a poof'. Such men have reported that they feel 'out of things' in the town because they neither drink nor play sport.[16]

Participants in the Gender Survey were twice as likely to report that women rather than men were disadvantaged by the community's lack of entertainment. The facilities that were most missed as far as women were concerned were cinemas, theatres and concerts. Hardly any women and no man saw these disadvantages as offsetting the marked advantages Smalltown was supposed to offer women, namely the opportunity for an easy-going, friendly life-style, and an outstanding physical and social environment in which to raise their children. In the light of these findings it is not surprising that women who are perceived to be too dependent on what are caricatured as leisure activities for 'city types' are strongly criticized. Single women schoolteachers who frequently spend a weekend in the city are subjected to this type of criticism. 'Smalltown is not a town for the high fliers, for girls looking for a fling. It's a town for those girls who like an easy-going rural life-style and for whom family is important: it's a family town (40-year-old woman clerk). There is, in fact, little that faintly resembles 'high-flying' in Smalltown. There is likely to be a dinner dance or cabaret held three or four times a year. Women are keener than men on such activities and will take the initiative in organizing several of their friends to persuade their husbands to attend so that they can 'make up a table'. For their part, however, men will not willingly forfeit one of their prized sporting activities with their mates, such as a weekend's duck shooting, for a dinner dance or a cabaret.

Of the three restaurants in Smalltown, two are attached to motels. The view seems to be that attending a restaurant is an activity reserved for very special occasions: birthdays, engagements, wedding anniversaries, etc. The alternative to a restaurant meal is a counter tea at one of the pubs in the main street. The women are probably keener on the 'counter meal' than their menfolk. It is one of the few ways of getting out for an evening's entertainment. Some husbands view taking their wives for a counter tea as a major concession. One man who, during an interview, was quite defensive about his practice of preferring the company of his mates to that of his wife said rather triumphantly, 'I take her for a counter tea at the Palace at least once a month and I tell her to order the best drink in the house!' Although wives may welcome the night out for a counter tea, it is not such a great treat. The food is adequate but the menus are limited and rarely change. Frequently husbands abandon their wives for the company of mates in the bar at least for a part of the night and the wives are left to make conversation among themselves.[17] One of the pubs occasionally hires a dance band and another occasionally stages a disco.

The only assured entertainment is a juke box with video attachment and the billiard-like game of kelley pool. This too is a men's game. Each pub sports a men-only pool team which competes with the teams from the other pubs.

Informal interaction and friendship

The segregation and the subordination of women also occurs in the area of personal friendship and informal interaction. More than 95 per cent of the friendships reported by participants in the Friendship Survey were with members of the same sex. With only a handful of exceptions, cross-sex friendships were restricted to friends of one's marriage partner. In Smalltown, interaction with a friend of the opposite sex should only occur in the presence of one's partner. The local norms supporting these practices, however, apply more to women than to men. Hence it is permissible for a man to attend a mixed social function without his wife and to dance with the wives of his male friends, but it is unacceptable for women to do the same thing. Even when attending a social function in the company of her husband, a woman must be more cautious about the amount of time she spends talking to her husband's mates than her husband has to be about talking to her women friends. Any protracted conversation with a man may spark off the rumour that she is chasing him.

Women, it seems, are anxious to spend time in the company of males and will seek ways to break down the gender segregation that occurs so frequently, but within the social parameters set by the norms governing female respectability. To achieve this end they will organize card evenings in their homes, or have friends around for dinner, or 'get up' a table for a dinner dance. They prefer dinner dances to ordinary dances because the seating arrangements guarantee their partner's company, and that of their friends' partners for much of the evening. Men's company is guaranteed because drinking is done at the dinner table whereas at an ordinary dance men can escape to a bar. For similar reasons women enjoy card evenings and private dinner parties to larger social gatherings because at the latter it is more likely that the men will segregate themselves.

Notwithstanding the resistance of women, the segregation occurring at the football, the pub, and the occasional ball occurs in many other social contexts and among men and women of all ages. One 35-year-old tradesman explained how it happens: 'At any social function you walk in—someone throws a glass of beer in your hand and you end up keeping with the blokes for the evening.' Whether it is after church, down the main street, or during recreational activities, such as any afternoon at the Elderly Citizens Club, the practice is likely to occur. For instance, at the Elderly Citizens Club men and women play cards or carpet bowls together but when they stop for afternoon tea the men go to tables separate from the women.

Our surveying, as well as our casual conversations, showed that longstanding members of the community are conscious of the tradition and their participation in it. In the Gender Survey only 6 per cent of the 109 respondents said that at a social function they spend more time talking to a member of the opposite sex than to a member of their own sex, whereas 70 per cent of the women respondents and 67 per cent of the men said that they talked mainly or exclusively to members of their own sex.[18]

The segregation is more often than not of men's doing. For instance, some of the elderly men say they go to a separate table at the Elderly Citizens Club because they need some time to themselves. Smalltown is a community where members of both sexes 'joke' about the attempts of men to escape from women, and from women's attempts to trap them into shared outings and conversations. Hence, it is not surprising that the Gender Survey revealed much more support for the idea that men prefer the company of men to that of women, than that women prefer the company of women to that of men.[19] 'Men don't want to listen to women talking all the time about kids, their ailments, and whatever . . . so we just switch off or slip away' (33-year-old clerk). Because of the value they place on men's company, women will often go to considerable lengths to try to ensure that they gain access. The practice of organizing a table at a dinner dance is one example of this. Another is the propensity of women to allow men to dominate informal conversations. Many women defer in this manner at official functions, parties, in hotel lounges, and at informal gatherings of friends in a private home. Some women respondents made the observation during the course of an interview or a conversation, that any woman who is worth her salt is skilled in holding a man's attention by focusing the conversation on his interests.

Two-thirds of the women participating in the Status Survey reported that the conversations they have with women change, if men join them, to topics of interest to the men. However, only one-third of the male respondents reported that their conversations change if they are joined by women. Usually men keep talking about 'men's affairs' and the women play the role of listeners. The things men discuss include work, sport, politics, the relative merits of different makes of cars, trucks and tractors. Some of the more confident women will make the occasional comment and they may be listened to if 'they speak up on a subject they know something about'. Otherwise they will probably be ignored or talked down. 'Who's going to listen to what a woman's got to say about the relative merits of various brands of chemical spray, or of Mercedes trucks as opposed to say Volvo trucks?' (56-year-old farmer). On the other hand if men join a group of women, the women will break off their conversation and change the topic to one they know will interest the men. A lifetime experience of caring for, and deferring to, men encourages this behaviour. Our analysis of the reported content of women's conversations reveals that sport and men's work are three times as likely to be discussed if men join women than if the women talk by themselves.

In these ways women become accomplices in the inferiorization processes which help maintain men's superordination. Men's ideological hegemony was made explicit in the responses we were given when we asked residents to explain why things worked out this way. Women, as well as men, frequently expressed the view that women's activities are inferior to men's activities (see Ch. 8).

In the light of such ideological hegemony it is not surprising that men succeed in using women to facilitate their major leisure and status-enhancing activities, and that when women participate in men's activities it is usually as their supporters and subordinates rather than as their equals. The next chapter demonstrates how marriage serves as the mechanism for incorporating women into the leisure activities of men both individually and collectively.

CHAPTER 4

Married to the game

In her book *Married to the Job*, Janet Finch (1983) demonstrates how the paid work of both working-class and middle-class men structures and constrains the lives of their wives. In this chapter I show that the leisure and status-enchancing activities, as well as the paid work of husbands, shape the lives of their wives. In Smalltown wives are expected to free husbands for play and they are as obliged to present them 'fit for play' as they are to present them fit for work. Husbands also pressure wives to serve as additional players and to provide what Finch (1983) calls 'back-up' services for their own leisure activities and those of the men's groups and clubs to which they belong. The husbands view the latter as altruistic activities—which in part they are—but they are also opportunities for husbands to cover themselves in glory while enjoying the company of other men unhampered by 'a wife and kids'.

Wives are incorporated in the leisure, public-service and status-seeking activities of men of all classes, but the most demanding marriages are to men holding down leadership positions in one or more of the town's sporting, political or public-service organizations. These male leaders are nearly always drawn from the middle class. This chapter demonstrates that the incorporation of wives in many of their husbands' leisure and service activities often occurs at the expense of the leisure activities of the wives themselves. As

Roth (1963:112–14, cited by Finch, 1983:24) shows, in family life there are a series of overlapping and interacting timetables. These are generated by a husband's work, the children's needs, a wife's work, a husband's leisure, a wife's leisure, and so forth. But, as several British feminists have shown, the impact of the leisure timetable of a man on his wife is, as a rule, much greater than the impact of her leisure timetable on his.[1] For instance, in her account of the lives of a sample of young British women Griffin observes: 'Women are an integral part of men's leisure, as 'escorts' whether paid or unpaid, or in relation to the myriad ways in which women must present and construct themselves for men, both materially and psychologically (1981:122 cited by Deem, 1986:13).

The relationships that husbands establish individually or collectively with their wives about the husband's leisure activities are so palpably one-sided that we are justified in describing them as exploitative. Exploitation entails what Ossowski describes as 'Constant compulsory labour "for someone else's benefit" ' (1963:26), or what Delphy describes as gratuitous labour (1976:80). In the present context, the unpaid labour of a woman rather than of a man is compulsory, constant, and, by and large, for particular others (see Ch. 5). Exploitation entails an unequal exchange; both partners do not benefit equally. In the present study exploitation occurs if the labour of one party is used to enhance the resources, prestige or recreational activities of another without adequate reciprocity (Barbalet, 1982:490; Macpherson, 1973:53–4).

The domestic labour of wives plays a key role in the exploitative processes.[2] It frequently creates a leisure gap between marital partners which almost invariably works to the advantage of husbands and to the detriment of wives.[3] This study shows that a substantial part of the domestic labour wives perform feeds directly into the leisure activity of husbands and into the performance of their 'good works'.

Free and fit for play

Wives free their husbands for play. The marriage relationship is predicated on the assumption that a husband's claim to leisure is superior to a wife's. 'Men see leisure as a right; women do not and are not encouraged by men to do so' (Deem, 1986:13). Smalltowners of both sexes believe that because a husband is the family's principal or sole breadwinner a wife should happily surrender his companionship and free him from domestic duties and child care so that he can engage in recreational activities, especially ones away from the home.[4]

Men do not perform domestic duties so that their wives can engage in leisure activities, although, on occasions, men mind children so that women can engage in leisure activity. Usually they only do so if the child care does not interfere with their own work or regular recreation pastimes.[5] Edgell (1980), Bryson (1984), Pleck (1985), and others affirm that the division of labour facilitates freeing husbands for leisure while inhibiting the leisure activities of wives (see also McRae, 1986; and Griffin *et al.*, 1982).[6]

As well as presenting husbands fit for work wives also present them fit for play. It is a wife's responsibility to cook, and it is a short step from cooking a roast for a husband to sit down to at the dining table to cooking a casserole for him to take for a 'stag's night' at his club. Wives feed husbands before and after their game of golf or cricket, or their evening at the service club. They send along their afternoon tea for their game of tennis, cricket, or bowls. Wives wash and iron and there is no demarcation zone between a man's work clothes and his leisure gear. Wives provide them with clean and pressed cricket or bowling flannels, or shirt and tie. It is also a wife's responsibility to ensure that a husband's physical needs are met after play: that there is a clean change of clothes and a meal ready to eat when he returns exhausted at the end of a day's play; perhaps unfit for anything but 'a good feed and a beer followed by a sleep in front of the TV'.

Ensuring that a husband is fit to play, and caring for him after he has played, entails a woman being available at irregular hours to provide a range of services on demand (Deem, 1982). These may include a rushed ironing job for a game of tennis that a husband forgot to mention; sewing a missing button on a cricket shirt; providing refreshments for a husband to take to a special function at his service club, and so forth.

Lending moral support

In her study of the incorporation of wives in their husband's paid work, Finch shows that wives are expected to facilitate their husband's work by lending their moral support. In a similar fashion Smalltown husbands expect their wives to lend moral support to their leisure activities and 'good works'. A wife should listen attentively as her husband recounts last week's sporting triumph: the boundary that clinched the game for the team or the glorious three iron he hit onto the fourteenth green. She is expected to be attentive as he foretells in detail the crucial part he will play in his team's winning next Saturday's football match. Wives report that husbands often assume that they will lend moral support by attending the performance itself: the one-day cricket match, the pennant bowls final, 'the change-over dinner' when a husband is installed in an executive position in his club, etc. Wives who fail to attend may be rebuked and have to cope with a sulky partner.

Wives bring their expressive and supportive skills to bear in the face of sporting losses or unhappy outcomes to other status-seeking pursuits. They are usually expected to tend the wounds acquired in the pursuit of glory and care for the husband who has drunk to excess. Sometimes these activities demand exceptional behaviour on the part of wives. For instance, I and other researchers witnessed a young wife speaking in reassuring tones to her drunken husband as she struggled to get him into a car parked outside a pub; he was too drunk to manage the manoeuvre unaided. Providing support of the kind just described is not something most Smalltown wives ever do. However, in meeting the expectation that they will facilitate the play or 'good works' of a husband, wives frequently perform extraordinary feats. On a number of occasions I have been present in a home where a scene of the following kind was being acted out. The wife prepares a Saturday lunch while her husband and teenage sons watch a cricket or tennis match on television. She moves repeatedly between the stove and the ironing board so that the cricket gear will look fine for the afternoon's game. Following the meal she transports one of the sons to his competition game. The husband departs for his game and she returns to clear away the dishes and wash up. Then she prepares a plate of savouries which she takes to the ground her husband is playing at in time for afternoon tea. Often this hectic and demanding routine occurs at the end of a week in which the wife herself has been out at paid work.

Serving as additional 'players'

Men view women as inferior players of most sports and they avoid playing with them if possible. When questioned on this matter husbands repeatedly made the following type of comment. 'You just can't play the game seriously when women are around and you can't be as free in what you say.' Yet wives may be called upon to participate in a range of social activities that require a female partner, especially those activities staged by their men's organization. These activities include musical evenings, 'change-over dinners' and lectures by visiting speakers. These are occasional events usually staged by organizations—such as the Rotary and Lions Clubs—which exclude wives from their regular meetings. This pattern highlights the exploitative character of the incorporation of wives in their husbands' leisure activities, and the implementation of the process of inferiorization. The women are admitted in order to witness the display of men's achievements and superiority.

Supporting the main players

While incorporation in the leisure activities of husbands affects the lives of virtually all wives it probably has the greatest impact on the wives of men in leadership positions in the town's major organizations, including the service clubs, the Town Council, and the Shire Council. The incorporation and exploitation of these wives is facilitated by the prestige of such organizations and the widely held view that many of their activities are morally worthy. For example, when, during the course of the Community Survey, respondents were asked to nominate the organizations they believed were doing the most for the community, more than 90 per cent of the nominations went to the men's service clubs. The more prestigious or morally worthy the role of a husband in leading organizations the more pressure is applied to his wife to play a 'help meet' role (Finch, 1983:86).

In Smalltown recreational leaders and service club organizers are expected to be always available. Consequently spontaneous visits and phone calls penetrate the privacy of the homes of such leaders, ensuring the incorporation of their wives in their leisure activities in an open-ended and sometimes demanding manner. As Young and Wilmott point out, the telephone provides 'a means of trespass': in this instance between a man's sporting and service club activities and his home (1973:167).

There are other technological devices that serve as 'means of trespass' in Smalltown. For example, several members of the golf club committee have burglar alarm extensions to their homes from the club to signal an illegal entry. Some husbands interfere with their families' timetables and often their leisure activities by holding committee meetings for their club in the lounge room of the family home. Their wives often hold meetings at home, but they are more likely to do so during the day or on evenings that do not inconvenience their spouses.

All wives provide what Finch (1983:94) calls 'back-up services' for their husband's leisure activities but leaders' wives are expected to provide a comprehensive and demanding range of such services. These wives are easily incorporated and exploited because so many of a leisure leader's activities occur within the home or are organized from the home. The back-up services provided include such things as: entertaining members of a husband's committee as they arrive and possibly providing supper at an appropriate point in the evening;[7] helping a husband construct the draw for a forthcoming sporting event; taking messages concerning who will play or who will be unable to attend a particular meeting; doing 'the banking' for his club; providing accommodation for members from other clubs 'paying a visit' to the Smalltown club; and using her home as a base for organizing the wives of other members to help with catering for a special event.

A woman who is married to a man who is the president of a service club or of any one of a number of leading sporting organizations, or who serves as a local government councillor, will be expected to accompany her husband to a wide range of social activities and civic functions. These expectations are usually held by the organization as well as by the husband. The activities she will be expected to attend include such things as the annual round of Christmas break-up parties staged by numerous Smalltown organizations, special community functions such as the opening of a library or the farewell to a prominent community member, and special functions of related clubs in other rural centres.

Attending the latter will often entail round trips that last several hours.

Wives frequently serve as 'sounding boards' for husbands who rehearse their plans to revamp their club, or who are devising tactics to get rid of an opponent. In some instances wives assist husbands to develop a strategy to handle a difficult situation that has arisen among members of a club's committee, or to help ensure that a husband does a good job as the incoming president of his club. There are husbands who reciprocate and provide moral support for the leisure or status-enhancing activities of wives, but husbands are less likely to provide the degree of support that wives customarily do. This is not surprising for, after all, wives *not* husbands are the designated carers and nurturers; there is not as much importance attached to their activities as to those of their menfolk, so the implicit assumption is that their activities are less deserving of support (see Ch. 8), and there is not a highly institutionalized role for husbands to play in the organized activities of wives.

The wife of a leisure leader may be expected to facilitate the success of a husband's leisure activity by both disseminating and collecting information that is useful to him. In a community with a small and stable population where people play where they live and work it is relatively easy for a wife to garner information concerning such things as the attitudes particular sectors of the community have to the activities of her husband's organization. This can be picked up as she goes about her weekly shopping, at school functions, during casual conversations in the main street and at meetings of her own organizations. Similarly, she can, if she chooses, feed the appropriate community grapevines with information her husband wants transmitted.

The provision of 'back-up' services for husbands who are leisure leaders goes still further. In Smalltown, male members of leading organizations often form close friendships with other members of their particular organizations. Their wives may be expected to form friendships with the wives of their husband's 'leisure friends'. The reverse also happens but, the data suggest, with considerably less frequency. For example, among the participants in the Gender Survey, 34 per cent of the wives were incorporated in some of the activities husbands engaged in with at least two of their three closest friends. By contrast, only 6 per cent of husbands were incorporated in any of the activities their wives engaged in with at least two of their three closest friends. Derivative friendship of this kind invariably puts at least some wives in situations where they have to engage in leisure activities that do not interest them and spend time with women with whom they feel no natural affinity or whom they may personally dislike. In the process wives may have their personal autonomy reduced.[8] The phenomenon is more common among members of the middle classes, especially farmers, businessmen and professionals. Married males of these classes are almost three times as likely as married working-class males to incorporate their wives in couple 'friendship' activities with their work or leisure associates (45 per cent compared with 16 per cent).

In the interests of presenting as balanced a picture as possible it needs to be stressed that wives of both middle-class and working-class men are not necessarily hapless victims of the leisure and mateship activities of their spouses. Discussions we had with women of the Gender Survey indicated that many and possibly most wives who were participating in couple relationships their husbands had initiated, were doing so willingly. Once these relationships were established some wives became friends in their own right with the wife of their husband's friend, and the women organized activities that brought the two couples together. Through this survey we also learnt of wives (it seems a small minority) who altogether resisted participation of the kind I have described, while others were selective about which of their husband's leisure friends (and the spouses of those friends) they had 'around to the house' or with whom they formed close relationships.

On occasion the incorporation of a wife by a male leader in activities designed to make a success of his term of office are taken to greater lengths than those already described: some husbands who are serving as presidents of sporting or charity organizations prevail upon their wives to accept a position as secretary or treasurer of the same organization. A spring 1990 edition of the *Smalltown News* carried the story that John Brownlow was again going to lead one of the local charity clubs. The article spoke at length of the tireless service he had given the club for many years. It made no reference to his wife other than to mention that she had been elected treasurer. This is a position she has held for a number of years of her husband's presidency.

The Brownlow situation is but one example of a long-standing tradition in Smalltown. For a number of years in the 1970s the wife of the president of the Elderly Citizens Club served as secretary of the club and in the late 1980s the wife of the president of the Table Tennis Club was elected as secretary of the club. In the same decade the wife of the president of the Smalltown Football Club served as the club's treasurer during her husband's term of office. The appointment of a wife as treasurer or as secretary is often viewed as a 'natural' extension of a husband's selection as president, but it does not necessarily mean that the wife participates in the same way as the males on the committee or that she is accepted as an equal. For instance, the wife of the president of the Football Club rarely, if ever, attended meetings. Instead she did the 'bookwork' at home. Adopting this approach allowed her to support her husband in his leisure activity without the job interfering with her child care. Her presence at the meetings (which at the time were held at one of the pubs) would have contaminated the male space and placed a dampener on the mateship activities of the men.

The wife of a leisure leader must give a public performance. She must be tastefully dressed, capable of engaging in interesting conversation with strangers, able to publicly thank other women for their help and support of her work on behalf of her husband's organization, and to do everything possible to make her husband's time in office highly successful. The social identity of such a woman is largely shaped by her husband's public status as a leading figure in Smalltown's community life. Because she is 'the wife of the president of the such and such club' she may be stopped in the street, or while shopping or attending a sporting event, and asked to relay messages to her husband. On occasion she has to listen to complaints about the administration of the organization he presides over. These are signs of her identity becoming an extension of his recreational or public service identity. The position of the wife of the mayor is an excellent example of this process. In Smalltown the mayor's position is voluntary and unpaid, but his wife has a highly institutionalized and also unpaid role to play. The title 'mayoress' symbolizes the level of institutionalization of the role of mayor's wife and accurately suggests that her public identity is an extension of his. Her social persona is at least partially submerged by his public persona. The same process occurs, if not usually to the same degree, to the wives of other public figures and recreational leaders.

Is incorporation in a man's leisure class-linked?

The women whose incorporation I have just discussed have been mainly the wives of men engaged in jobs at the higher end of the middle-class spectrum. In reality, wives of all classes are incorporated principally through providing domestic labour and moral support for their husbands' leisure activities. Similarly, wives of all classes work for the benefit of men's organizations. Working-class women, for example, participate in the fund-raising activities of the auxiliaries attached to the RSL (Returned Services League), the voluntary fire brigade, the brass band and the football club. The Community and Organizational Surveys indicated that middle-class men are ten times more likely than working-class men to hold committee positions in political, service and sporting organizations.[9] Consequently, it is more likely that a middle-class rather than a working-class wife will be incorporated in the public leisure activities and 'good works' of her husband and his friends or fellow club members.

Benefiting husbands collectively

Although wives are often excluded from the clubs and organizations their husbands belong to, their exclusion does not prevent the husbands and their fellow club members expecting wives (and often girlfriends and mothers) to use their skills as cooks, knitters, expert caterers and sewers to raise money for their organizations. The labour is provided free and is available when required. These clubs establish relationships with women which according to the criteria adopted in this study are as exploitative as the incorporation by individual husbands of their wives in their informal leisure activities.

The process of incorporating not just the wives of presidents and mayors but women generally as supporters and subordinates of men's collective activities is highly institutionalized in Smalltown. Attached to many of the men's organizations are women's auxiliaries.[10] The auxiliaries exist primarily to raise money for the superordinate organization. Numbers of them have come and gone during the years of field-work, but at some stage, or throughout the entire period, there have been auxiliaries or auxiliary-type organizations for the brass band (a predominantly male organization), the voluntary fire brigade, the hospital, ambulance, the RSL, the football club, the schools, and the churches (usually called guilds). The guilds of the Anglican and Uniting Churches exist primarily to raise money, much of which is handed to the boards of management of these churches to spend. Women certainly 'have a say' on these administrative bodies but they are numerically dominated by men. Most members of the guilds are the wives of members or widows of former members. These women run street stalls and fêtes. There is no men's group given over to raising money for either church.

Most women participating in the ladies guilds are sixty-five years of age or older. Some of the older women are hopeful that when the young women are more advanced in years they will join the church organizations and ensure their continuity. This is probably a false hope, in part because there is a much smaller group of younger women actively associated with the churches now than at the time that the current older women were young themselves, but more importantly the hope will probably go unfulfilled because hardly any of the younger Protestant women are prepared to devote the time and effort their mothers and mothers-in-law have to raise money for the churches. This response should not be interpreted so much as a rebellion against patriarchy as a statement of the perceived irrelevance of the churches and their organizations to younger women (Dempsey, 1989b; Dempsey, 1991). Despite younger women's complaints of the futility of emulating their mothers by joining a guild or auxiliary, many of them are still using their domestic skills for the benefit of men's organizations such as the Rotary, Lions and Jaycees Clubs.

Wives are expected to work alongside their husbands in some of the fund-raising activities of these clubs. I have witnessed Rotarians' wives assisting their husbands in serving dinner at a banquet for several hundred people, but the prestige that these activities attracts devolves on the men, not their wives. Wives of Jaycees members are also expected to watch men enhance their status when they assume office as members of the new executive at the annual 'change-over' dinners. These are social and ritualistic functions during which the retiring executive of the club hands over its control to the incoming executive. Probably most—but not all—wives are eager to attend because of the opportunity the dinner offers for a night out for which they do not have to cater, and time with friends.[11] The women do not share equal billing with their husbands; the night's activities focus on the men. The men recount lengthy stories about each other's misdemeanours, or alleged misdemeanours which are accompanied by much mirth. They speak in glowing terms about the achievements of the retiring executive committee and congratulate the incoming executive on their election to office. The wives are there to applaud the men for the antics of the evening, their good works throughout the year, and elevation to office in the club. There is a certain irony to all of this because many married male members view their service-club activities as a release from the demands and constraints of family life as well as from the demands of a middle-class job.

Facilitating men's sporting activities

Many sporting organizations also expect their women members, or the wives and girlfriends of male members, to use their domestic skills for the benefit of the club. For example, each week one of the teams participating in the Saturday tennis competition is rostered to provide afternoon tea for all the teams competing. Both male and female members of the rostered team are expected to bring along food.[12] However, it is the women members who nearly always place the food on the tables, prepare and serve the drinks, and who usually clear away and wash up afterwards.

At a weekend tennis tournament, lunch is provided for participants. Female not male members contribute either a salad or a sweet (at their own expense), serve a knife and fork meal to the players and 'clean up the mess afterwards'. The male members of the local club will be expected to perform certain tasks such as putting up the nets and 'looking after the barbecue' if one is held, but these are less time-consuming tasks than those performed by women. Women members also operate a kiosk to raise money for the tennis club both at tournaments and at regular Saturday competitions.

Tennis is a mixed sporting activity providing some opportunity for women to play and socialize with men, but football is a man's game. The mechanisms for incorporating women to facilitate this leisure activity are more elaborate than those for tennis. Of all the sports, football provides the best example of the way in which women facilitate the leisure activity of men, sometimes to the point of being exploited.

There are two organizations associated with the town's football club—the football committee itself and the women's auxiliary. The football committee runs the club: appoints coaches, selects teams, and dispenses the funds at its disposal. It is a committee comprised mainly of men and controlled by men. For instance, in 1991 only four of the twenty members were women. In the mid-1980s it was suggested that a woman be elected to the position of secretary of the football club but the men decided against this because it would be necessary for the secretary, on occasions, to enter the men's changing rooms during the half-time interval of a match and this was, of course, unacceptable. Like public bars, changing rooms are men-only territories. If a woman entered, men would have to 'cover up' and curb their tongues and horseplay. In Imray and Middleton's terms, if women were found inside, both the symbolic quality of the space and its utilization as a place where men could 'be themselves' would be placed in jeopardy. In order to retain the distinctive maleness of the place, a woman secretary would need to be re-classified as a man or treated as invisible (1983:18–19). Men invoked the notion of female respectability to preserve the gender homogeneity of the changing room. If a woman entered the changing room, men said her respectability would be placed in jeopardy.

There were further reasons why it would have been difficult for a woman to hold a position on this committee at the time this proposal was made. The meetings of the committee were being held in the back room of one of the town's hotels.[13] The meetings began at 8 o'clock but committee members arrived at least half an hour earlier to drink in the public bar.[14] The meeting lasted about one hour, and football tactics and the selection of the team for next week's game were discussed. These are things that men are expert in. After the meeting the men returned to the bar to drink, perhaps for a couple of hours.

Football committee meetings, like cricket committee meetings, and many other men's committee meetings are, in fact, a lot of fun. They provide a legitimate excuse for men to engage in their mateship behaviour, often 'over a few drinks'. 'Men are always looking for a chance to sneak out for a drink. The meetings provide them with a legitimate excuse for doing so' (a former football club president). That kind of comment was made repeatedly during the course of interviews and conversations about a range of men's activities in Smalltown.

In contrast to the men's committee, meetings of the women's committee attached to the football club—the women's football auxiliary—are business-like affairs. This club exists primarily, virtually exclusively, to raise money for the men's club. It recruits members by drawing on the kinship, marriage, and potential marriage ties (girlfriends and fiancées) of players. These women are expected and pressured to work for the club by raising money. Just before the 1986 season began, the local newspaper carried a prominent story calling on women to support the club. Here are some pertinent extracts from the story:

Smalltown Football Club ladies are ready to stir after a well-deserved off-season break with their annual meeting set down for next Friday night . . . Big in fund raising the small committee would like to see some new faces . . . Ideal candidates would be the mothers, wives or girl-friends of players . . . a few of the older ladies who had 'done their bit' felt they needed a spell . . . Good support [of women] would give the club added impetus in its all-out drive for premiership success this year . . . Main activity throughout the season would be the stocking and manning [sic] of the canteen at the Smalltown Football ground. Last year the ladies handed a record $7,000 to the club.

The women's football auxiliary has to be business-like largely because women often lack men's autonomy and they are more subject to mores restricting their ability to have 'a good time'. For at least some members, domestic duty and child care preclude open-ended socializing. Such members are away from home for as short a period of time as possible. The code of respectability that influences much of married women's behaviour keeps them away from pubs and drinking.

While they are meeting, the women discuss their next fund-raising activity. For example, one meeting of the football club auxiliary was called to arrange catering for a special function for the pacing club, another male-dominated organization. The money the women raise by such activities is handed over to the men's committee. The women may recommend that some of the money be spent in a specific way, say on insurance for players, but men make the final decision.

Exploitation of women by men's organizations

Much of the contribution that wives make to the leisure and status-seeking activity of husbands and their organizations is conducted at home (cooking, answering phones, writing up minutes, etc.) so that the extent to which wives are incorporated without adequate reciprocity is not always visible. However, there are a range of situations in which exploitation is clear, such as the repeated and public use a club or institution makes of the time and social skills of a leader's wife without offering anything of significance in return. This process is well illustrated in the story told by Mrs Margaret Riddle. Its essentials were corroborated by her husband, David. David Riddle was a leading entrepreneur who held an executive position in one of the community's service clubs. Work and the club so dominated David Riddle's life that there was little time left for the family. Much of Margaret Riddle's life pivoted around David's club activities. She accompanied him to barbecues, change-over dinners, and a range of other social activities associated with his club. She also helped with fund raising for his organization. Because he held an executive position with his club he travelled hundreds of miles each month visiting neighbouring clubs. She was usually expected to accompany him on these trips. Margaret complained that she found it difficult to devote time to her one sporting interest—netball—and that she was sometimes prevented from attending practice by her husband's failure to free her by minding the children. Apart from her sporting team she belonged to only one organization: the local kindergarten. She said that fathers were free to join this organization but none, including her own husband, had. She went on to say, 'Even if David did choose to come along to the kindergarten, we lack the baby-sitting resources to allow him to do so. We use all our baby-sitting resources up on functions in connection with his club.' She also explained how her husband's leisure activities impinged on her friendships:

I don't have much time now to see my friends because I am busy with David's friends. Like David almost all of them belong to the X Club. It is also difficult because David does not like my two closest friends or their husbands. So I have to see them on my own and that proves difficult. I now sometimes go weeks without seeing them.

In instances where the wife's support for her husband's leisure activity is of this order it usually ensures that her 'identity becomes an extension of his and as his adjunct she proclaims his good work through her own' (Fowlkes, 1980:46, cited by Finch, 1983:90).

The wives of men in a variety of public positions are incorporated in their husbands' activities: mayors and shire presidents, the presidents of service clubs and of a number of sporting organizations. The relationship between the organization and the wife of the office-holder may also serve as an instance of patriarchal dominance, in the sense that the individual wife is not consulted about whether she wishes to participate, or in what ways she wishes to participate. Rather, it is taken for granted by members of the organization that, because she is the wife of the man who has been elected as president, or to some other executive position, she will play a well-orchestrated part in more or less the same way as wives of former executives.

Exploitation is also palpable in those instances in which the husbands themselves provide little practical assistance to the women in their money-making activities on behalf of their husbands' organization. Wives and girlfriends do not play football, but principally through the activities of their auxiliary the women provide a major part of the funds raised for the football club with little assistance from the male members.

One of the more demanding ways in which women frequently raise money for a men's organization or committee is by catering for weddings, twenty-first birthday celebrations, and the special functions of various men's organizations.[15] The women members of the golf club are one group operating in this way. An organization, such as the Jaycees Club will, for example, arrange to hold their Christmas party at the golf club. A couple of the male golf club members will serve drinks but the real work will be done by 'the golf club ladies'. They will buy, prepare, and serve the food, and wash up afterwards. During the second half of the 1980s the golf club men's committee decided to build a new clubhouse. The women's catering was a principal form of fund raising for the new facilities. The men pointed out that the women would also enjoy the facilities, which may be true, but it is the male-dominated committee that controls their use. Until recently, women were only associate members of the club. Now they have been admitted to full membership.[16] However, in 1991 there were only two women on the committee, and all three executive positions were held by men.

The exploitation of members' wives by clubs is clearly manifested when the wives' labour produces good works or money for good works which enhances the prestige of the club and its male members rather than the public standing of the wives themselves. When, in the mid-1980s, the Governor-General of Australia visited Smalltown, the Rotary Club catered for a banquet held in his honour, at which the Rotarians were assisted by their wives. The Governor-General stated publicly how impressed he was that the Rotarians, as leading citizens of the community, waited on tables. No reference was made—at least in my hearing—to the Rotarians' wives, either by the Governor-General or by the local councils that co-sponsored the occasion.

The Lions and Jaycees Clubs staff stalls selling drinks and confectionary at the Smalltown Agricultural Show—one of the ways such clubs raise money to spend on community-service projects. Wives who are *not* members of these clubs will be asked to assist in these activities. Although wives toil as industriously as husbands, the public recognition, flowing from the club's investment of the profits in community services, goes exclusively to the husbands. So, for example, it is the male president of the

Lions Club and not his wife whose photograph appears in the *Smalltown News* accompanying a story about the club's latest 'good deed'. In such instances, wives are physically present and their labour indispensable to the success of the enterprise, but their public persona is submerged by that of their husband's club: they are, in effect, socially invisible.

Exploitation is also demonstrated by the failure of the men's organizations, as of individual husbands, to reciprocate by supporting the leisure activities or the 'good works' of their wives' organizations. There are those husbands who assist a wife's organization with fund-raising activities by, for example, putting up trestles for a street stall, or helping erect a marquee for a fête, or by ferrying goods from home to the site of the fête. Wives value this kind of assistance but it is not commensurate with that given by women's auxiliaries attached to men's organizations or even by wives who help out in an informal manner by, say, preparing food for their husband's organization.

Although it benefits club members generally, much of what women do for their husbands' organizations is at best marked by a token gesture of appreciation. For example, a half-page article singing the praises of the X Men's Club for its sporting successes may contain at or near the end the following type of brief gratuitous recognition: 'The Ladies Auxiliary did themselves proud when they provided a delicious luncheon for the host club and the visiting players. Many very favourable comments were passed by appreciative males.'

Wives attend any mixed social function arranged by their husband's organization, but far fewer husbands attend comparable entertainments arranged by organizations their wives belong to. Consequently, the social functions of women's groups are often of necessity, rather than by choice, single-sex activities. Whenever men are engaged in a major sporting activity their wives will be present in large numbers to cheer them on, but few husbands watch their womenfolk play sport. Men are more likely to attend a final of a women's competition than a weekly match. Nevertheless, only twenty or so men watched the Smalltown Women's Hockey Team win the 1991 district grand final; on the same day several hundred women joined men in watching the Smalltown Men's Football Team lose the grand final.

Wives and girlfriends attend the social function held for the football team after every home game. Many of these women belong to the hockey club or the netball club but these clubs do not run comparable Saturday night functions because the pool of potential supporters is too small to make a second function economically or socially viable. Even if such a function were viable, staging it would create a conflict of interests for some women players: because they are the girlfriends or wives of footballers, they are expected by their partners to support the football function. In short, men's activities take precedence and women are incorporated to facilitate their success socially and economically. My research indicates that if sportswomen sponsored a competing social function it would be perceived as 'bitchy' and divisive.

The precedence that a husband's organization takes over a wife's organization is demonstrated by seating arrangements at public functions to which the town's organizations have been invited to send representatives. If a wife is invited to represent a women's organization—such as the Red Cross or the CWA—and a husband is invited to represent a men's organization—such as the Jaycees or the Lions Club—she will sit with her husband at the table allocated for members of his organization rather than at the table reserved for members of her organization. Even if a husband does not belong to a men's organization that is represented at the function and his wife does, he will not accompany her. If he is not invited 'in his own right' he will not attend the function. Consequently, on such occasions the tables of the women's organizations are occupied by women only, whereas the tables of the men's organizations that are represented are occupied by couples (that is husbands and the wives that have been incorporated for the occasion). Yet very few of the women who have been socially deprived in the ways just described would not have been working to ensure the success of at least one men's organization.

The irony is that, no matter how hard women work for a men's organization—often harder than the men themselves—they do not through their labour become members of their husband's club.[17] What Finch observes regarding the gains for wives who contribute to the productivity of their husbands' corporations applies to the wives who contribute to the 'productivity' of Smalltown's men's organizations, especially the more prestigious ones. She says such wives merely bask in the reflected glory, and in so doing affirm their dependent status (1983:116–17). Abrams makes a related observation when he says: 'Women are indirectly denied recognition as autonomous individuals and viewed as merely complimentary to men . . . they appear as part of a male defined social unit: the family' (1978:160). It follows that 'women's work in caring for children and husbands does not appear as necessary labour; it appears as a natural part of family life' (1978:160). The same can be said for the labour that a wife performs for a husband's leisure and that of his fellow club members. This labour increases the effectiveness (that is the productivity) of husbands' clubs as well as enhancing the performance of individual husbands in their roles as presidents or secretaries, and it contributes to the public acclaim that the husbands receive for their efforts.

Effects on wives

In deciding whether exploitation is occurring the perceptions of neither the exploiters nor the exploited can be the decisive factor. In the present instance few, if any, husbands, or organizations comprised of husbands, would acknowledge that they are taking advantage of wives. It is also the case that wives are often willing accomplices in the usurpation of their time and talents by individual husbands, as well as by their organizations. As I have already acknowledged, many wives report that they enjoy 'helping the men out', etc. Yet exploitation has an objective quality and it occurs whether or not it is perceived to occur by the participants themselves. It may also occur when those who are being exploited gain tangible and valued rewards from their participation. The issue is: are those rewards commensurate with the labour and resources that are contributed? In the present instance I would argue that exploitation occurs because, by using wives as domestic workers, sales people, and as facilitators of social activities, husbands, boyfriends and their organizations increase their productivity of 'good times' and of 'good works' without any increased cost to the men or their clubs, and without the men adequately recompensing the women. Because it is the labour of wives it is not viewed as something that should be paid for or reciprocated.[18]

Some of Smalltown's men's organizations are aptly described as 'greedy institutions' (Coser, 1974, cited by Finch, 1983:109). The demands these organizations make, not only on male members but on wives as occasional participants, are almost unlimited. Furthermore, like other greedy institutions they encompass the whole person in their activities. In the present instance this means they draw on the skills of wives as domestic workers and sales people and on their social skills.

As the foregoing account shows, exploitation occurs not only because men individually and collectively use up the resources of women, usually partners, for their leisure activities but also because they, at best, only partially reciprocate by supporting the leisure activities of women.

It also occurs because the incorporation of women in these leisure activities restricts and sometimes precludes the leisure activity of the women themselves.

Constraining women's leisure

It takes time and energy to wash and iron sporting gear and to prepare meals for a man returning late from a drinking session at the pub or to send food for a meeting of his club. It also takes time to attend the games, meetings, and social functions associated with a husband's or boyfriend's leisure activities. Many women perceive some of these as leisure activities for themselves, but not all women do. The intrusion of men's leisure into the lives of their wives is exacerbated by the open-ended character of the service that their wives provide them—meals, clothes and moral support for their leisure activities. Deem found in her study of women's leisure in the British community of Milton Keynes that, 'Where men worked unsocial or irregular hours the times of their households had to be adjusted to suit' (1982:33). In Smalltown, husbands often play as well as work at irregular hours, so the practice has evolved of wives making such services available more or less on demand. Members of both sexes acknowledge that men take advantage of their wives' domestic captivity to come and go as they please. Many husbands think nothing of arriving late for the evening meal after a game of golf or an extended drinking session at one of the pubs, but, at the same time, they reserve the right to chastise a wife if a meal is not ready when they want it (see also Dennis *et al.*, 1969).

While a woman's responsibilities can intrude on her husband's leisure, our observations indicated that it is much more likely that the reverse will happen. This was corroborated by data we collected during the course of the Gender Survey. We asked respondents several questions aimed at establishing which partner, if either, had more opportunity to engage in leisure activities. The survey showed that 72 per cent of husbands participating in the Gender Survey were better able to pursue their outside leisure interests than their wives. Only 5 per cent of wives were better able than their husbands to engage in leisure interests outside the home. The remaining couples in the study (about 25 per cent of the sample) reported that each spouse had about the same ability to pursue their individual leisure interests. Just over 50 per cent of the husbands compared with less than 5 per cent of wives had more freedom than their partners 'to come and go as they please, that is without needing the permission or co-operation of their partner. Forty-four per cent of the partners had the same ability as each other 'to come and go as they please'. Finally, about 45 per cent of the husbands compared with 10 per cent of wives spent more money then their partner on their leisure activities. There were no significant differences in the amount of money spent on leisure among the remaining 45 per cent of couples.

In the light of these findings it is not surprising that wives are much more likely than husbands to report surrendering their sporting activities after marriage, especially when they have dependent children. Deem (1987b:423, 429) and Bryson (1983:415–20, 424–5) have shown that this is often because wives lack support from their families and they no longer have the energy once they have met their work responsibilities. In this study the mode of wives' incorporation into their husband's leisure—largely through work in the home—also reduced their external leisure, including participation in sport.

Many Smalltown men are obsessive about their leisure or status-enhancing activities. For some it is an all-consuming passion that 'contaminates the whole of their lives' (Finch, 1983:133). Such men are found in all classes and may be of any age. They may include local government councillors, leading members of service clubs, owners and trainers of thoroughbred horses and pacers, amateur coaches of various sporting clubs, golfing, bowling, football, hunting, fishing, and vintage car enthusiasts. These men are often so preoccupied with their obsession that there is little time for companionship with their wives (except that demanded by the pursuit of the obsession itself) or for helping with tasks around the home. Their wives are often drawn into facilitating the obsession and perhaps 'sharing' it as well. Facilitating the obsession means ensuring the appropriate leisure clothing is always ready and, if necessary, immaculately presented, and entertaining other enthusiasts. It may also extend to contributing from the 'housekeeping' or the wife's own earnings to the husband's leisure activity, serving as a companion for long trips away from home while a husband pursues his obsession, and serving as an interested 'sounding board' as he talks about it repeatedly. The demands for practical service and moral support from these men can be insatiable. Women married to them find their lives shaped by their husband's leisure activity in a manner that, at most, only a handful of Smalltown husbands would have experienced as a result of their wives' leisure activities.

The impact on a wife's life and leisure of this type of one-sided relationship was articulated repeatedly during interviews not only by wives married to men in leadership positions, but also by the wives of men who did not occupy an executive position in a local men's organization. One such wife was Jan Davidson. Her husband, John, was employed as a clerk in a 9 to 5 job. This left him with plenty of time, he said, for indulging the two greatest passions in his life: football and cricket. He and his wife had two children of primary-school age and she worked on a part-time basis. She washed and ironed her husband's sporting gear and helped on occasions with fund raising for his sporting activities. She also took their two children to watch her husband play football, and, on occasions, cricket. Mrs Davidson was a keen basketball and hockey player. Husband John never watched her participate in sporting activities even though she sometimes had to forgo one of her leisure activities to watch him play. He did sometimes mind the children so that Jan could join other women in leisure activity. His ability to do so was partly due to his working regular hours, but it was also due to his decision not to accept an executive position in the sporting organizations he belongs to, or join any of the town's leading service or political organizations. His contribution to his wife's leisure activities fell far short of complete reciprocity.

While the impact John Davidson's leisure activities had on his wife and her activities was not as disruptive of his wife's life as David Riddle's activities were of Margaret Riddle's life, nevertheless the relationship he had with Jan Davidson remained sufficiently asymmetrical to warrant describing it as exploitative.

Conclusion

The data presented in the foregoing pages confirm the claim of Griffin and her colleagues that 'women's work produces leisure for men' (1982:91). They also show that their incorporation frequently reduces the leisure activity of wives.[19] At one level of analysis the inequitable outcomes are brought about by husbands taking the initiative and incorporating their wives in the preparation for and the aftermath of their leisure activities and often in the leisure activities themselves. In some instances the incorporation does take the form of recreational activity for the wife, but often it takes the form of unpaid labour, or it produces a more passive form of leisure than that enjoyed by the husband, or it entails a subservient role for the wife in the activity her husband initiated. The data demonstrate that at least some wives are locked into exploitative relationships with their own husbands and often with the husbands of other women.

Historically, there is nothing new in the situation I have been describing in Smalltown. Lown stresses that since pre-industrial times wives have been 'expected to provide services for men' (1983:35). Lown attributes the exploitation of women to their lack of a work identity. In the present instance, few wives earn enough from their paid work to be financially independent. In Chapter 6 I show that men dominate the better paying jobs, control farming land, the major resource for generating wealth and income, and have bigger incomes than women. Consequently, the great majority of wives are partially or entirely dependent on husbands for money for leisure activities. This dependence extends beyond the need for small change for a few leisure pursuits to dependence for major life necessities and for ensuring a reasonable life-style and education for their children. Such a dependence provides husbands with a great deal of leverage, especially when a wife's support for a man's leisure activities is viewed as desirable as in this community.

McRobbie joins Lown in affirming that the material position of women plays a crucial role in their oppression (1978:96–7), but, as many writers have argued, economic dependence is one of a complex and interdependent set of factors responsible for the oppression of women.[20] The factors include men's superior physical power, legitimated power (authority), ideological hegemony, their fewer domestic responsibilities, and women's socialization, and at least partial domestic captivity. In Smalltown they also include certain demographic and spatial factors: a small and stable population coupled with geographical isolation make it easier for superordinates to control subordinates.

We would have jeopardized the entire Smalltown project if we had attempted to investigate whether husbands used force to achieve their way with their wives.[21] There were many indications in interviews and during periods of observations that husbands invoke superior power and probably authority over wives to incorporate them in their leisure activities. For instance, husbands often tell rather than request wives to provide food and clothing or attend a function in which they are participating. Many wives comply, at least in part because they believe in the right of husbands to take charge in such ways, rather than because they fear economic sanctions or an emotional outburst, although these possibilities are often considerations. Wives also appear more likely than husbands to seek permission to engage in an external leisure activity. The practice is another acknowledgement of the superior power of husbands. It will be recalled that a much larger number of husbands than of wives are free 'to come and go as they please' and to pursue their own interests.

It was possible to investigate in more detail the part that ideology plays in the maintenance and reproduction of men's leisure advantages. I will also describe the socialization experiences that prepare women to facilitate men's leisure and cause men to expect women to do so (see Ch. 8). I made an extensive study of domestic labour, and the next chapter describes how women are responsible for carrying out most domestic tasks.

CHAPTER 5

Dividing the jobs: unpaid work

In 1960, American sociologist Leonard Benson wrote in a book on fatherhood, 'the old pattern of male-dominated, female-serviced family life is . . . being replaced by a new and more symmetrical pattern' (cited by Oakley, 1974:136). Thirteen years later the British community sociologists Michael Young and Peter Wilmott observed, 'this century . . . a more symmetrical relationship has been created within marriage . . . in the majority of families there is some role-segregation along with a greater degree of equality' (1973:32).[1] The authors claimed that while there was still some way to go to reach a state of egalitarianism, there was more equality in the division of domestic tasks than in the past. They believed that this trend would continue to grow in strength.

Subsequent research in the USA, the UK, and Australia has failed to confirm the observations and predictions of Benson, and Young and Wilmott.[2] Rather, it has lent support to the view of those feminists who argue that, in the context of marriage, a male who is *the* provider exploits his wife by appropriating her unpaid work. For instance, Barrett cites the domestic division of labour and the familial ideology supporting it in her short list of the factors responsible for women's oppression and exploitation (1980:32). Yet while this is true, it needs to be borne in mind that women's inequality is mediated by personal relationships rather than emanating directly from structural arrangements or ideological processes (Abrams and McCulloch, 1976). Delphy (1984: Ch. 3) and Davidoff (1976) affirm that it is men, as well as the capitalist system, who benefit from women's unpaid labour. In this chapter our principal concern is establishing the extent to which Smalltown husbands (rather than capitalism) benefit from the unpaid labour of their wives and whether the contribution husbands make 'in and around the home' establishes equity. In this examination we will take into account whether or not a wife is engaged in paid work or whether a husband has retired from paid work.

In the previous chapter I stressed that exploitation occurs where the labour of one partner is appropriated by the other without adequate reciprocity. To assess the extent of exploitation, it is useful to distinguish tasks from one another according to: (1) the frequency and regularity of their performance; (2) the extent to which they impede leisure and paid work; and (3) their propensity for placing the performer into a subordinate relationship to other actors in the situation. To help assess tasks according to the first criterion, I am adopting Thomas and Zmroczek's (1985:115) convention of using the term 'routine' to refer to tasks which have to be performed at least weekly, and mostly several times or more a week throughout the year. The term 'non-routine' refers to tasks which are performed irregularly. Non-routine tasks include such things as gardening, cleaning windows, painting, etc. The principal routine tasks are cooking, washing clothes, washing up, cleaning, shopping, and child care. Such tasks are not as easily postponed or anticipated as non-routine tasks and they are less likely to have definite time boundaries (Deem, 1982). Accordingly, they are more likely to seriously interfere with leisure, paid work, and career advancement. They are more likely to entail the provision of personal services; this is a trait which, in combination with their relentless and open-ended character, usually places the performer in a subordinate and servant-like role.

The division of labour among young and middle-aged adults

As far back as the available historical evidence goes, child-rearing and domestic labour have been primarily feminine tasks (Eliot, 1986:73).

We conducted two surveys in Smalltown of the domestic division of labour among young and middle-aged adults. The first was made in 1974, the year after the publication of Young and Wilmott's study claiming that the division of labour was becoming more equitable. Our study failed to produce any evidence whatsoever of the blurring of the old distinctions between 'women's work and men's work'. Although a decade elapsed before we made the second study, it too produced no significant evidence that the domestic division of labour was becoming more symmetrical.

Both surveys showed that more than 95 per cent of wives had major and usually sole responsibility for cooking, washing clothes, house cleaning and ironing.[3] In both decades husbands were more likely to wash up than perform any other traditional 'women's tasks'. Yet, in the mid-1980s, we found that two-thirds of husbands either never washed up or only washed up occasionally. The 1974 Family Study showed that 80 per cent of husbands never washed clothes, 90 per cent never ironed, and more than 70 per cent never helped with the vacuuming. In the Gender Survey (1984–86) the proportions were slightly higher: 75 per cent of the husbands never performed any of these three tasks, and over 90 per cent never ironed or washed clothes. There were no class differences in our findings. Men in middle-class occupations, such as traditional professionals, were more likely than working-class respondents to display egalitarian attitudes in interviews, but as (Edgell, 1980:64) points out, men in these occupations can trade on the open-ended and the prestigious nature of their employment to avoid the more tedious and domestic jobs. We also found that farmers and businessmen, as well as professionals, sometimes cited the physically and emotionally demanding nature of their employment as a reason for not assisting their wives more, while the open-ended nature of their work schedule was put forward as an explanation for not making a regular commitment to certain jobs.

The Smalltown study confirms Oakley's (1974), Collins's (1985), McRae's (1986), and Hochschild's (1988) research in showing that if men participate in routine household tasks, it is usually as their wives' helpers rather than as people equally responsible for seeing that the tasks are done. As Collins (1985:77–8) observes, 'help' is the operative word. Repeatedly, during the Smalltown interviews, husbands responded to a question such as: 'Do you do any of the washing?' with an answer such as the following: 'No I never help her with that. I'd only muck the job up.' Or a wife would say: 'Yes, he helps me occasionally.' Such comments exemplify the perception by both sexes that the traditional routine tasks are 'women's work', and if a husband performs them it is not because he is under any obligation to do so, but because he wants to 'help his wife out in that way'. A substantial minority of respondents made it clear that they viewed the division of labour as natural and consistent with biological differences between men and women. A social arrangement which is viewed as biologically determined is, says Willis, virtually unchallengeable (1982, cited by Bryson, 1990). This would explain why Smalltown men displayed no shame when they said they could not do what their wives did because they would 'only muck up' such jobs or when they indicated that performing them was not compatible with their masculinity: 'It's hardly a man's job.'

Insofar as men choose to help with routine tasks they usually select the less demanding or the more interesting of them (Oakley, 1974:Ch. 8; Edgell, 1980:Ch. 4). One of the less time consuming of the routine household jobs is washing up. As we have already seen, men are much more likely to assist with this job than, say, washing clothes or vacuuming. In the Gender Survey about one-third of husbands reported that they helped, or were reported by their wives to help, at least several times a week with the washing up. The typical comment made by such a husband was: 'I give her a hand if I am home in the evening.' However, if he chooses not to come home, his wife has to do the job or enlist the services of a child—after all, it is her task 'to see the job gets done'.

As a rule, men of all classes only help out with such tasks as washing or ironing if their wives are ill or away, and most Smalltown women do not make a habit of absenting themselves. Many see it as their responsibility to look after their husbands. They are also aware that husbands do not like being left 'to fend for themselves'. If, however, a wife is absent, husbands are frequently saved by the intervention of female relatives or friends who ensure that they do not have to prepare their main meal of the day or do their washing or ironing (more than two-thirds of Smalltown people have immediate kin living locally and more than 95 per cent claim to have close friends in the neighbourhood).

Despite their predilection for leaving the housework to their wives, cooking is one task with which husbands may 'assist'. About two-thirds of the husbands we gathered data on during the Family Survey (1974) were reported to be doing some cooking. In the Elderly Survey, which was conducted in the following year, 44 per cent of the male participants stated that they had cooked on at least one occasion during the previous week. These findings require further comment because they may suggest that men are more tied to the house by this, the most frequent of the routine jobs, than our interviews and observations suggest.

It seems that only a handful of Smalltown men assume responsibility for all or for a substantial part of the cooking. Usually these are men who either live alone or are married to incapacitated wives. The Gender Survey (1984–86) produced only one instance of a husband taking responsibility for about half the cooking (his wife was an invalid), a second who usually cooked at least one main meal per week, and a third who cooked several. The last man's wife was in good health; he cooked and shared other routine domestic tasks because he believed the burden should not fall disproportionately on women.

It is becoming fashionable for middle-class husbands to play chef at barbecues to which friends are invited, but they cook the meat their wives have bought. Furthermore, the women will usually continue to prepare the salads and the sweets. The praise these men receive for their efforts at a barbecue, and the frequent absence of praise for the efforts of their wives, underlines the inverted and exceptional nature of the situation. The comments of one wife describe well the realities of men's cooking in Smalltown:

> When husbands cook at barbecues they do little more than turn the meat. The wives get it all ready and they clean up the mess after the barbecue. They also usually clean up the mess after any husband who cooks a regular meal. No, when a husband says he does some cooking it's got to be seen as a bit of a joke.

In some instances, solo cooking for Smalltown men means getting a quick snack by, for example, heating a can of baked beans or by 'shoving in the oven a casserole the wife prepared before she went out'. Thomas and Zmroczek's study showed that cooking of this nature makes very different demands from the day-to-day cooking for which Smalltown women assume responsibility (1985). The authors found that whereas women devoted between 77 and 134 minutes a day to cooking and washing up (depending on whether they were engaged in paid employment or not) men, on average, devoted only 10 minutes per day to these tasks (1985:115). Neither the comments made in interviews, nor our own observations during field-work, suggest that Smalltown men give to cooking substantially greater time than their British counterparts.

Taking care of the children

Child care is a major part of domestic life entailing the performance of routine tasks.[4] Our study confirmed earlier research that husbands are, in fact, more likely to choose to participate in child care than housework (Edgell, 1980:104; Sharpe, 1984:177). In Smalltown they seem to prefer the fun parts of child care—playing with the children or taking them to sport—rather than helping them with their homework, or looking after them when they are sick. Yet their help in even the fun tasks is often conditional on it not interfering with their paid work or leisure activities: 'He's happy to take the kids to their sporting fixtures providing they don't clash with one of his fishing trips or something else that comes up. Mum always has to be available as the backstop.' Many of the sports in which children participate occur during working hours and this precludes many fathers taking their children along. The Gender Survey showed that mothers were much more likely to take their children to their sporting activities than were fathers. More than 50 per cent of mothers took sole responsibility for getting their children to sporting activities compared with only about 10 per cent of fathers. Fathers were more inclined to take their sons to football because they were interested in the football themselves. The responsibility was shared, but not necessarily equally, by the remaining members of the sample.

The responsibility for caring for the children impinges on the organized leisure activity of mothers. As a rule, wives with younger children who wish to play sport take the children with them to, say, a women's mid-week game of tennis. Husbands do not usually reciprocate by taking the children with them to their game of cricket or football. It is far more likely that the wives of such men will free husbands for sport by staying home and minding the children (see Ch. 4).

Child care, then, is yet another area in which men help or assist their wives rather than share responsibility and in which their participation has a voluntary character. Of the fathers with young children who participated in the Gender Survey, only 3 per cent helped with their children's homework on a regular basis, fewer than 10 per cent helped with or took responsibility for putting them to bed most nights, and only 18 per cent had a significant involvement in their discipline. This survey showed that no father took major responsibility for seeing that a child's homework was done, and only about 1 per cent took major responsibility for disciplining the children or for seeing that the children were put to bed. By contrast, more than 90 per cent of mothers helped with homework on a regular basis, and just under 50 per cent took sole responsibility for seeing that homework was completed. Approximately 50 per cent of the mothers took entire responsibility for disciplining the children, and 66 per cent for putting them to bed. Where child-care tasks were reported as being shared by mothers and fathers, interview data revealed that wives were usually performing them more frequently than husbands. Comments such as: 'He helps if he is at home, but that's not very often of an evening' (wife of farmer), or 'I helped when they were very little' (businessman), were commonplace. As Oakley so aptly put it: 'husbands are housewives' aids' (1974:159).

The data collected in School Survey 11 from a sample of teenage boys and girls in the 1970s confirmed the general thrust of the findings from the survey of parents. Both sons and daughters reported that mothers spent more time with them than fathers. They were more likely to say that mothers (not fathers) assisted with homework, and influenced how much time they gave to study.

In the second half of the 1980s we met up with a dozen or more younger husbands who claimed that they and some of their male friends were playing a much greater part in child care than husbands had a few years earlier. The men making the claims were in their thirties and mostly engaged in professional or semi-professional occupations. Most were members of close-knit friendship networks of four or more couples. Some wives were pressing their husbands to participate more in child care, and a number claimed their husbands were 'starting to do more'. These respondents were convincing talkers, so we were surprised to find that the hard data we gathered about the extent and nature of their involvement in child care did not support their claim. Our data indicated that none of these men took a substantially greater share of child care than other husbands in our sample.

While some of the younger women said things were starting to change, a greater number of them were claiming that men were only *talking* about equality. As recently as 1990 one of these rather disenchanted wives observed, 'The reality is that there has been little or no change. Small-town husbands are as chauvinist as ever.' This woman supported her claim with anecdotal information about the attitudes displayed by a number of married men where she worked. She said that, on more than one occasion when a male colleague excused himself from a social gathering on the grounds that he had to mind the children, several of the other men present quickly chided him for being 'under his wife's thumb'. There were numerous indications during daily interaction that her male colleagues, most of whom were professional men with young families, believed that the children were 'a wife's worry, not a husband's', even if the wife herself was engaged in paid employment. The data we gathered on child care in homes where the mother worked were consistent with these claims.

Another woman who was working as a nurse at the time and married to a businessman corroborated these claims:

> In this community if a kid is in trouble or just has untidy clothes the mother is always blamed. 'It's her fault.' That's my husband's attitude too. He won't take responsibility for Bill [their 18-month-old child]. After a lot of effort I've got his father doing things like taking Bill for a walk, but he won't bathe him or put him to bed. I confront Don [the father] about it every couple of months because I believe he should be as involved as me. He does a little bit more for a while but it is not sustained. He sees Bill as my responsibility. He's got most of the town's backing on that.

There is nothing in the Smalltown research findings to corroborate Curthoys's optimism, expressed a decade and a half ago, that there are positive signs that Australian men are substantially increasing their share of child care (Curthoys, 1976, cited by Bryson, 1985:91). Instead, it seems from the data collected in several surveys that the great majority of Smalltown husbands are at most helpers rather than taking equal responsibility for children. As Oakley emphasizes, *who* takes responsibility is the crucial issue. Unless this is being shared, she says, any suggestion that equity exists is mythical (1974:160–1).

The situation of women in paid employment

The research conducted by Blood and Wolfe (1960) in the USA and by Wearing (1984) in Australia suggest that when wives enter the paid work-force their husbands devote more time to domestic tasks. The Smalltown study fails to confirm these findings but rather corroborates those of other studies conducted in this country, as well as overseas, which show that both working-class and middle-class women entering the paid work-force shoulder a greater increased work-load.[5] Smalltown's wives in paid work, like those in the studies just cited, face 'double duty'. During the Gender Survey we collected data on the domestic labour of fifty-two wives engaged in paid work. In excess of 90 per cent of these wives took all or most of the responsibility for cooking, washing clothes, and ironing, and more than 80 per cent were responsible for vacuuming.[6]

Only one of the husbands (who was married to a woman working part-time) was contributing to the housework and child care in the way that 'assertions of equality in modern marriage imply' (Oakley, 1974:138). This man cooked several of the main meals each week and did some of the cleaning and washing.[7] Of the husbands married to wives who worked full time (N = 27), only one was reported by his wife to be 'doing much of the washing'; a second shared the ironing but not equally; and a third 'looked after the vacuuming'. A further two husbands of women working full time assisted, on occasions, with the vacuuming.

As a rule, husbands of women engaged in paid work on a part-time basis (N = 25) did even less. Leaving to one side the man referred to earlier, none took responsibility for the ironing, washing, cleaning or cooking. These men were no more likely than the husbands of wives *not* engaged in paid employment to perform such tasks. Most of both the full-time and part-time working wives participating in this Gender Survey had dependent children, but the husbands of these women did not play a discernibly greater part in child rearing than the husbands of wives who were not employed, and none of them took major responsibility for child care.[8]

The division of domestic labour among the elderly

The inequitable division of domestic labour between husbands and wives persists into old age (Dempsey, 1989a; see also Bittman, 1991:3 for similar recent Australian findings). One hundred per cent of the married women in the Elderly Survey compared with only 16 per cent of the married men reported cooking, cleaning, and washing clothes on at least one day per week. Furthermore, only 18 per cent of married men compared with 100 per cent of married women reported cooking on all seven days. These results strongly suggest that elderly married men fail to assume an equitable share of routine domestic tasks. Our research also showed that older wives—like younger wives—were left with responsibility for household management. This means they ensure that clothes are washed and ironed and available when a husband requires them, and the house is clean and tidy. It also means that they take charge of all stages of the provision of food: planning meals, buying and preparing food, and ensuring that meals are delivered on time, and are enjoyable to eat.

In summary, older husbands are, in the great majority of cases, their wives' helpers rather than sharing equally the responsibility for seeing that the tasks are done. The only exceptions to this were where a wife was so ill that it was no longer possible for her to perform routine tasks. Even in some of these instances a daughter or other women relatives relieved an older husband of much of the responsibility for household management and the completion of routine domestic tasks. When they do help, older husbands like younger husbands select the less demanding tasks and leave their wives with the more repetitious jobs, and which exercise the greatest constraints on the performer's freedom to come and go as they please, and on their leisure activity. Retired husbands are twice as likely as their wives to say that they pursue most of their leisure activities outside the home.

Davidoff considers that the ability of men to delegate domestic labour to their wives, as we have seen in Smalltown, is a significant index of patriarchal power (1976). The Smalltown findings show that this power is still palpable when men are no longer serving as family breadwinners: that is, when they are no longer at least partially reciprocating their wives' unpaid work by providing some or all of the family's income. This was illustrated by a story that appeared in a 1990 edition of the *Smalltown News*. The story concerned the retirement of one of the town's leading male citizens. The man was reported to have said during an interview with the newspaper: 'It's good to have a lie in until eight thirty and have time to go fishing, read the paper and go to the trotting races every week.' He was also doing some odd jobs around the house, including some painting. His wife had not retired but was cooking, cleaning and washing as she had done before her husband's retirement. She said that she was using the increase in leisure time (since her husband's retirement) to look after the house, garden, and engage in voluntary work. She announced enthusiastically, 'I've just about got the house the way I've always wanted it!'

The persistence of the system of gender inequality in the domestic sphere after men cease to be providers is facilitated by an ideology which 'perpetuates broad social definitions of male and female roles' (Collins, 1985:68). It prescribes that women must go on forever doing what they have always done around the house. Consequently, unless an elderly woman is physically incapacitated, it is assumed by both male and female members of the community that she will cook and clean for herself and for her husband if she has one. By contrast, it is viewed as legitimate for men of retirement age or even younger to voluntarily give up paid labour, provided they can afford to. Once they do so, they are not expected to increase their unpaid labour in or around the home to compensate for their withdrawal from the work-force.[9]

Are husbands making a different but equal contribution?

In previous sections of this chapter I have demonstrated that an inequitable division of labour exists between husbands and wives of all ages in Smalltown households. However, Edgell says that if we restrict our examination of equity in domestic labour to the tasks traditionally performed by women, we exclude a range of activities that men have traditionally engaged in and through which they can 'equal things up' (1980:10–11). Edgell continues, 'it may well be that the husbands who performed only a token amount of [women's] domestic work . . . were busy painting, decorating, building shelves, gardening and so on' (1980:10–11).

The survey data we collected and the direct observations we made showed that Smalltown men usually do perform the kinds of tasks that Edgell describes. Yet, despite his claims, they are not the best mechanisms for achieving equity: they are what Thomas and Zmroczek call non-routine tasks. They are distinguished from routine tasks—such as cooking and laundering—which are the tasks that women normally perform, usually at least weekly, but often several times a week throughout the year. Non-routine tasks can usually be performed at different times, or postponed for a time, so they do not interfere to the same extent with what their performer does away from home (Deem, 1986:64).

Previous research strongly suggests that men's input of time through non-routine tasks is far less than women's input through routine ones (Thomas and Zmroczek, 1985). In their research on a British sample, Thomas and Zmroczek demonstrated that, in a typical week, non-routine tasks take about one-quarter of the time that routine tasks require. Bittman's (1991) Australian study indicates that they take about one-third of the time required for routine tasks. There is no reason to believe that Smalltown men devote more time to non-routine jobs than the men who participate in either Thomas and Zmroczek's or Bittman's study. Although Smalltown men see themselves as practical and capable with their hands, they do not usually tackle the more complex jobs such as renovating a kitchen or stripping down a car engine. These are tasks that demand a similar amount of time to that devoted by women to domestic chores. Because men usually serve as their families' principal or sole bread-winner, they command the financial resources to hire the appropriate tradesmen to perform such tasks and they have community approval for doing so.

When we asked Smalltown men to nominate the jobs they performed in or around the house they most frequently cited gardening, doing small repairs, chopping firewood, washing the car, and painting. According to the Gender Survey about two-thirds of husbands frequently carried out one or more maintenance tasks. These included painting, mending a broken flyscreen or a faulty piece of electrical equipment. Gardening and mowing lawns were, however, the most frequently cited activities. In 1974 it was reported that in 68 per cent of households, husbands frequently mowed the lawns and in 78 per cent they gardened at least occasionally. A decade later about 65 per cent of husbands reported gardening frequently.

In the British study, Thomas and Zmroczek found that, on average, men spent about one and a quarter hours per week gardening. None of our evidence suggests that Smalltown men put in a greater period of time. Our observations indicate that the majority of householders choose to have gardens requiring little maintenance, with grass, a few shrubs, and perhaps one or two beds of flowers and a patch of vegetables. They are not dissimilar to those maintained in countries such as Canada with much colder climates.

Mowing the grass (as opposed to caring for an English lawn) is the major gardening activity. The grass is allowed to die off during the hotter months of summer and to grow during the winter months. Accordingly, it is not uncommon for gardening to cease for a period of several weeks at a time. According to the Gender Survey, about one-third of Smalltown husbands never garden or only garden occasionally. Even if we double the figure provided by Thomas and Zmroczek for the performance of non-routine tasks by men, we produce a result which amounts to only one-sixth of the time women engaged in full-time employment were giving to cooking and washing up, and less than one-tenth of the time women not in paid employment were giving to cleaning and washing. Again, if we allow double the time Thomas and Zmroczek found that male members of their sample were giving to all domestic tasks, and add to this the time we have allowed for gardening, this only amounts to one-quarter of the time that British women devoted to routine tasks. There is no reason to believe that Smalltown women allocate less time to these tasks.

In comparing the contribution of husbands and wives, it needs to be borne in mind that wives also perform non-routine tasks. Thomas and Zmroczek found that wives spent almost as much time as husbands on non-routine tasks. In both the 1970s and 1980s knitting, sewing and gardening were the non-routine tasks most often cited by Smalltown women. Data collected during the Gender Survey showed that just under one-half of the women were gardening frequently, and about one-sixth of them took major, or entire responsibility, for their family's garden.

It is unlikely that elderly men could achieve equity with their wives through their gardening because the Elderly Survey revealed that husbands were only slightly more likely than wives (61 per cent compared to 56 per cent) to have gardened on at least one day during the previous week. By contrast, wives were much more likely than husbands to have cooked, cleaned and washed. Nor were elderly husbands usually approaching equity through their paid work, for only 18 per cent of them were engaged in paid work for at least one day in the week before being interviewed. There was an ironical twist to all this: it was older husbands who were the most likely to cite gardening, or gardening combined with odd jobs, as comprising their major activity in life (husbands 70 per cent, wives 15 per cent) whereas wives were much more likely to cite housework as their major activity (wives 77 per cent, husbands 15 per cent). In summary: the evidence gathered from young, middle-aged and elderly Smalltown respondents fails to corroborate Edgell's hypothesis that men are making a different yet equal contribution to domestic labour. Rather the detailed analysis and comparison of the tasks that men and women perform suggests strongly that the division of labour in the domestic sphere is inequitable.

To what extent are Smalltown housewives being exploited?

In Smalltown the domestic labour of a woman rather than that of a man is compulsory, constant, and, by and large, for particular others. When it exhibits such characteristics, it is, in Ossowski's (1963) terms, exploitative. A majority of Smalltown men, and probably a majority of Smalltown women, would reject this conclusion. They would claim that men more than compensate for the labour their wives perform for them through the contribution they make to the marriage as the family's principal or sole bread-winner. Several things can be said in reply. First, unlike much of women's domestic labour, a man's paid labour does not bring him into a subordinate or servant-like relationship to his wife. In Smalltown, where such a substantial proportion of men work for themselves, it does not bring the man into a subordinate relationship to anyone, but if it does, it is usually to somebody outside his immediate family. Second, while Smalltown menfolk often work long hours, it is not necessarily the case that the total number of hours they work is equal to that worked by wives, especially by wives who have responsibility for young children.[10]

Third, what is at issue here is not only the amount of time that is worked, but, as we have already seen, the nature of the relationship to one's spouse that work creates and the impact that work has on an individual's autonomy and on their leisure activity. The tasks wives perform are more likely to interfere seriously with leisure, especially leisure outside the home, and with an individual's ability to come and go as he or she pleases (Deem, 1986; Green *et al.*, 1987b; McRae, 1986; Woodward and Green, 1988). Many Smalltown men are engaged in activities which do at times restrict their autonomy. This applies, for example, to farmers at special times of the year such as shearing and harvesting, but there are few men whose paid work constrains their freedom as much as the household chores and child care of women, especially women with young children. We have seen in Chapter 4, for example, that Smalltown wives often organize their recreational activity around their husband's timetables. We have also seen that a much larger proportion of Smalltown husbands than of wives have greater freedom than their partners to pursue their own interests. Accordingly, I would contend that many of the wives, even those who are not themselves engaged in paid employment, are exploited by their husbands. If we leave to one side those households where only the husband is engaged in paid employment and focus on those where the wife is also engaged in paid employment, or neither the wife nor the husband is engaged in paid employment, then the argument that wives are exploited by their husbands appears incontrovertible. It seems that such wives are making a far greater contribution to the marriage in terms of labour then are their husbands.

Conclusion

During the 1980s we came across a number of younger men who talked enthusiastically about lightening the domestic load of their wives and playing a greater part in child care. Our research failed to produce any hard evidence that talk was being translated into action: wives—including those with young children and in a paid job—continue to do most of the more demanding and repetitive jobs in and around the house and most of those entailed with raising children. It may be the case that in the 1990s some husbands are doing marginally more than husbands were doing, say, in the 1970s, but, as Edgell found in England, the great majority of Smalltown men tend 'to "give" a token amount of help on a discretionary basis' (1980:93). Furthermore, we have seen that they are more likely to choose to help with the tasks which both sexes prefer: the care of children. Yet, even in this sphere, their help is usually contingent on it not interfering with their paid work or leisure activity, whereas a wife is obliged to care for children and perform household tasks.

I have argued throughout this account that the critical issue is not just the sharing of tasks but the equitable sharing of responsibility. In Smalltown it is women who retain overall responsibility for household management. It remains a woman's job to ensure that the pantry is adequately stocked, that a hot and appealing meal is available when a husband comes home at the end of the day or at lunch-time; that his clothes are washed and ironed and ready when required, and that the house is clean and presentable at all times. Where there are children it also means that the mother takes responsibility for their proper care; sees that they attend their school, do their homework, are looked after when ill, and that the thousand and one things that children need are provided. One of the women participating in Williams's study of an Australian mining town accurately described a common situation in Smalltown when she said, 'My responsibility is to bring the kids up, he provides for them, but it's up to me to keep the house clean. His part of the marriage is just bringing home money' (1981:146).

Beginning in the 1970s an increasing number of wives began bringing home at least some of the money as they entered the paid work-force. If wives went out to work it was on the premise that their paid work accommodated both the demands of the home and the children, and often the husbands' work. These conditions prevailed even in those unusual instances in which a wife earned as much or more than her husband. By contrast, husbands were freed from the regular demands of domestic life and child care by their wives in order to engage in their paid employment. We have also seen that when a husband ceases earning the family income, his privileges within the marriage remain intact.

Oakley concluded her examination of the domestic division of labour in some British households with this observation: 'There is a long way to go before equality even appears on the horizon' (1974:164). This observation applies to the division of tasks in most Smalltown households. If we leave to one side the issue of men's paid work, adult women of all ages are making a greater contribution to the marriage in terms of labour than are their husbands. That is not the same thing as saying that all wives are being exploited. It is possible that in many households equity is achieved in the total division of labour through the contribution that husbands make through their paid work. The case for exploitation is strongest in those households in which the women themselves are engaged in paid employment or in which the husbands have retired from paid employment. These husbands appropriate an inordinate share of a wife's labour without offering a reciprocal expenditure of energy or time.

Two of the major obstacles to greater equality being achieved domestically are women's financial dependence and men's ideological hegemony. The following chapters show that the chances of women reducing their financial dependence are slim because of men's control of the main productive resource in this community—farming land—and their dominance of a disproportionate share of the better-paying jobs. We shall also see that when women do enter the paid work-force it is often to use skills that help define them as women, consequently their participation confirms their identities as home-makers and as the carers and servants of others. These activities are viewed as inferior to men's bread-winning role (see Ch. 8). The gender ideology that prevails in Smalltown reinforces men's superordinate position in both the domestic and economic spheres.[11]

CHAPTER 6

Dividing the jobs: paid work

Men gain much of their power to delegate domestic labour and child care to women from their dominance of paid work and from the economic resources that result from this dominance. Their considerable ability to usurp the domestic and social skills of women to facilitate their leisure and status-seeking activities also flows, in large measure, from their superior access to jobs. Men control at least two out of three jobs in the paid work-force and, in some years, as many as four out of five jobs. In 1986 only one-fifth of the women aged fifteen or older were engaged in full-time paid employment compared to more than half the men of a similar age.[1] These disparities are indicative of long-term trends in Smalltown. In 1871 only one in eleven Smalltown women had a paying job; ninety years later there was still only one woman in eight in the work-force compared with more than 50 per cent of men.[2]

In Smalltown, as throughout Australian society, there are two job markets: a male and a female (Power:1975a). Women are grossly over-represented in jobs stereotyped as female jobs and under-represented, or even absent, from those labelled male jobs. Men's jobs are stereotyped as ones which it is 'natural' for men to pursue and for which men are more suited than women (Donaldson, 1991:Ch. 1). Conversely, women are employed in jobs for which, it is argued, they are best suited temperamentally and which give expression to the skills they have acquired in the home.

> Women are crowded into a small range of occupational niches, which are often extensions of domestic roles—caring for the sick (nurses), socializing the young (teachers), cleaning office blocks (cleaners), providing clerical support for males in positions of authority (stenographers), making clothes (apparel workers) (Jones, 1983:135).

Hartmann (1979) argues that job segregation contributes more to the oppression of women than any other factor by ensuring that women's wages are low. Low wages make women dependent on men, which pushes them into marriage, which in turn locks them into performing domestic tasks for men. Men gain from both women's domestic tasks and their own higher incomes while women's domestic responsibilities weaken their position in the labour market. Australia is recognized as having the most sex-segregated work-force of the more advanced OECD countries.[3] Smalltown displays the same tendencies. While men comprise 70 per cent of the total work-force they comprise more than 95 per cent of farmers and tradespeople. Conversely, although women comprise only 30 per cent of the work-force, they comprise more than 95 per cent of nurses, cleaners, typists and garment machinists. Over 90 per cent of women in the work-force are concentrated in female jobs. The specific jobs in which women predominate in Smalltown are those which can be rationalized as giving women the chance to express their capacity for caring, selfless service, and for being followers rather than leaders. These are not nearly as well rewarded materially as men's jobs, nor are they as prestigious.

The social processes which give rise to gender segregation and stereotyping of jobs are far from well understood (Curthoys, 1986; Siltanen, 1986). Curthoys says, 'Since about 1970 a vast literature attempting to describe, measure and explain this phenomenon [that is segregation] has emerged . . . but there has been . . . remarkably little progress in explaining why [it] exists and persists' (1986: 319).[4] There certainly cannot be any doubt about its persistence and intractability. Its historical roots predate industrialism and modern capitalism. 'Historically, it has been rare for a sex label not to be attached to any given job by both workers and employees' (Yeandle, 1984:8). With industrialism the sexual division of tasks that prevailed in an agrarian society 'spread into the new workplace' (Yeandle, 1984:9). Mann stresses that at that time, as economic life increasingly became a part of the public realm, there was, in theory at least, the possibility of men and women becoming 'interchangeable as labourers . . . [and] so ending gender particularism in the economy [however employers and male labourers] . . . contrived to create a labour market, in which priority was given to males' (1986:44). Those women who entered the waged labour-force at the time of the emergence of industrialism worked in open 'semi-domesticated' occupations—that is ones that entailed preparing and serving food, making clothes, and caring for the young, elderly, and infirm (Mann, 1986:44–5). They have recently worked in service-sector occupations, especially retail and commerce.

The same pattern of female employment has probably been present in Smalltown throughout its history. In 1871, just twenty years after the township was settled, 54 per cent of the women in paid employment were preparing and serving food or cleaning houses and public buildings, 18 per cent were making clothes, and 10 per cent were caring for the young. The remainder were working as sales assistants, or educators of the young.[5] By contrast, men dominated traditional professional, managerial and administrative posts. They owned most of the town's small business enterprises, were the enforcers of law and order, dominated skilled manual work, and monopolized the gold-mining that had been responsible for the establishment of the town. Gold gave men the opportunity to accumulate the capital necessary to establish a farm, or some other business enterprise. Both mining and farming were stereotyped as male occupations. In 1871 roughly 90 per cent of adult women were engaged in unpaid domestic work whereas about 90 per cent of adult men were engaged in paid employment.

It seems, from the data available, that not a great deal has changed since the last century.[6] While the ratio of women to men in the paid work-force rose from about 1 to 10 to 1 to 5 (both full-time and part-time workers) there have not been any marked changes in the patterns of segregation and concentration, or of men's domination of the better-paying and more prestigious jobs. For instance, in 1933 women and men were both present in considerable numbers in only one of the eleven industries to which workers were allocated by the Australian Bureau of Statistics: the retail trade. The heaviest concentration of women was in personal and domestic services, as it had been in the 1870s: women comprised more than 75 per cent of the work-force in this industry. By contrast, 75 per cent of the male work-force was engaged in agriculture, construction, property, and retailing.

During the course of the Community Survey in 1973 we collected information on the occupational activities of 75 men and 41 women who had been employed in the Smalltown district during the 1920s and 1930s. If the patterns of employment that we deduced from these interviews were fairly representative of the actual occupational distribution of women and men workers in these decades then the work-force was segregated in a similar manner to the segregation occurring in the 1870s, and which still prevails. The majority of the women in our 1973 sample who had been employed in the 1930s had worked at jobs that were extensions of their domestic roles: they worked as cooks, cleaners, and hairdressers. Most of the remainder worked as instructors of the young (primary teachers) or carers of the sick (nurses) or in service industries as sales assistants or typists. None of them reported working in occupations men had traditionally dominated or in occupations perceived to require masculine traits: labouring, the higher professions (such as law and medicine), farming, or trades other than hairdressing. Whereas, according to the data provided by members of our sample, women in the 1930s were concentrated in jobs stereotyped as 'suitable for women', most men were employed in occupations perceived as demanding such masculine traits as physical strength and long-term commitment. They were working as tradesmen (mainly in the building industry), town and farm labourers, and as farmers. The only occupations any of the male and female members of our sample had in common were jobs as shop assistants and clerks.

In the 1960s, 1970s and 1980s, more than 90 per cent of the Smalltown women's work-force were, as in the past, employed in jobs entailing caring for or socializing others, providing support services, or ones utilizing domestic skills. These women were working as teachers, nurses, cleaners, typists, garment makers (seamstresses), packers, and shop assistants. By contrast, 90 per cent of the male work-force were employed in jobs which could be stereotyped as requiring several of the following 'masculine' traits: considerable physical strength, initiative, resourcefulness, leadership and management skills, and a willingness and ability to make paid work the centrepiece of one's life. These men were engaged principally in industries where they either worked on their own account (farming, building, etc.), or they occupied administrative positions, or they were employed as metal workers, labourers, road and rail transport officials, operatives of one kind or another, and carpenters and plumbers.

The allocation of the occupations of men and women to class categories based on market power and job status shows the lower ranking of women's occupations. At the beginning of the 1980s men occupied 95 per cent of the class 1, 2 and 3 positions in the non-manual sector of the work-force and 99 per cent of the trade positions in the

Table 6.1 The class position of Smalltown men and women in paid employment

	Men %	Women %	Total %	Women as % of total
Middle classes				
1 Higher-level professionals and administrators	2	0	2	0
2 Farmers	36	1**	26	1
3 Business proprietors	14	5	12	13
4 Semi-professionals and administrators	6	21	10	57
Lower middle class				
5 Ordinary white-collar workers and sales	9	43*	19	66
Working classes				
6 Skilled manual workers and foremen	16	1	11	1
7 Semi-skilled or unskilled manual workers	17	29	21	41
Total %	100	100	101	
N	924	370	1294	

* 28 per cent of these women report that they are self-employed as clerks and shop assistants but they are in fact working in their husband's businesses and not necessarily receiving an independent wage or salary for doing so. They are shown as employees because to show them as self-employed indicates that women are better placed in this class structure than is in fact the case.

** For similar reasons I have excluded from the analysis all but three of the wives of farmers who list themselves as farmers on the census return. The numbers vary but according to leading members of the industry there are never more than half a dozen women who are farming 'in their own right'.

manual sector.[7] By contrast, women held 63 per cent of the class 4 and 5 positions in the non-manual sector and 41 per cent of the class 7 positions at the bottom of the manual sector.

Now (1992), as in the past, men monopolize the more financially rewarding positions in the workforce. They are the community's farmers, they dominate community business, professional and administrative activities, and they comprise virtually all of the tradespeople. There are only a handful of women who own small businesses and until recently one woman managed a medium-sized business employing approximately forty-five workers.[8] The great majority of businesses including the largest—the stock feed company—are owned or managed by men. Until its closure in the middle of 1991, the largest employer of women was a knitting mill; it too was managed by a man. Men are in charge of several small processing industries in which women are employed in semi-skilled and unskilled labour. Women are found in ordinary white-collar jobs and semi-professional jobs in both the private and public sectors under the management of men.

With only three exceptions, Smalltown's lawyers, doctors, engineers, clergy, accountants, and research scientists are men, as are the community's dentist and veterinary surgeon. Virtually all of the community's senior administrators are also men: the town clerk, the shire secretary, the principals of the state primary and state secondary schools and the Roman Catholic secondary college, and the manager of the Smalltown District Hospital. The exceptions are: one woman practising medicine; two women working as lawyers, a fourth employed as director of nursing at the hospital, a fifth and sixth serving as principals of smaller schools, and a seventh working as the unpaid editor of a newspaper managed by a man. The great majority of women are employed as teachers, nurses, clerks, typists, sales assistants, domestic workers, and cooks.

In these patterns, Smalltown exemplifies both international (Murgatroyd, 1982; Bradley, 1989) and national norms (Power, 1975a; Western, 1983; Jones, 1983; Williams, 1988). It has been demonstrated repeatedly that men gain the lion's share of the superior occupational positions in both the manual and non-manual sectors of the Australian work-force. Williams shows that in the 1980s women comprised only 17 per cent of managerial positions but 73 per cent of clerical ones (1988:93). A study carried out in 1986 in Victoria showed that although 18 per cent of female employees were engaged in professional and technical jobs, approximately 66 per cent of these women were employed either as nurses or teachers (Williams, 1988:93). According to Western's criteria, only 19 per cent of the male Australian work-force but 56 per cent of the female work-force are found in inferior positions—ordinary white-collar, semi-skilled, and unskilled jobs (1983:150–1).

Status and income hierarchies

Murgatroyd points out that the notions of higher grade and lower grade occupations can refer to rankings of life-styles, prestige, or economic-class positions:

> It is not that men and women 'most commonly work in different types of occupations . . . [but that] . . . men are most commonly working in higher grade occupations and women are most commonly working in lower grade occupations' (Hakim, 1979:19, cited by Murgatroyd, 1982:576–7).

I have already shown that men dominate the higher economic-class positions in Smalltown's work-force. In this section I will concentrate on hierarchies of status and in the following section on those of income. Murgatroyd found in her examination of gender and occupational stratification in the UK that women ranked lower than men on scales of occupational prestige. In the Australian context Broom and Jones have demonstrated that for much of this century women have been greatly over-represented in jobs of lower prestige in both the non-manual and manual sectors of the work-force (1976). Their analysis ends in 1966. In a more recent study of occupational prestige, Daniels demonstrates that the long-term trends delineated by Broom and Jones persist (Daniels, 1983:186–92). The research of Broom and Jones, and Daniels, shows that the Australian work-force can be ranked in terms of prestige or status from the highest—professional and administrative positions—through farming and small businesses, teaching and nursing, clerical and secretarial work, trades, to the lowest—process work or labouring.

It has already been shown that in Smalltown women are under-represented in the higher professional positions, farming, and the trades positions, and over-represented in the ordinary white-collar, semi-skilled and unskilled positions. If, in Smalltown, the social status of these occupations mirrors or at least approximates their social status in the wider society then it means that women are occupying

Table 6.2 Voluntary ranking of occupations

Occupation	Ranking	Percentage nominating
Higher professionals (especially doctors and lawyers)	1	57
Executives (e.g. town clerk, hospital manager)	2	13
Managers (e.g. bank manager, mill manager)	3	10
Farmers	4	7
Business people, shop owners	5	4
Schoolteachers	6	2
Tradesmen	7	0.05
Shop assistants	7	0.05
Miscellaneous		6
Total (N = 247*)		100

*Respondents could make more than one nomination.

positions attracting less prestige than those occupied by men.

In order to establish whether, in the view of local community members, women's and men's jobs differ substantially in prestige, we asked participants in the Status Survey (1983–85) to nominate the occupations which had the highest social standing in Smalltown. About one-fifth of respondents said the occupations could not be ranked because occupations did not vary in social standing. A common response to our question was, 'There are no classes here mate . . . it's not like the city you know.' However, the majority of respondents did agree to nominate the occupations they believed had the most prestige. There was a high degree of agreement within the sample on occupations nominated for the highest social standing in the community. There was also a high level of agreement between these results and those obtained in national surveys of occupational prestige (Broom and Jones 1976; Daniels, 1983). For instance, more than 90 per cent of the responses to our question on highest occupational status fell within the first three categories of the sixteen-point occupational prestige scale developed by Broom and Jones from a national sample of respondents (1976).

The jobs to which Smalltown respondents gave the highest rankings were all dominated by men (Table 6:2). They were upper professional jobs (especially lawyers and doctors), government executive positions, business managerial positions, and farming. Only two jobs in which women were and still are found in any numbers were nominated: schoolteacher and sales assistant. The first was nominated by six people and the second by one person. The negligible degree of support for teaching and the lack of any support for nursing (another female professional occupation) occurred despite the fact that there were, at the time, far more teachers and nurses than members of any other profession working in the Smalltown community.

Women were just as likely as men to cite male-dominated occupations as ones with the highest social standing.

Entering the paid work-force may be for women an indispensable step towards equity and greater autonomy, but it is certainly not sufficient in itself to achieve these ends. For Smalltown women it has not produced public esteem equal to that enjoyed by men, nor has it brought equal gains in income.

Table 6.3 The average annual taxable incomes of Smalltown's classes by gender, 1981*

	Men N		Women N		Total N	
Middle classes						
1 Higher-level professionals and administrators	20	$20 600	0	———	20	$20 600
2 Farmers	333	$11 600	3	$11 000	336	$11 600
3 Business proprietors	130	$ 8000	20	$ 6600	150	$ 7900
4 Semi-professionals and administrators	56	$18 000	76	$12 200	132	$14 700
Lower middle class						
5 Ordinary white-collar workers and sales	82	$13 500	160	$ 8300	242	$10 000
Working classes						
6 Skilled manual workers and foremen	145	$ 9900	2	$ 7000	147	$ 9900
7 Semi-skilled or unskilled manual workers	158	$ 9800	109	$ 6700	267	$ 8600
N	924	$11 300	370	$ 8600	1294	$10 500

*This is the latest year for which income data are available in this form.

The inferior income of women workers

In 1981 men in the Smalltown work-force received incomes that on average were 20 per cent higher than those received by women (Table 6.3). Furthermore, 19 per cent of men compared with only 10 per cent of women received an income in excess of $15 000. The data on occupation and its relationship to income are presented in occupationally-based classes (Table 6.3).[9] It is evident that within all classes women earn less than men. At one level of explanation, women's inferior incomes reflect the fact that they are more likely to be engaged in part-time work and that they spend more time than men out of the paid work-force. The prevailing values of the work-force reflect the point of view 'that broken experience of paid work is bad and indicates lack of commitment . . . part-time work creates . . . second class status [and economic rewards] for women workers' (Moir, 1984:97).

At another level of explanation the inferior incomes of women exemplify the fact that their economic oppression is often mediated through their interpersonal relationships. For instance, many women teachers and nurses have surrendered their careers to bear and raise children, or to enable husbands to advance their careers; they work only on a part-time basis, or, in some instances, they obtain only emergency work. With the exception of those wives working as emergency teachers, most of these women have a measure of job security, but of course they receive smaller incomes than full-time workers. Part-time or casual work also precludes any significant career advancement and attracts less status. The subordination of women's paid work to the demands of husbands' careers and their domestic and child-care responsibilities help explain why semi-professional women earn incomes that are 50 per cent less than those of semi-professional men.

Probably the most disadvantaged paid women workers are those employed in part-time unskilled occupations as cleaners and cooks in hotels, motels, and private homes. Also penalized financially are women who 'take in' ironing and washing, or who mind children so that other women can work. Some of these women are employed under appropriate awards, but in many instances wages are set by personal negotiation. In 1985 several of these casual workers reported receiving as little as $2 per hour, and many only $5 per hour.

Of course the gender-based differentials in wages and salaries reported here are but one further manifestation of an international phenomenon. Throughout the Western world women receive less money than men for doing similar work (Abercrombie *et al.*, 1988:111; Pearson and Thorns, 1983:178–81). In Australia there is a long history of income discrimination against women. It was institutionalized by legislation in the first decade of the twentieth century when women's wages were fixed at 54 per cent of men's wages. Although during World War II women's wages rose to approximately 75 per cent of men's wages, it was not until the equal pay for equal work legislation was passed in the 1960s that, at least in theory, direct wage discrimination against women was eliminated (Jones, 1984:102).

The introduction of equal pay for equal work legislation did benefit certain sections of the Smalltown women's work-force, especially those engaged in government and semi-government employment. Unfortunately, domestic work and child care prevented many women taking advantage of the wage equity the legislation promised. In addition, a large proportion of Smalltown women are also disadvantaged because the legislation does not apply to them. As Jones stresses, the concept of equality incorporated in the legislation is a limited one applying only to the 'minority of women who work alongside men in mixed occupations' (1984:104). It has been estimated that, for Australia as a whole, about one in five women workers have benefited from the equal pay legislation. In Smalltown the ratio of women beneficiaries is even lower: probably about one in seven. This is in part because there are fewer jobs in the local tertiary sector of the work-force than in the Australian work-force generally, and it is tertiary jobs which are most likely to be affected by equal-pay legislation.[10] It is also because there is such a high proportion of Smalltown women working in semi-skilled and unskilled women's jobs, especially domestic work and, until 1991, garment manufacture. The following example illustrates the discriminatory impact of the legislation on Smalltown women. In early 1986 Smalltown male process workers employed on a full-time basis were earning over $300 a week, while female process workers, also employed on a full-time basis but under a different award, were earning less than $250 a week.[11] The next chapter shows that, at another level, the lower incomes of women in the work-force are also due to gender-based discrimination that is commonplace in Australian society.

Economic dependence

Bryson argues that obtaining a measure of economic independence through entering the paid work-force is a prerequisite for women establishing greater equality with men (1984). Wearing offers a similar argument in the context of her examination of the part that ideology plays in challenging the prevailing gender division of labour. She says wives will not achieve a more equitable division of labour unless they also achieve 'greater material resources' (1984:104).[12] However, throughout Smalltown's history, so few women have engaged in full-time paid work that most Smalltown women have been denied the chance to see if Wearing's and Bryson's hopes can be realized.[13] Even as recently as 1986, only about one in three married women worked on either a part-time or full-time basis.[14] With the closure of the knitting mill in May 1991 the proportion working dropped further. The mill was the largest employer of women engaged in manual work in the community. Its closure reduced the number of full-time jobs available to women by about one-sixth and the number of married women in the work-force by between 10 and 15 per cent.[15] By 7 August 1991, only four of the sixty-nine sacked women had gained alternative employment.[16] A further three had enrolled in a twelve-week personal computer course conducted in a town some 80 kilometres away, but without any hope of translating the training into a paying job in Smalltown. Six of the married women who lost their jobs were the sole providers for their families. Despite the intense efforts of the local council to attract a replacement industry to the town, there is no real prospect in the foreseeable future of a new industry supplying employment for women. Consequently, most of those who have been dismissed will remain jobless. As for the long-term future, employment prospects are in this, as in other small towns throughout Australia, bleak (Baxter *et al.*, 1988:23).[17]

As shown in Chapter 5, instead of getting a paying job, the typical Smalltown wife labours at home without a wage for 'love', keep, and out of a sense of duty. Except when too ill to leave her bed, or confined to give birth to a child, she rarely escapes cooking, cleaning, and 'picking up after others' virtually every day of her married life. By contrast, as the family's bread-winner, a husband not only gains a considerable measure of financial independence but solidifies his position as the head of the household. Many wives are totally dependent on their husbands financially, and most are at least partially dependent.

Income data collected during the 1981 census indicate the extent to which most Smalltown wives are financially dependent upon their husbands. The average income of wives was less than half that of husbands (approximately 48 per cent). Table 6.4 shows that married women were three times as likely as married men to have an income of less

Table 6.4 Distribution of income according to marital status for males and females, Smalltown 1981 (column percentages)

Income	Females			Males		
	Never married	Now married	Separated, divorced, or widowed	Never married	Now married	Separated, divorced, or widowed
$0–4000	52.3	60.7	59.9	37.5	20.3	42.0
$4001–10 000	34.3	23.2	32.3	43.1	35.9	27.3
$10 001–15 000	11.9	10.3	4.2	1.1	26.7	18.2
$15 001 +	1.5	5.8	3.6	5.3	17.1	12.5
Average annual income	$5231	$5540	$4836	$6739	$10 306	$8869
N	268	771	217	341	847	88

than $4000.[18] If we focus on those married people between twenty and sixty-four years of age (these years encompass the greater part of working life[19]) then the potential for women's financial dependency is highlighted. Married women in this age range were five times as likely as married men to have no income at all, or an income of less than $4000. Such a low income guarantees financial dependency upon their partners. More than half of the wives, compared with one-tenth of the husbands, were in this category.

It is probable that, in reality, the proportion of men with such a low income was even less because two-thirds of those reporting an income in this category were self-employed. Such people commonly understate their disposable income by practising 'income splitting' in order to reduce their taxation burden. Income splitting entails 'paying' a proportion of their income to their wives. Our research suggests that, in this community, the man who actually earns the income is believed to have the right to control it and to treat at least some of it as his personal income as opposed to family income. These rights apply to the income that has been 'earned' but which for taxation purposes is being declared as a wife's income (compare with Whitehead, 1981:105). The practice also means that the declared incomes of the women who, in 1981, were married to self-employed men, exaggerate the true income of married women collectively (Table 6.4). But even if these income data are accepted as valid, they still reveal the significant disadvantage experienced by women. For example, in 1981 married men between the ages of twenty and sixty-four were more than twice as likely as married women of a comparable age to have an income in excess of $10 000.

Differential access to the means of production or to wages and salaries largely explains the dramatic differences in male and female incomes in Smalltown (see Table 6.4).[20] However, in the 1980s, whether or not they were in the paid work-force, men enjoyed an income advantage over women. More specifically, in both the non-paid work-force and the paid work-force categories, men's incomes were on average 20 per cent higher than those of women. Presumably, the higher income of men in the non-paid work-force category reflected their superior gains from such things as superannuation and dividends, which in turn reflected their greater rate of participation at an earlier stage in their life in the paid work-force.

The data on the incomes of men and women of retirement age indicate that husbands were not sharing the benefits of their previous employment equitably with their wives. These findings suggest that, not only do the marked gender inequities in access to finance persist into old age but, in many instances, it is the explicit action of husbands as controllers of a couple's finances which ensure their persistence. It appears that husbands keep an inequitable share of the income for themselves, or the husband continues in retirement to be the sole recipient of income, even though he is no longer engaged in paid employment. The wife continues in her position of financial dependence, reliant on what her husband chooses to pass on to her. The data presented in Table 6.4 show that incomes of widowers were on average twice that of widows. Sixty per cent of women in this situation had an income of less than $4000, compared with 42 per cent of men. This difference may have been due to husbands disposing of much of their income-producing resources before death. Presumably, the vast majority of the 130 women who had lost their partners and had such a low income had exchanged financial dependency on their husbands for financial dependency on the state. While they had probably been freed—through the death or divorce of their spouses—from the subordination that tends to accompany financial dependency within a marriage, it is highly likely that their standard of living had declined. Furthermore, many of them were likely to be too old, or insufficiently qualified or experienced, or too committed to taking care of children, to enter or re-enter the work-force.[21] In short, these women's past or present caring commitments reduced, or negated entirely, the capacity of many of them to earn an adequate income once the patronage of their husbands had been deliberately or inadvertently withdrawn, or, alternatively, once a wife had chosen to leave a husband.

In the 1970s and 1980s our enquiries indicated that the majority of Smalltowners were aware of the financial dependence of wives of all ages. For instance, 74 per cent of the participants in the Gender Survey said Smalltown women were very dependent financially, or that most women were dependent financially on their husbands. By contrast, only 3 per cent of the respondents said men were financially dependent on their wives. Not one respondent unequivocally denied women's financial dependence, whereas just half of them did unequivocally deny the financial dependence of husbands.[22] Women respondents were as likely as men respondents to acknowledge the financial dependence of wives, and middle-class respondents were as likely as those of the working class to endorse its occurrence.

Economic dependence declares women inferior because of the supreme value of money, reinforces the superordinate position of men in marriages, and often produces powerlessness (Tulloch, 1984). It informs and reinforces men's authority in the eyes of partners and community members of both gender. 'Men are entitled to take the big decisions', it was often said, 'because it is their money'. Some also said that men, rather than their wives, were equipped to take such decisions because their paid-work experience qualified them to do so. A minority of women strenuously disagreed with this judgement, but many Smalltown women accepted it. Some of the wives who accepted its validity believed that decision-making in their particular marriage was equitable, but they tended to the view that if a husband chose to 'take the big decisions' it was, for the reasons just canvassed, his prerogative.

In short, a woman's economic dependence not only enhances a man's economic power but legitimates his use of that power to maintain a superordinate position in marriage. It also makes it highly likely that a husband rather than a wife will exercise more control over the choices a partner makes about such things as whether or not to enter the paid work-force, or to spend considerable sums of money on leisure activities.

CHAPTER 7

Excluding women from paid work

Male dominance in any particular institutional sphere 'is part of a wider system of male power' (Ferree, 1990:866). It will be shown in this chapter that men often prevent women entering paid work altogether, or they impede their participation to such a degree that it is impossible for them to gain substantial autonomy, either economic or social, through employment. Men do this in one or more of several ways: establishing sons rather than daughters in farming or town businesses; employer discrimination; withholding permission for wives to work; making permission for wives to work conditional on their retaining overall responsibility for domestic work and child care; leaving wives with so much domestic work and child care that it is impossible for them to take a paid job; and incorporating wives in their own paid work.[1]

Excluding daughters from farming and town businesses

The possibility of women engaging in paid work, especially in more economically rewarding and prestigious jobs, is substantially reduced by farmers and town businessmen taking sons rather than daughters into the family enterprise or, alternatively, of providing a son rather than his sister with the capital to farm or go into business 'in his own right'. Gender-based priority of this kind makes a marked difference to employment patterns in a community where approximately 40 per cent of the paid work-force are engaged in some form of petit-bourgeois enterprise. The practice effectively excludes women from more than one-third of the jobs in the total work-force, and approximately three-quarters of all middle-class jobs in Smalltown. This means that Smalltown men have roughly four times the chance of Smalltown women of gaining a middle-class position (other than an ordinary white-collar job) in the local community.

The impact of gender discrimination by families organizing (or failing to organize) jobs for their children is most noticeable in farming. Farming land has been the principal economic resource in the Smalltown district for the last 120 years, and farming the commonest form of petit-bourgeois enterprise. However, farming land is not freely available on the open market and when it becomes available from time to time it is too expensive for a younger person to buy without family assistance. Estimations vary but it probably costs more than one million dollars to establish a viable farming enterprise in the Smalltown district.

As a rule, farms are not bought but transmitted through the kinship system from father to son. Of the 220 or so farms in the district, probably less than 5 per cent have been inherited by daughters.[2] When a daughter inherits a property it is usually because there is no son to succeed the father. Few women farm the property they inherit: some of them sell it; others employ a manager. It is not uncommon for the husband of an inheriting daughter to 'run' the farm and to be viewed as the farmer by the local community.[3] Consequently, it is the son or sons of such a marriage who are most likely to inherit the farm and in that way to bring about the establishment of a new male line. The practices of inheritance and succession I have just described are not usually questioned. Why would they be? After all they are consistent with the prevailing view that a man, not a woman, serves as '*the* provider'. Farming has always been a 'man's job' and as such it requires the abilities, especially the physical strength and entrepreneurial skills, men are believed to possess. Furthermore, it is difficult to reconcile the Smalltown notions of femininity with a career in farming for women (see Ch. 9).

The deliberate exclusion of women from farming is the most clear-cut example we found of patriarchal control of paid work in Smalltown, and the acceptance of this practice by the great majority of farmers' wives one of the most convincing demonstrations of patriarchal authority. The practice reinforces men's dominance of one of the more lucrative forms of employment in the district, reduces the number of women engaged in paid work, and, as Chapter 10 will show in more detail, prevents them gaining the jobs that offer locally-born young people their best chance of achieving economic autonomy and considerable status without leaving the district.

By favouring sons over daughters, town businessmen—like farmers—also limit women's opportunities to gain a level of economic autonomy that might make for a more equitable marriage. In 1987, 41 per cent of the families with small businesses had sons and 33 per cent had daughters of a suitable age to participate in the family business. However, whereas 44 per cent of the sons had been taken into the business, less than 10 per cent of the daughters had been. For instance, at about this time, one prosperous business family took their only son into the business whereas his sister worked as a sales assistant in someone else's business. Her class position declined and only by making the 'right' marriage will she partially restore it. I say partially because it is misleading to equate the vicarious class position marriage bestows on the wife of a farmer or businessman with the class position the husband himself gains through inheritance or the gift of capital to establish a business. The wife usually gains only indirect and partial access to the economic benefits of her husband's occupation. As Delphy and Leonard stress, 'Inheritance is a system which . . . very often is based on inequality, on some being advantaged and others disadvantaged' (1986:69). Clearly, in this community, it is women who are disadvantaged. Gender overrides class: because of their gender, the vast majority of daughters of farming and business families are excluded from the major benefits of their family class position—a partnership in the family business or the capital to go into business for themselves—while often their brothers are assured of such positions. The inheritance practices occurring among the community's petit-bourgeois families reduce the competition from women for the scarce resource of property and, as stressed earlier, in a community where family enterprises comprise much of the economic activity (more than 40 per cent of the male work-force is self-employed), it savagely reduces the opportunities for women to enter employment and makes their economic dependence on their husbands inevitable. The same practices exploit wives by ensuring that their child-bearing and child-rearing labour are appropriated in the economic interests of men, or of their male offspring, and they also ensure that the cycle of gender discrimination in access to family economic enterprises is repeated.

Whenever, in the course of casual conversation with parents from petit-bourgeois families, we asked why sons appear to be favoured over daughters, our respondents usually offered one of two explanations and sometimes both. The explanation offered most frequently was that parents feel a greater responsibility to provide a job future for a son than for a daughter because it is the son who has to be the provider. 'After all, a daughter is going to be her future husband's problem [laughter]. We've got more than enough to worry about with two sons who need to be given a start' (45-year-old businessman). Such a parent invariably hastens to add that nowadays it is as important (or almost as important) for a daughter as for a son to have a career and that they intend to help their daughter get a 'good education', but in reality daughters are not given the same opportunities. After all they are excluded from access to the families' best assets for facilitating a career for them: property and a business enterprise.

When asked why boys rather than girls inherited, some respondents also said that family businesses get passed on to boys because they're based on 'a man's trade'. The data we collected corroborated this second 'explanation'.[4] In 1987, 68 per cent of non-farming businesses were based on so-called 'male' occupations and only 7 per cent were based on 'female' occupations. The remaining 25 per cent could not be categorized easily as businesses based exclusively on either 'male' or 'female' occupations.

The male occupations most likely to serve as the base for starting a business are the traditional trades, such as carpentry, plumbing, bricklaying and electrical work, and truck driving and operating heavy equipment of various kinds, such as that used for dam building. These are seen as men's jobs, principally because it is customary for men to perform them. It is always a short step from customary to natural and right, and Smalltowners take this step readily. When pressed, they say that it is natural (and therefore right) for men to engage in these jobs because they demand male characteristics such as their superior muscle power, and 'unnatural' for a woman because she lacks the physical characteristics to perform them adequately. Occasionally a respondent also points out that it is inappropriate for a woman to engage in many of these jobs because they entail working in a 'man's world' where dirty jokes and sexual innuendo are an integral part of interaction 'on the job' and harassment is possible. Entering such employment may call into question a woman's respectability, her feminine identity in the eyes of the community, and her suitability as a marriage partner in the eyes of younger men.[5]

There are far fewer 'female' than 'male' jobs that can serve as the basis for the establishment of a business enterprise. In the 1990s hairdressing and dressmaking are the only female trades being practised.[6] Several women practise dressmaking on a part-time basis. There are three hairdressing businesses in Smalltown's main street and a further three businesses run by women 'out of their homes'.

If women want to 'go into business for themselves', they can set up a retail business in the main street, provided they have the capital. They are most likely to attract custom if they choose a business perceived as appropriate for a woman to run. In 1991 two women owned or managed shoe shops, another two dress shops, and one each a coffee shop, tea rooms, a travel agency, a draper, a motel, and a garden centre. Two women were in partnership with their husbands in cafés and another woman partnered her husband in a drapery. This is a minuscule number of enterprises compared to the 150 or so businesses based on a 'man's' occupation.

In a community in which petit-bourgeois enterprises account for the great majority of available middle-class jobs, and in which there is so little opportunity for women to establish a business based on a traditional woman's job, the decision of fathers to take sons and not daughters into either a town business or a farming enterprise assumes great significance.

We only very occasionally heard this gender favouritism questioned during field-work. For fathers, mothers, and adolescent children it was taken for granted. The women most likely to question the system were some of those who had pursued a professional career before their marriage to a Smalltown man. One of these women told me that she pleads repeatedly with her husband to vary the traditional practice of favouring the son over the daughter. The following exchange occurred after the birth of their third son.

Husband: We now have three boys to provide for. It's a real worry. We are just going to have to expand our holdings.
Wife: No, we have four children to provide for. Don't forget we have a daughter too. She has to be looked after just as much as the boys.
Husband: It's the boys I have to worry about. They are the ones who'll have to come on to the farm if they want to.

This wife reported that all her attempts to persuade her husband came to nothing. She is powerless, she said, to ensure that her daughter is treated like her sons.

In Chapter 9 we will see that, because adolescent girls do not aspire to jobs currently dominated by men, there is unlikely to be any serious challenge to men's exclusion of them from most of the more rewarding positions in the local work-force.

The possibility of employer and community discrimination

A comprehensive examination of this form of direct discrimination is beyond the scope of the research from which this book was developed; and even if it had been feasible, such an investigation would probably have placed the entire project in jeopardy. However, it is important to make reference to its possible occurrence. Two of the larger employers did volunteer the information that they believed men were, by nature, endowed to lead and women to play supportive roles. One of them reported that, after what he regarded as a disastrous appointment of a tertiary-qualified woman to an executive level, he would 'avoid like the plague appointing another such woman in the future'. He went on to stress that women were better suited to centring their lives on the home and family. 'It's fighting nature for the man to stay home and the woman to go out to work. The whole idea feels odd.' The second said: 'I'm a bit old-fashioned, but it's proper for a man to look after a woman.'

Men occupy all senior positions in local government; they serve as principals for the three largest schools, and a man is manager of the District Hospital. I do not possess evidence to establish one way or the other whether men were preferred for these positions. I do know that a substantial minority and possibly a majority of community members believe that men are qualified by temperament and experience, while women are disqualified by their housekeeping roles to assume responsibility for the more important leadership positions in community life (see Ch. 8). When we raised with Smalltowners the matter of the absence of women from senior administrative positions, we were sometimes told that women had no grounds for complaint because they lacked the formal qualifications required for these jobs. This was an accurate assessment in so far as senior executive positions in local government and hospital management were concerned, but it has to be said that these were occupations that women had neither been encouraged to identify with nor trained for in Australian society. Consequently, the absence of women from such positions in Smalltown is an expression of what Jones (1984) calls societal discrimination.

There were, during the 1980s, women present in Smalltown who were sufficiently qualified to occupy positions as principals of the state primary and secondary schools. None has served as a principal of these schools. As far as I am aware, none of them has put herself forward as a candidate when a principal's position has become vacant. One of the women who was sufficiently qualified to compete said that she would not apply for a principalship because she believed she would risk being labelled as a 'bitch' for doing so. Another stressed that it would be impossible to combine the demands of such a job with her domestic commitments and her responsibility as a mother.

Withholding permission

In the studies that Sharpe (1984) and Yeandle (1984) made of working mothers it emerges that most wives need their husband's approval in order to engage in paid work. Sharpe reports that the husband of only one in ten of the wives in her sample explicitly disapproved of her working (1984:166). Yeandle states that a small minority of the husbands of working wives in her sample were opposed to their wives working. It appears that the majority approved even if approval was often conditional on the wives attending to traditional domestic tasks and child care (1984:145–7). Unfortunately neither researcher interviewed wives who were not engaged in paid work (or their husbands) to elicit the attitudes of those husbands to their possible employment.

In Smalltown we asked participants in the Gender Survey whose decision it would be as to whether or not a wife worked. Eighty-three per cent of respondents said either it had been a wife's decision at some time in the past, or it would be if the decision were taken at some time in the future. However, when in a subsequent round of interviews we enquired whether husbands had given their approval to work for wives who were working, or whether husbands had withheld approval from those who were *not* working, a different picture emerged. First, all fifteen husbands whose wives were *not* working said explicitly that they were opposed to them working. We also asked the sixteen different wives in this sample who were not working how they believed their husbands viewed the possibility of them entering paid employment, and only two said their husbands would approve. In sum, it appears that 94 per cent of the husbands of non-employed wives were opposed to their wives participating in the paid work-force. Conversely,

90 per cent of wives who were working had their husbands' approval (N = 48).

It was clear from the comments made during these interviews that, although the decision was perceived as the wife's, she did not take it unilaterally. Without exception, wives were well aware of their husbands' attitude to their taking paid employment, and many husbands couched their answers to our questions in terms that left us in no doubt that they were exercising considerable power or authority in this matter. Expressions such as, 'I would only agree if such and such' and 'She can go to work *provided*, etc.' were frequently used. Many of the wives used expressions such as: 'He'd never agree to me going to work.' We witnessed interactions in which wives pleaded their case to be allowed to work. A number of wives participating in the Gender Survey volunteered the information that they would not work without the consent of their husbands.

Domestic work

In Smalltown, domestic work is organized to facilitate the participation of men in paid work. Both the Family and Gender Surveys showed that in more than 90 per cent of cases, married women have major and usually sole responsibility for most routine domestic tasks and for child care.[7] In this community, the domestic jobs that men are normally in charge of are those that are compatible with paid work. These are the tasks that occur less frequently, and are more easily postponed than those women perform. Furthermore, the participation of husbands in domestic work and child care is optional, whereas the wife's performance is pivotal and indispensable (see Ch. 5). The nature and extent of a wife's unpaid work invariably impedes her paid work and often precludes her taking it up.[8] As the American writer Kessler-Harris observes, 'Given the realities of work in the home . . . women could not be expected to perform effectively in the labour force' (1987:521).

Women also lack work experience because of the time they have been out of the work-force bearing and raising children, or facilitating a husband's career, or both. As Crompton points out, 'the explanation for women's lack of success in career terms may be sought in the near impossibility of combining the demands and requirements of a successful career with the gender assigned responsibilities of the domestic role' (1986:124). The Smalltown women themselves are well aware of the impact their domestic activities have on their ability to engage in outside employment. For instance, a majority of the wives participating in the Gender Survey (sub-sample) who were *not* at the time of the survey engaged in paid work, said that their home-making responsibilities and the needs of young children were the major reasons for their staying out of the paid work-force.

Some feminists hold husbands responsible for preventing women entering paid work by delegating to them responsibility for domestic work (Davidoff, 1976). In Smalltown there are a number of indicators that husbands possess superior power and that at least some of them use it to insist on their wives giving priority to domestic duties rather than engaging in paid work. A minority of women participants in the Gender Survey who were in their twenties and thirties reported that their husbands resisted all their efforts to get them to help with domestic work and child care enough to allow them to participate in paid work. They pointed out that when their husbands withheld assistance they had no alternative but to do the housework and mind the children themselves. 'It's expected of us by our husbands and by everybody else. If we don't do it then it's not done' (farmer's wife). There were no indications in the course of our field-work in either the 1970s or 1980s that a wife could delegate domestic work to a husband but there was a great deal of evidence that husbands could delegate domestic work and child care to their wives.

Wives spoke explicitly of the impediments husbands placed in the way of their working. One wife said, 'Men expect women to have the housework done when they get home. So if they take a job they have to somehow keep things up to scratch at home (woman with part-time job married to a professional man). Another wife said that her husband was vigorously discouraging her from returning to work on a full-time basis. She was also deterred by what she described as her complete responsibility for 'everything that has to be done around here'. She said, 'What would be the point of going back to work when I would still have total responsibility here. Bill would not lift a finger to help. I will have to find other outlets for stimulation' (a farmer's wife).

Very few Smalltown husbands, if any, offer to increase their share of domestic tasks so that a wife may work. For example, not one of the husbands participating in the Gender Survey volunteered the comment that he was prepared to help so that his wife might work (N = 54). Given that going out to work full-time doubles the number of hours a wife works, unless her domestic load is substantially reduced, this unwillingness makes a nonsense of the claim of 90 per cent of the husbands in the Gender Survey that it was their wife's decision whether or not she entered the paid work-force. Indeed most of these husbands demonstrated during our interviews with them that it was *not* a wife's unilateral decision. These men said their wives could work provided neither the children nor the housework was neglected. For instance, a foreman in his forties said:

It's OK for my wife to work because she is able to set her own hours that she is at work so as to ensure that the kids are at school before she starts work and that she finishes before they get home. She is able to take time off when they are sick and she doesn't work during the school holidays. She would *not* take on a full time job because of the kids, although she might when they are older.

No husband in this sample said, 'Yes she can work and I will help by cooking the evening meal twice a week', or doing the washing, or anything of that nature.

If a wife is trying to decide whether or not to engage in paid work she cannot assume that her husband will necessarily continue to perform any tasks that he had customarily performed (for example washing up after the evening meal). Most husbands see themselves having the right to withdraw assistance if it interferes with their work. Their view is that their paid work takes priority because they are *the* providers. If a wife works she becomes a supplemental earner rather than a 'co-provider'.[9] Wives report that husbands think nothing of saying, 'I'm working back tonight so I won't be able to help put the kids to bed', or something similar. In direct contrast, a wife who does work will try to organize her working hours so that she is available when needed by children or husband. It surely has happened, but it is difficult to envisage any Smalltown wife phoning her husband late in the day and simply announcing, 'I'm working back tonight so please feed the children and put them to bed.' Some wives told us that their husband's unreliability in the home, and especially in 'helping with the children', deterred them from taking a job. 'You can never be certain that George will show up to mind the kids. He may phone five minutes before he is due home to say "something's come up", or he may just forget.'

The conclusion Leonard drew from her study of a sample of British couples aptly describes the situation prevailing in Smalltown. Paid employment for wives is seen as something the woman may *choose* to undertake '[it is] seen as her responsibility to organize her domestic work around her outside duties if she wishes to do it' (Leonard, 1980: 243–4, cited by Finch, 1983:138).

Many husbands also linked their opposition to wives working to the view that it would reduce the quality of family life and threaten the well-being of children. More than four-fifths of the husbands of wives who were *not* working at all, or working only occasionally, stated that they believed that a wife's engagement in paid employment would have a negative impact on their marriage. The great majority of the same sample of husbands (85 per cent) expressed the view that children would pay the price if a mother worked.[10]

You cannot have a stable family life if a woman is working . . . a woman cannot be a good mother and work (an administrator in his late twenties whose wife did not work).

Wives should stay home and mind the children. Some of the most disturbed kids in this town are from families where the mother works (a 36-year-old professional man whose wife worked very occasionally).

In summary, the evidence produced in this section shows how patriarchal power is at once pervasive and subtly exercised. One cannot go so far as to say that any wife who is not engaged in paid work is being directly prevented from doing so by her husband, but what seems irrefutable is that husbands are able, if they choose, to impede their wives working both by withholding permission for them to work, and by delegating to them such a degree of responsibility for domestic work and child care that it is often impossible for them to work.

Community opposition to working wives

The likelihood of the husband preventing his wife working is enhanced by community opposition to working wives. One wife who was pushing her husband to help more in the home in the mid-1980s in the hope that she could resume a professional career (if only on a part-time basis) articulated the type of community support that exists for a husband such as hers who is resisting this kind of pressure: 'When he digs his heels in and refuses to offer more than token help he has the whole community backing him up (30-year-old wife of a businessman with a child of pre-school age). A majority of community members of both sexes oppose, in principle, wives engaging in paid work. The opposition is most likely to come from the middle classes—particularly from farmers, businessmen and many professionals, and the spouses of these men, but it also comes from the working classes, especially from those in secure jobs. The opposition stems in large measure from the widespread acceptance in Smalltown of the notion of the dual spheres: it is a husband's job to be the provider and a wife's to be a home-maker, to care for the children and support her husband in his work. We were told repeatedly, 'It's a wife's job to look after things at home'. Smalltowners of both genders and all classes believe that good family life is difficult, if not impossible to achieve unless a wife gives herself full-time to the tasks around the home, especially 'when the children are still growing up'.

In the 1970s respondents also opposed wives working because they believed that, by working, they deprived single girls leaving school of a job. This deprivation was seen as producing unnecessary hardship for many of the community's constituent families. It was argued that, because married women were taking jobs, families were being forced to provide economically for daughters for a longer period than they should, or losing the company of a daughter who had no alternative than to emigrate to the city in order to find work. This was believed to reduce the pool of potential marriage partners, which interfered with the orderly progression of females from school to paid work and ultimately to marriage with a 'local boy'.[11] If, by entering the job market, married women were setting in train these interrelated processes, clearly it was potentially de-stabilizing demographically and socially for a community with a steadily declining population.

So vocal and sometimes vindictive was the opposition to married women working that in 1974 I made a survey of wives in paid employment to establish what proportion of them were depriving girls leaving school of jobs. This survey was conducted at a time of relatively high employment in Smalltown as well as throughout Australia, and at a time when school leavers could reasonably expect to gain full-time employment. The survey showed that married women were, in the vast majority of cases, employed in jobs either that females leaving school did not want—such as part-time work as domestics—or jobs which required tertiary qualifications that could not be obtained locally, such as nursing or teaching.[12] In the 1970s the opposition to a wife working was strongest if she had dependent children (I return to this issue below). It was also fierce if she were married to a man who was believed to be able to provide adequately for his wife and children. In the 1970s it was widely assumed that men in business for themselves—farmers, professionals, administrators, and permanently employed skilled manual workers—were able to support a wife and family.

By the early 1980s the opposition to wives working had lessened in the face of the evident growing inability of many families to 'make ends meet' on a single income. It was now viewed as permissible, but not desirable, for a wife to work if her working was materially essential for her family and provided she was not jeopardizing her children's well-being by doing so. Working so as to help a farmer or businessman husband who was struggling to 'keep his head above water' was viewed as falling within the parameters of working for the family. Our surveying indicated that most Smalltowners were still opposed to a wife working if it was not financially necessary for her family. This was the position taken by 84 per cent of the members of the Gender Survey (sub-sample) (N = 48).

If a husband has a good job, his wife should *not* work (retired semi-skilled manual worker).[13]

In this town if a woman goes out to work we all assume at the start at least that things are not going well financially for her family (38-year-old wife of an equipment operator who herself worked on a part-time basis).

If a woman took up a paid job to protect the economic well-being of her family it was seen as acceptable behaviour, but some respondents, including the woman just quoted, were sceptical about the claim that wives were going out to work out of financial necessity. During the same interview she went on to say, 'If, however, it turns out that a woman's family does not really need the money then people are going to start criticizing her.'[14] A 55-year-old employee tradesman with a government job said, 'There is no need for wives to work. One income is enough for any family in this town. We have raised our family and educated them on my income. The younger wives who are going out to work now are just greedy!

While going out to work in order to raise your standard of living was *not* viewed as justifiable behaviour, during the 1980s women were increasingly taking a job for this purpose. Some of our respondents argued that, because of the expenses associated with participation in the paid workforce, these wives were not increasing their standard of living substantially. If they had young children it was claimed that by going out to work they were jeopardizing their children's well-being. They were also possibly putting their marriage at risk.

They're working so they can have parties, buy a second TV and two cars. I reckon that they're not that much better off by the time they pay for someone to baby sit and buy 'take-aways'.

They wouldn't be any worse off [financially] staying home, cooking their meals and looking after kids. But they go out and become independent and the marriage becomes rocky. When only the husband works she's dependent on him for money and he's dependent on her to have the house tidy and his meals ready when he gets home. When they both work they both become independent. That's what happening around here and we are getting some big shocks with marriages breaking up (67-year-old wealthy businessman).

This respondent then cited the recent breakup of the marriage of a well-known middle-class couple to support his argument. He linked the dissolution to the wife's working. Men were more likely than women to say that if a wife works it may have a detrimental impact on a marriage—more than 80 per cent of the husbands participating in the Gender Survey took this position—but the view was expressed by members of both sexes.

A majority of community members also disapproved of a woman going out to work to achieve financial independence or self-fulfilment. More than four-fifths of the participants in the Gender Survey said that a married woman who worked for such reasons would be viewed as selfish. Women respondents were almost as likely as men to offer the assessment that community members generally would disapprove of a woman working in order to achieve personal fulfilment (81 per cent of female respondents compared to 88 per cent of male respondents). The following extract from an interview with a 45-year-old driver in a secure government job whose wife worked full-time is a rather extreme example of the attitude expressed frequently, if usually in a more muted manner, during interviews.

Interviewer: Do you think that a wife should go out to work if it is not financially necessary for the well-being of her family?
Respondent: If it is not financially necessary why is she working?
Interviewer: Some women say that working is necessary for their emotional well-being.

Respondent: That's a lot of bloody bullshit! If they don't need the money they should be at home, making sure everything is OK. That's where they belong. They can get their emotional needs met there.

Opposition to women working for such reasons was expressed by men of all classes and ages. 'The world would be a better place if women would find their fulfilment in the home' (33-year-old professional whose wife was not working). Only five of the 104 respondents participating in the Gender Survey, most of whom were under the age of fifty, said that wives should be free to choose to 'take an outside job' in order to find fulfilment. Most participants in this survey took the view that the satisfactions that home and family offer should provide enough fulfilment for a wife and mother, or, failing that, the rewards of home and family, supplemented by such things as the sense of well-being that came from contact with friends, and participation in voluntary organizations or sporting activities should suffice.

As already indicated, there was a small minority who dissented from the dominant view. One of these, a man, said home coupled with 'a bit of work' should provide enough satisfaction for a wife. Four women respondents offered a range of comments which amounted to saying that wives should be free to find fulfilment through work if they choose to do so. They made clear their position in answer to an explicit question about paid work being used by women to express themselves or achieve independence.

In this community if a husband is bringing in a good wage a wife is criticized for going out to work. But they forget that a woman has a right to go out to work. She might be a better housewife and mother because of going out to work (farmer's wife who had a professional qualification).

Three of these four women were tertiary educated and were themselves engaged in paid work. None of them was a woman who had grown up in Smalltown. All had emigrated to Smalltown after gaining professional qualifications elsewhere.[15] Nevertheless, they were reluctant to press their view publicly because they wished to retain the goodwill of the people they associated with daily in this small and tightly-knit community.

In both the 1970s and 1980s the opposition to wives taking outside employment was fiercest when they had very young children. In this regard the community reinforces the position taken by those husbands who say they do not want their wives to work because it will be detrimental for the children. 'If you go out to work people will probably say it will be hard on your kids' (mother of two young children). Seventy-nine per cent of the participants in the Gender Survey (sub-sample) said a wife should not work if her children are of pre-school age. 'Unless mothers stay home and mind the kids until they go to school they'll get grandmother's view of life and end up a generation behind (32-year-old businessman with two young children whose wife stayed home but kept the family business books). Sixty per cent of respondents in this survey also disapproved of a wife working if she had a child of primary-school age (approximately five to eleven years). However, a majority of respondents said it was all right for a wife to work if her children were of high-school age. 'High school kids can fend for themselves when they get home.' But there were those who made the following type of comment:

> A lot of people would say mothers should be home when kids get home to bring them news and stuff like that (farmer's wife).

> Kids shouldn't have to come home to an empty house. A woman shouldn't have kids if she is going to work (professional man's wife).

Even those who did approve of mothers with older children working usually did so on condition that their paid work did not disadvantage their offspring. The following type of comment was made frequently: 'If a kid gets into trouble then the finger is pointed at the working mother' (female teacher). In Smalltown the view prevails that a working mother should ideally arrange her hours of employment so that she is available 'when the children need her', such as during school holidays, at the end of the school day, and when 'they are ill'. Accommodating such views is clearly going to impede the development of a career and push women in the direction of part-time employment.

Older women are the most likely to be cited by younger women as the persons who disapprove of mothers working. The survey data we collected confirm the accuracy of this perception. Almost without exception the older women in the Gender Survey did disapprove. Younger women are possibly more aware of the disapproval of older women because the latter voice their opposition in public as well as in private conversations, but if older women act as the police, they are supported in their action by many of Smalltown's younger men and women.

The discussions we had with respondents on the subject of a wife working when she has young children demonstrated how widespread is the acceptance of the notion that the husband is the primary bread-winner. Its acceptance discourages women from competing with men for jobs the latter have traditionally dominated. Even those women who reject the validity of the traditional sexual division of labour accept that, in the Smalltown community, males are and will remain the major or sole providers. These respondents concede that this is a structural given which sets parameters on the choices of wives. Furthermore, several of the women holding feminist views on this issue argue that, in certain circumstances, the demands of the provider role may excuse husbands from playing the part in domestic affairs that these women, as radicals, believed they *should* ideally play. So, for example, some of the more radical women said husbands engaged in such jobs as farming could not be available on a regular basis to assist with child care. At the same time, none of the women suggested that a husband should take over a woman's domestic duties and child care and allow her to work. Very few of them even went as far as to say a husband should curtail his participation in paid work if he has a child who needs him.[16]

Community opposition to wives working, or of conditional approval, placed at least some who contemplated going out to work in a defensive position. The prospect of having to cope with direct criticism if they did work deterred some. The occurrence of such criticism was most likely to be reported to us by women married to men in well-paid positions. One of these wives said that one man had made critical comments to her face about her working on at least six occasions. The essence of his criticism was that she should not work because her husband had a well-paying job. A second woman, who was the wife of a prominent administrator, said she had to cope with the same kind of criticisms being offered by women and men when she entered the work-force. Some women respondents cited the response to the administrator's wife and other similar instances as proof of local opposition to women working. We have no way of knowing how many wives are deterred from working because of this criticism but at least a few are.

What is probably more common is the decision by wives not to work because they are sensitive to criticisms about the negative impact that a mother's paid employment might have on her children's well-being. Hearing such criticisms voiced often triggers feelings of guilt in women strongly committed to motherhood, including those who have joined the work-force, especially when husbands are making similar criticisms.

In this community women's work [that is paid work] is justified or condemned according to its impact on women's roles as wives and mothers. I myself feel guilty because I have to leave the kids with the baby-sitter and I just cannot keep the home as nice as I would like (38-year-old wife of a self-employed tradesman).

Another woman, who gave up a semi-professional job to bear a child, reiterated the comments she received from 'a number of people during the first few months following the child's birth. She said: 'Quite a few people said to me, "Are you back at work yet?"; when I said "No", they said, "Oh that's good. You're looking after your little boy properly then", or that sort of thing.' This woman's husband was unemployed during part of the time these remarks were being made.

Incorporating wives in husbands' jobs

The impression we gained from numerous conversations and interviews is that a husband is often likely to withhold permission for his wife to work, or at least place hurdles in her way because he believes her employment will reduce his effectiveness as a bread-winner. Husbands have community support for this stance also. Such husbands wish to be free of domestic tasks and child care so that they can devote long hours to their job. They also want a wife to be available to assist them with their paid work by serving as a 'substitute worker' or by providing 'back-up services' of several kinds (Finch, 1983). They reason that if a wife is busy with a paid job of her own she will not be available when needed. These husbands repeatedly try to gain their wives' compliance by urging them to find their fulfilment partly through the home and partly by helping with their business or farming.

On one occasion I was present during a protracted discussion between a businessman and his wife over her need to work. He said that he could not understand at all why she would want to return to work. The following conversation ensued.

Husband: You really have enough to do here [meaning in the home]. Anyhow you are really my partner in the business.
Wife: I know that dear. But wives need interests of their own. I would like something in addition to what I have here. Jill Collins is very happy now she is going out to work. It has given her a real interest and her situation is similar to mine. [She was about the same age—mid-thirties—she also had two children of primary-school age and was married to a businessman who worked long hours].
Husband: You haven't heard what Tom Collins thinks of his wife working. He is very opposed. I can't see why you are not like Ruth Finch [another businessman's wife]. She gives her husband so much help with his business and that's enough for her. She's not looking for anything more! A man needs his wife's help these days when the going is getting so tough.

The longer the conversation went on the angrier and the more hurt the husband became. He interpreted his wife's wishes to take a paid job as a reflection on him as a provider. It appeared, from the interaction and his tone of voice, that her desire to have an outside interest that would reduce her availability to him was viewed as a lack of appreciation of what he was doing for her, and perhaps as a sign of insufficient affection on her part. Love, it seems, is to be expressed by being an attentive and enthusiastic supporter of a husband's *provider* activities. In this instance, she decided to let the matter drop—intending, she said, out of the hearing of her husband, to raise it again at some future time. She also indicated that she would need his agreement to re-enter the paid work-force. This woman was not seriously challenging her husband. She was petitioning him. Her demeanour confirmed her husband's superior power and his authority.

Many wives are prevented from taking a paid job in part at least (or they are forced to work on a part-time or casual basis) by their husbands' practice of incorporating them in their paid work. In Smalltown, all wives, including those who engage in paid work themselves, made a substantial contribution to their husbands' job. The contribution is so great that it interferes significantly with the activities of the wives themselves. They facilitate their husband's work by ensuring they are fit physically, mentally, and emotionally for work, by freeing them from virtually all domestic work, and taking major responsibility for child care.[17] The women most affected by incorporation are the wives of men with careers as opposed to 'dead-end' jobs. The occupations of these men are so designed that they can only be carried out successfully if their wives are available to assist directly with various aspects of the business or career itself. In addition to feeding a husband, providing him with clean clothes, caring for the children and keeping them quiet so he can rest and relax, these wives provide 'back-up' services, or they serve as 'substitute' or 'additional' workers for husbands.[18] The expectations of such support are 'built into the structure of the job(s)' (Ferree, 1990:873) especially of businessmen, farmers and traditional professionals.

The businessman's wife

As Powell and Jensen point out, the typical small town firm is 'operated by an owner and (largely unpaid) family labour' (1981:27). In these settlements 'the firm is seen primarily as a means of support for the family; survival becomes the primary objective, particularly if survival is threatened' (1981:37). Smalltown exhibits the demographics and economic structure of the typical rural settlements that Powell and Jensen are generalizing about, consequently it is not surprising to find that local businessmen take it for granted that a wife will do 'a spot of typing', answer the phone and deal with callers to the front door ('back-up services'). Those with a 'main street' business assume that, if necessary, a wife will relieve in the shop or office for a couple of hours a day, or for one or two days a week ('substitute worker') or assist on a more or less a full-time basis ('additional worker'). There is an economic advantage to incorporating a wife: whereas a hired worker has to be paid a regular wage or salary, a wife does not. She is more than likely to work 'for her keep' and to achieve the economic security for herself and her children that a viable family business offers. Yet, wives' incorporation makes it difficult or impossible for them to work on a full-time basis for an employer who would be legally bound to pay them an award wage for their labour.[19]

The farmer's wife

Farmers comprise about 30 per cent of Smalltown's male work-force. The great majority of their wives are impeded in taking a job off the farm by their husbands' expectations that they will help on the farm. These expectations are not peculiar to the Smalltown farming district. For example, Baxter and her colleagues, studying a sample of ninety-eight farm and town women living in rural Queensland and New South Wales, found that the opportunities for farmers' wives to engage in off-farm work were often limited by the need for wives' labour to supplement husbands' farm work (1988:2).

Many of the Smalltown farmers claim in conversations and interviews that their farming enterprise is only viable if a wife provides what has been described here as 'back-up services'. Fewer farmers than businessmen want their wives to assist on a full-time basis. As Bradley observes: 'In industrialized societies where farming has become highly mechanized woman's role has usually diminished' (1989: 92).[20] However, in Smalltown farmers do expect wives to free them to do the 'actual farming' by taking responsibility for domestic work and child care seven days a week and providing meals on demand and at irregular hours. Wives are also expected to be available to perform a range of 'back up services' such as driving to town to get a part for a tractor that has broken down, or shifting a piece of machinery from one paddock to another.[21] A handful of wives assist by carting grain to the silo at harvest time.[22] Many farmers also expect their wives to take responsibility for the farm's accounts, work out breakdowns of farm costs, arrange the registration of vehicles, and so forth.

All farmers are loath to lose the contribution wives make to their farming activities. If they do lose them, they may be forced to replace unpaid labour with paid labour (see Baxter *et al.*, 1988:22). Even if they do hire labour they would not be able to afford to hire sufficient labour to provide the 'around the clock' availability that wives provide. We were present at several lengthy exchanges between farmers and their wives that were stimulated by a wife claiming that she needed a 'job of her own'. In each instance the husband rejected the suggestion, claiming that the wife should be able to find all the fulfilment she needed by helping with the farm in the ways described above, and by 'looking after the children and me'. During one of these exchanges the farmer affirmed repeatedly that his wife's contribution was indispensable to the success of his enterprise. He also endeavoured to manipulate her sense of obligation and indebtedness by saying, 'After all I am not working day in and day out just for my benefit but especially for your benefit and for the future of our kids.' During the course of a similar conversation a second farmer said, 'A farmer needs his wife's help if he is going to be a successful farmer. Her place is at his side, not taking a job of her own' (35-year-old farmer).

The degree to which a husband's farming enterprise impacts on his wife's employment is demonstrated by examining the motivation of farmers' wives who do an off-farm job. Many of these women work in order to help out financially with a husband's ailing farming operation. As one local businessman who employed a number of farmers' wives put it, 'They are working for 'survival money'. Their wages pay the farm bills and keep the farm viable. That's why they're working for me.' This interpretation is corroborated by the observation Mason makes about the motivation of Australian rural wives generally for taking a paid job: 'many farms are now dependent on off-farm income—often the wife's—to survive . . . [this] can mean the difference between financial survival and failure for the farm' (1986:13, cited by Baxter, *et al.*, 1988:18). Most farmers' wives comply with the expectations of husbands, whether these are to facilitate the success of a farming enterprise by staying home and providing 'back-up services' or, in addition to helping at home, to take a paid job to service a farm debt. The great majority stay home. In the mid-1980s, when 30 per cent of Smalltown wives were engaged in paid work, only 15 per cent of a sample of 177 farmers' wives were employed off the farm, and most of these women were working on a part-time basis.

The professional's wife

The independent employment of the wives of men either engaged in traditional professional jobs or in executive positions is also impeded by the highly institutionalized roles these wives play in connection with their husbands' occupation. This generalization holds for the wives of doctors, lawyers, clergymen, school principals, local government executives, and policemen. The array of tasks assigned to the wives of men engaged in such occupations is diffuse and often demanding. It included at least several of the following: entertaining or explaining a husband's lateness (or absence) to other professionals, to clients, patients, members of the public, parents or parishioners; serving as confidante and adviser about his work; accompanying him to official functions (many of which are held during the normal hours of paid employment), providing a wide range of 'back-up services' such as phone answering, typing, 'looking after the books', and in some instances serving as 'substitute workers'. So, for example, a doctor's wife might be expected by a patient to give advice on a medical problem in her husband's absence, a school principal's wife to assist with a parent's problem, and a clergyman's wife to do such things as conduct worship, teach Sunday School, lead women's meetings and youth groups and counsel a parishioner in her husband's absence (Finch, 1983; Dempsey, 1986).

The responsibility entailed in being 'married to the job' of these husbands prevents or discourages most of their wives from taking any employment or causes them to settle for part-time employment. The reasons for the participation of wives in their husbands' work are complex. Clearly husbands apply a lot of pressure to wives. They never tire of reminding them that other wives help out and that they (that is the husbands) can expect a lot of help because after all they are working for the benefit of the wife and the kids.

The impact of living on or near the job

The ability of a wife to choose to be involved or not in her husband's work is also restricted by the physical proximity of that work to the family home. In Smalltown almost all husbands work at home or their work is located a few minutes from home. It is commonplace for a husband to return home for a lunch provided by his wife. Even some wives who are engaged in full-time paid employment rush home at lunchtime to feed their husbands. Many professionals use their home as their place of work, or organize much of their work from their home. The same holds for many businessmen. Bank managers wives, for instance, usually live on the bank premises and they report being subject to requests from husbands, their staff, and customers. Most farmers live on their farms, which facilitates their wives' exposure to the demands of their job. A farmer's home serves as his office so it is easy to use his wife as a 'Girl Friday': relayer of messages, typist, bookkeeper, and so forth. In an era when an increasing number of farmers have a two-way radio link from their work vehicle to their home, the chances of wives creating the temporal space to engage in paid work are being further reduced. Although a husband may be several kilometres away ploughing, harvesting, or carting wheat, he can instantly check on his wife's presence or absence.

Community pressure

Husbands usually get their way in their demands that wives give priority to their work, partly because they do not exercise their power in a social vacuum: they have the backing of a range of community members, especially those in the same line of work as themselves, for the stand they take. So, a farmer's wife is pressured by other farmers' wives to support her husband in his work and to put the farm above any job of her own in her hierarchy of priorities. One farmer's wife, who was complaining about the domestic captivity she experienced because of the inordinate hours her husband worked, said other farmers' wives expressed their resentment about her complaints. Awareness of this resentment was one fact which discouraged her from returning to a paid job on a full-time basis.

Frequently, community members oppose the wives of professionals and men in senior administrative positions taking paid employment. The opposition to a professional man's wife taking a paid job is most forthcoming if her husband is engaged in work which has aspects of community service to it. In Smalltown, the work of doctors, clergymen, school principals, and local government executive officers is viewed this way. Consequently community members will simultaneously criticize a wife who curtails her support for her husband by taking a paid job and sympathize with the husband. 'I really feel sorry for Reverend Jones. How can he possibly do his job properly when Mrs Jones works? If she didn't want to be a clergyman's wife she shouldn't have married him in the first place.'

Wives' acceptance of incorporation

Most Smalltown ministers' wives do not attract this kind of criticism because they willingly comply with the expectations that they will provide full-time support for their husbands. The following comment made by one of the ministers' wives in Finch's British study is similar to that offered by a number of Smalltown ministers' wives: 'My job is being Gordon's wife, and keeping the home running smoothly so that he can do his job better' (1975:295–6, cited by Finch, 1983:85).[23] Mrs Watson, a Smalltown minister's wife of the 1980s, epitomized this approach. 'I organize the home to help Tom in his work. I am happy to do his typing as well as entertain people who come to the manse to see him.' During my conversations with Mrs Watson she spoke of 'our ministry'. She reported how she had introduced one new organization to the church because she believed it would meet important needs of younger sections of the church community, and she began teaching Sunday School so that she might exercise a major influence on the quality of Sunday-School life. Hers was, in reality, a joint enterprise. She made her husband's work her own and the lay people praised her for her exemplary wifely behaviour. It is not surprising that Mrs Watson reported that taking paid employment was out of the question, but so did the wives of most other professionals and administrators with whom we discussed this matter. During the seventeen years of our field-work only a handful of these wives were employed, and most of these worked on a part-time basis.

The majority of farmers' and businessmen's wives also willingly supported their husbands in their work. They did this in part because, like the wives of professionals, they have been trained 'to merge their interests with those of the family [and therefore of the husband]' (Whitehead, 1981:105). For example, about one-third of the farmers' wives who participated in the Community Survey were, themselves, the daughters of farmers' wives who had witnessed their mothers' incorporation in their fathers' farming activities. Even if a wife were not the daughter of a man in the same occupation as her husband, the chances would be that her mother had made a substantial contribution to her father's work. Consequently, most wives had probably left their parents' home to establish their own home, committed to the view that they should support a husband in his work and skilled in at least some of the ways of doing so.

The compliance of wives with their husbands' expectations of support for them in their work also occurs because the wives perceive that it is in their best interests and those of their children to do so (Finch, 1983:Ch. 14). As Finch points out, once a woman has married she can probably best serve her own economic interest and that of her children by working to make a success of her husband's job.

> A higher standard of living can be gained over a lifetime by being a wife than most women could achieve in their own right. In those circumstances it may well sound the most sensible economic option for a wife to invest her energies in her husband's work, thus promoting his earning potential rather than to pursue her own (Finch, 1983:152).

Her observations apply doubly in a community such as Smalltown, where the job market is much more restricted for women than in the city, and especially where there are fewer middle-class career paths for women to pursue.

Yet, while wives' compliance with the demands husbands make of them for support in their work often enhances their standard of living, social status, and level of personal gratification, it also affirms their vicarious social status, reinforces their economic dependence, and bonds them tightly to a supportive and subordinate role in their marriages.

Unsuccessful dissidents

Despite the combined impact of the various factors and processes encouraging wives to accept the status quo and facilitate their husbands' work, there was, among the women we interviewed in the Gender Survey, a small minority who were hostile towards the prevailing sexual division of labour. Some were also hostile to being incorporated in their husbands' paid work. All of these women had repeatedly expressed their opposition to their husbands. They were resentful of what some of them described as their domestic captivity. Each argued that her husband could work less if he chose to and help more with the children and so free her to go out to work, if only on a part-time basis. With only two or three exceptions these women were married to professional men, farmers, businessmen, or administrators.

> Fred (and many other farmers are the same) works until the kids are fed and in bed so that he won't have to be bothered by them. He doesn't ask me to help with the farming but he expects me to free him by always being on duty at home. I'm trapped here.

Despite repeated protests to their respective husbands about feeling trapped and 'used up', not one of them has been able to achieve an equitable division of labour. All of them are married to men who do not want their wives to pursue careers on a full-time basis and who expect them to organize any employment around their responsibilities for the home, the children, and his job or business. A wife's paid work has to fit in with a timetable that the husband largely dictates, and which, as a rule, he does little or nothing to ease. Many Smalltown men will not compromise on this.

Several of these dissenting wives volunteered the observation that their husbands' work has a negative impact on their marriage or family life. However, it would be unthinkable for them to demand that their husbands cease work in order to improve 'things at home'. Wives are much more likely to be preoccupied with the impact of their work on their children and their husbands than vice versa. In one survey, fourteen of the thirty-one working wives who were engaged in paid work (most on a part-time basis) said that they were worried that their paid work was having a detrimental effect on their husbands, their husbands' jobs, or their children. They usually expressed a sense of guilt coupled with a determination to reduce the negative effects by such action as spending more time with the children or taking more interest in the husband's work and other activities, or reducing or ending their participation in paid work.[24]

Conclusion

The data presented in this and the previous chapter call into question the claim of more than three-quarters of the participants in the Gender Survey that women choose whether or not to engage in paid work. Any choice that women—particularly wives—make occurs within well-articulated cultural and structural parameters and is exercised in the face of pressure from husbands who have superior power to theirs and a social context where sanctions are readily invoked by a range of community members. The structures and processes occurring in Smalltown are biased against her working, especially in the jobs that have the potential to provide her with an economically independent existence. The jobs that are accessible, or the hours of and type of work that are compatible with the responsibilities assigned to wives by husbands and community, are much more limited than those available to men.

Men residing in Smalltown during the years this study was conducted did not initiate the system which works to their advantage and at the palpable expense of women, but their actions play a large part in ensuring its continuance. Men leave women with responsibility for an inordinate share of home-binding activities; often oppose their taking paid employment; insist that, if they do, they continue to look after things at home; and pressure them for support in their work as farmers, businessmen and professionals. Those men who are the community's entrepreneurs reduce drastically the access of women to middle-class jobs by transmitting their farms and town businesses to sons rather than daughters. The act of transmission inferiorizes women. It will be seen in the next chapter that men repeatedly inferiorize women when they advance justifications for excluding them from a variety of other activities or maintaining them in a subordinate position.

CHAPTER 8

Ideology and oppression

As Michelle Barrett (1980) has shown, men have two main mechanisms at their disposal to oppress women: their superior power, especially material, and their ideological hegemony. Throughout much of the foregoing account I have concentrated principally on men's superior power, and tried to elucidate the manner in which their greater power in one institutional sphere creates or reinforces advantages in other spheres.[1] We have seen that men's dominance of paid work facilitates their control of local political, religious and recreational activities and resources. It also ensures that women are financially dependent and allows men to delegate most domestic work and child care to women.

As Collins (1985:67–8) observes, male power and prerogative are always supported by a gender-specific ideology. In this chapter I focus on the content of the gender-specific ideology that supports male power and prerogative in Smalltown, and the manner in which it is transmitted and utilized in the creation of gendered identities and the inferiorizing of females (Bryson, 1990).

The ideological processes that help construct the social distinctions between men and women are akin to what Bennett, following Bourdieu (1984), calls value discourses (1985). In these discourses women and men are distinguished hierarchically by a process of evaluating various objects and activities that are perceived as signs for each gender. For instance, paid work is one of the key signs of male identity, and domestic work of female identity. Paid work is valued much more highly than domestic work, and through it men are valued more highly than women. The value discourses advance ideals of personality—physical, mental, and emotional—which are used by men to differentiate themselves from women and evaluate themselves as the superior sex, and which women are encouraged to use to evaluate themselves as inferior. These discourses serve as mechanisms for inferiorizing women because each message they convey about the superiority of men carries with it an implicit and often explicit message about the inferiority of women. They play a crucial role in creating what Rowbotham (1972) so aptly describes as the social secondariness of women.

Typifying women as wives and mothers

Members of both sexes in Smalltown regard wifehood and motherhood as the natural and ultimate roles for women. While men are typified as family providers, women are typified as child-raisers, home-makers, and husband-supporters. Smalltown comes closer to speaking with one voice on these matters and the universality of these ideas helps give the community's culture a monolithic quality. It also helps maintain male dominance because the roles of men are viewed as superior to the roles of women by members of both sexes. The typifications of men as providers and women as wives and mothers are constants in the meaning system of this community. This was shown by our failure to find any significant diminishment in Smalltown people's attachment to them in the course of nearly two decades of research in their community.

The strength of the attachment of Smalltown people to the traditional typifications of women's roles was conveyed in answers they gave in the Gender Survey to questions about the kind of woman who would feel at home in Smalltown:

> A woman who fits into Smalltown will be a woman who is happy with what she's got . . . I mean with children and a home. She'll not be looking to do such things as go to the theatre, the ballet, or restaurants (55-year-old farmer).

> A sophisticated city-oriented woman doesn't belong here. She must be a simple home-loving person who likes to be with her family (42-year-old male worker).

> A woman will be accepted in this town if she gets involved in anything her children are involved in . . . if she joins the mothers' club or the kindergarten committee, if she takes them along to swimming classes, things like that (40-year-old wife of a mechanic).

> A woman will fit in [in Smalltown] if she's a good home-maker (65-year-old farmer's wife).

> A woman will fit in if she is prepared to mix with people. Perhaps play sport or join the mothers' club or the kindergarten committee, or anything her kids were in (40-year-old wife of a self-employed businessman).

> Women fit in much more easily if they are married (33-year-old farmer's wife).

> Single girls are not going to be at home in Smalltown. Especially if they are very career-minded. The married mum with the young children is going to fit in the best (38-year-old professional's wife).

Respondents were three times as likely to say that the kind of woman who would feel at home in Smalltown was one who centred her life on the family or the children than they were to say that the kind of man who would feel at home in Smalltown was a family-centred person.

A large gap was perceived to exist between the caricature of the woman who would feel at home and 'fit in' in

Smalltown and the caricature of the sophisticated city woman who is always going to remain an outsider. The following extracts from an interview with a 44-year-old wife of a semi-skilled worker, who herself was employed as a secretary, catches something of these contrasting caricatures.

Interviewer: What kind of women are going to feel at home in Smalltown?
Respondent: Well not . . . I'm not sure how to put it. *Not* a socialite. If a socialite had to move from Melbourne to live here I don't think she would be very happy. This is not a very socialite sort of town. You can't go to the pictures because there aren't any. When they were here they were overrun by kids throwing jaffas.
Interviewer: So that wouldn't suit her?
Respondent: No. The only thing she would go to for a social night would be a counter tea or a cabaret. Well, that's not very socialite sort of stuff is it?
Interviewer: I suppose not.
Respondent: Then there is the Arts Council Group. They probably think they are the socialites of the town. I don't know if they are entitled to or not. That would be a group she could join. They get together and have a lot of fun. They put on their concerts and they get visiting artists. They do enjoy themselves. Apart from them there are groups like the Red Cross and the CWA which meet monthly. They seem to enjoy themselves a lot.
Interviewer: But would they suit the kind of woman from the city whom you have been talking about?
Respondent: No they wouldn't.
Interviewer: Who then do you think would feel at home?
Respondent: The homely type of woman.

In the Smalltown social consciousness a good woman is a good wife. A good wife supports her husband in his paid work, she helps him in his public office or in his sporting or service-club activity. The prevailing view is that in most, if not all things, wives are to put their husbands' interests before their own.

Some fellas do well in farming because of the input from their wives but more often farmers don't do well because of their wives. They fail to help during the busy times. But what's worse is that they lack foresight and common sense about spending money (46-year-old successful farmer).

While some farmers and businessmen only succeed because they have a 'good wife'—that is a wife with a lot of business sense—the common view is that men are much more likely than women to possess the acumen and experience to ensure that a business or a farm succeeds.

Wives who fail to provide the support for a husband occupying a leadership position in a town organization are chastized by men and women in ways that indicate their acceptance of the belief that wives ought to put their husbands' activities first. The wife of a businessman recounted one such incident:

Tim arranged for some of the fellas to come around from his club for a meeting. I prepared the supper but I told him they would have to help themselves because I was having a meeting of one of my committees that evening. The men made it very plain to me that they thought it was very poor of me to be tied up the night Tim was having the meeting here.

The following comment was made by a leader of an organization to another leader and both their wives at a dinner arranged by the organization:

You really feel sorry for Tom Brown. He has a real struggle to run this organization. It's surprising he has done as well as he has when Mary [his wife] gives him zero support. How can he hope to do a proper job for a club like this when his wife fails to come along and support him (committee member of a prominent organization).

The last two incidents are excellent examples of value discourses in which men seize upon a wife's failure to engage in the activities that symbolize her supportive and subordinate position to reaffirm the values that mark the divide between themselves and their inferiors: women.

Taking part in a husband's sporting or service-club activities was also cited by respondents as a way for the wife of a middle-class man to gain acceptance in Smalltown. 'If she is not prepared to do that she will *not* be "looked after" when she moves to this town' (40-year-old professional man).

I have never heard it said that the acceptance of a man who has moved to Smalltown is dependent on his joining in his wife's leisure activities, nor have I heard a 'local' man criticized for failing to support his wife's voluntary-organization activities. To do so would be to turn on its head the existing hierarchical arrangements in marriage and in community life. Rather, if a man is too zealous in his support of his wife he runs the risk of being described as a 'henpecked' husband.

Defining women as inferior

Subordinating, excluding and exploiting women is facilitated by Smalltown men successfully stereotyping women and their activities as inferior and having those definitions accepted by the community (Parkin, 1974:5). Presented below are numerous examples of the process of women's inferiorization, which Bryson (1990) argues contributes significantly to the maintenance of their oppression. Many of these examples show that women are men's accomplices in this process.

Eighty-four per cent of participants in the Gender Survey claimed that women were more critical of other women than men of other men. Comments made during a discussion of this issue—and in many informal conversations as well—demonstrated that women are perceived as men's goal keepers, as 'bitchy', untrustworthy, and more ready to hold grudges than men. Here is the type of comment made as frequently by female as male respondents:

> Basically, women are catty—they've all got that nature . . . they're born with it. If they see another woman down the street they say in a spiteful manner: 'Did you see what she was wearing!'

Blokes don't give a bugger what their mates are wearing (32-year-old tradesman).

Women are more bitchy than men (70-year-old tradesman's widow).

Men tend to be accepting of other men's shortcomings unless it disadvantages them personally. Women compare how people dress and things like that. They seem to have nothing better to occupy their time with (a professional man's wife in her thirties).

Women are perceived by each other as very competitive, and compete as mothers, home-makers, wives, and men's sex objects. Women said repeatedly that women compete over men.

During the Gender Survey some women expressed the view that many women were very materialistic and money-hungry, wanting to spend all their husband's money in order to 'keep up with the Jones's'. Sometimes they offered this comment to justify the observation that women were more competitive than men. They believed that women reveal their inferiority by competing over things of minor importance while men compete over significant matters. Men compete over employment, and in the town's top sporting events, while women compete over hairstyles and the latest gadgets. One farmer's wife said:

There are those women who like the best of everything. They want their husband's money as well as their own to get what they want: to get a new car because a friend has got one. If a neighbour builds a new room at the back of their house you can bet your bottom dollar they'll have to get their husband to build one too.
Interviewer: Are you sure it is the wives who prompt their husbands to do these things?
Farmer's wife: Yes definitely. Men don't worry about a lot of status. They enjoy having a beer with their mates. They know their friends will take them the way they are no matter what kind of home they have. The women are very much the other way. They want the better life, the better everything. It is stupid.

By transmitting such negative evaluations in the course of daily interaction the women are contributing to the maintenance of their subordination.

In Smalltown a woman's worth depends far more on a man's accepting her as a marriage partner than vice versa:

I think that if a man is single it is assumed that he is single by choice where if it's a single woman they [i.e. other community members] feel she has been left on the shelf. If a woman has not married it's assumed that she hasn't had the opportunity, not that she chooses not to marry (self-employed tradesman's wife).

A woman's inferiority is sometimes symbolized by the view that her thinking, values and life-style are a reflection of her husband's, rather than an expression of her own convictions and interests:

A woman's life revolves around more of a man's life rather than his life around hers. It revolves around his likes, his occupation and generally his ideas . . . If Joan [the speaker's wife] was married to someone else she would think differently . . . She'd have different ideas about politics, different ideas about where to send the kids to school, think differently about other people. The husband I think has a really strong bearing in most cases I reckon on what ideas the wife has (town businessman).

There were also those respondents who claimed that women demonstrated their inferiority by being contented with less from life than men:

A man is often ambitious to get on but a woman finds it much easier to be contented with ordinary things. That is the way she is made. When she gets married she is willing to do anything to survive. My daughter just got married and she took a job as a machinist at the knitting mill. Anything for a bit of money. She is happy but he [that is her husband] is determined to go places and she will help him get there [middle-aged wife of semi-skilled worker who herself was employed part time in a sales position).

At the same time it is not appropriate for a woman to be too ambitious. That is not compatible with the prevailing notion of femininity:

> If a woman wants to fit in and be accepted in this town the last thing she must do is try and compete with men. They [meaning other women] will tear her to pieces for that (40-year-old female typist).

> If she is to fit in she must not be too ambitious. She shouldn't make a career that takes on the significance of a bread-winner's career. She shouldn't achieve too much that rivals men in their activities, such as in town politics. It's OK for her to be the best cake-maker because that's maintaining her feminine role (39-year-old businessman's wife).

In the value discourses that help reproduce boundaries between men and women, cake-making, along with such activities as ironing and washing clothes, function as signs of women's inferior position. Men do not bake cakes and only in extreme circumstances iron or wash clothes.

Some women are said to display the inferiority of their sex by engaging in paid work for base motives. If a wife works when it is not financially necessary she will probably be denigrated in casual conversation by members of both sexes. Rather than acknowledge that—as for a man—paid work may be intrinsically interesting, Smalltowners assert that by going to work she is chasing a 'bit of glamour' or 'big-noting' herself. Women are perceived to fall into such traps when they neglect their true calling to be proper mothers and wives: 'That stupid bitch—she'd be better off at home looking after her kids' (male worker referring in pub conversation to the wife of a well-off businessman who had recently taken a full-time job).

The inferior status of women is revealed in the common practice of using a female gender label to talk about a member of either sex in a derogatory way. For example, community members are often heard to say, 'Isn't he an old woman?' Many Smalltowners believe that women are innately inferior to men: where men are rational and predictable, women are irrational and capricious. They frequently conveyed these beliefs in the comment, 'You're a dope if you think you can ever understand a woman!'

Men in casual conversation in pubs, in the street, and at sporting fixtures—as well as in surveys—talk frequently about the power of women in ways that suggest that they are genetically endowed with a darker, dissembling side which sets them apart from men and shows that they are morally inferior to men:

> A woman has got terrible power. It is so easy for her to manipulate a man to get her way with him and he doesn't even know it is happening and the next thing he is buying her something that she doesn't need. He doesn't even realize it is happening to him (35-year-old tradesman).

Men occasionally portrayed women as less trustworthy than themselves. A 45-year-old farmer remarked, 'Women can't be trusted. You could say a lot of things to a bloke and he would never pass it on but if you said the same thing to a woman it would get back out somewhere [*sic*]'. Unlike men, women are believed to be capable of unfair play in the things that matter. They are creatures obsessed with trapping a man into marriage and then holding him captive for the rest of his days.

Defining women's leisure and work as inferior

Members of both sexes play sport, but men's sport is seen as superior to women's sport. Men resist playing sport with women because, they say, 'they are all hit and giggle'. Men's sporting activities generally attract more public attention and prestige: they are the ones on which the community's collective ego rides. This is evidenced by the space given to men's sport compared with women's sport in the Smalltown newspaper. A content analysis we made of a random sample of the newspaper from 1986 showed that men received 83 per cent of the space devoted to sex-specific sport (which accounted for 77 per cent of all sports coverage) and women 17 per cent. Men's sport received a remarkable 95 per cent of the space on the major sporting page.

When the Smalltown football team were the district premiers in the late 1980s, the news was trumpeted on the front page of the local paper in a two-colour presentation. However, when the Smalltown women's hockey team won the district premiership in 1991, not only did the news fail to make the front page, it did not even make the main sport's page which featured the football team that was beaten in the grand final. A social function was organized for the evening on which the grand final was played—hopefully to celebrate a victory for the senior football team. It was held in the town hall and all community members were invited to attend. The victorious women hockey players attended the function with 'We won' written on their foreheads. While their victory attracted some congratulatory comments, the tone and mood of the evening—one of despair and disappointment—was set by the second failure in a row of the town's football team to win a grand final.

Perhaps the typifications that play the most crucial cultural role in the subordination and exploitation of women are those that deal with the relative merits of their work. As I pointed out earlier, men's work is viewed as decidedly superior to women's domestic labour and, as a rule, to women's paid labour as well: superior in the sense of being more important economically to the well-being of the family and future viability of the community, more physically and emotionally demanding, and usually entailing greater responsibilities. In short, in the eyes of most members of this community, men's work symbolizes their superiority and women's work their inferiority. These evaluations are reflected in the common practice of men ignoring women when they are discussing their work at such social functions as dances and parties. They ignore the women, they say, because they believe women have little or nothing of significance to say on this topic because they lead home-centred lives.

Some husbands manifest their sense of superiority by belittling the significance of their wives' knowledge and activities. For instance, during one survey in which one middle-aged businessman and his wife were being interviewed in separate rooms, the wife became so concerned over the direction the questioning was taking that she went to her husband and asked if she should answer the questions. He said: 'Don't you worry. What could you say that is dangerous. Just answer the questions. I am the one who has to be careful!' The same man explained that it was difficult to conduct an interesting conversation with women because their lives revolved around their families and their homes. A second man belittled women's domestic responsibilities:

> What a hard life these wives have. What, with their automatic dishwashers, their washing-machines and microwave stoves. I don't know why they are always complaining. If I took on their job I would have it all done by nine in the morning and leave the rest of the day free for golf and going to the races. Men don't get out of it nearly as easily. They have to perform if they are going to keep supporting their wives up to the standard they have got used to. Some wives in our circle work on a part-time basis, but they can always give up and spend their lives being housewives. Men cannot—they have to keep working! (40-year-old professional man).

Not participating in paid work in a community where working for a living is regarded as the most important thing any person can do, automatically places most Smalltown women in an inferior position to men. Wives are socially located on the basis of their husband's occupation, whether or not they work, and of those who do, many work on a part-time basis, and most have jobs of inferior status to those of men. A wife who attempts to gain status by taking paid work may actually lose status if, in the eyes of the community, it impedes her effectiveness as a wife and mother. In this ideological climate, going out to work is likely to confirm and reinforce a woman's subordinate and supportive roles as wife and mother rather than to establish for her an independent position in the local social structure: the process locks her into what Finch (1983:2) calls her pre-ordained roles. Hence, as Barrett points out, even when women make a considerable contribution to the family budget, their subordination and oppression will probably persist because the ideology of women's dependence is so strong (1980:214).

The community judgements on the relative significance of men's and women's work are reflected in the news coverage of the *Smalltown News*. The paper devotes about one-third of its space to men's paid work but only one-twentieth to women's paid work. Women's domestic labour receives no coverage at all, but one-twentieth of the space is given over to pictures and accounts of their child-bearing activities and another one-twentieth to reports of family reunions and celebrations in which women feature exclusively or predominantly. On occasions it carries stories of middle-aged and older women serving refreshments to men at public functions, while more frequently it presents pictures of men as business decision-makers. For example, an issue of the *Smalltown News* for early 1991 that arrived during the week I was drafting this chapter was typical of those that were published throughout the years of this study. On the front page there were three stories featuring men and none featuring women. The main story (with accompanying photograph) featured two of the community's leading businessmen discussing plans for the establishment of new business premises. A second story (also accompanied by a large photograph) tells of the impending retirement of a professional man, and the third reports an appeal for funds for the voluntary fire brigade: a men's organization whose members exhibit some of the key traits of the culture of masculinity, such as physical strength, resourcefulness and courage in the face of danger. By contrast, page 5 featured two photographs of mothers with their newborn babies, on a subsequent page there was a photograph of a mother collecting her young son at the end of his first day of school, and another page carried the story of members of a leading women's organization serving refreshments to male and female participants in a public celebration.[2] In such ways the paper reinforces the stereotypical view that all things to do with children and kin are women's matters; because such things are viewed by the principal power holders—men—as much less significant than their own work activities, women's inferior status and identities are reaffirmed. Less than one-fifth of the local media coverage of family activities makes any reference to men.[3]

The view that men's part in the division of labour is superior to women's was revealed during interviews with male and female participants in the Gender Survey. Some of the male interviewees recounted incidents from conversations in which they, or their male companions, symbolically affirmed the boundaries between themselves and women by denigrating women's activities. Nappies and cooking become stigmatized signs of women's principal tasks and ultimately of women themselves. This sort of discourse is found among men of all classes and ages. A 42-year-old schoolteacher's report of how he and his mates deal with what they regard as women's domestic obsessions demonstrates both inferiorization and boundary maintenance.

To tell you the truth we [that is he and his mates] get sick and tired of what we call their nappy talk. We're interested in the children but the women are positively obsessed with them. Now, when one of the wives joins us I pull out my watch [and he gestures to indicate he does it with a flourish so all can see] and time how long it takes before she starts talking about babies and their problems. Invariably it happens in less than one minute. We go out to escape that. We want to talk about things of interest to us.

A farmer reported in an interview that he and some of his farming and business associates discussed together the gulf between the less serious interests of their womenfolk and their own more important interests.

Women talk all the time about their cooking and children. I think it is something they have grown up doing so when you get with women all you can have is fairly idle talk isn't it? It is more or less a pastime talking with women because you can't talk seriously to them. If you want to have a worthwhile talk you have to talk with men. After all, they [that is women] take decisions over spending a few dollars and we take them over spending hundreds of thousands (55-year-old farmer).

This sort of discourse, repeated constantly when good mates get together, facilitates the maintenance and reproduction of the gendered social differentiation that pervades all of private and public life in this community (Bourdieu, 1984).

Because of their position of dominance and authority, it is highly likely that men's negative discourse about women encourages women to engage in negative self-evaluation. Certainly, many of our female respondents offered such evaluations. For example, the explanation most frequently given by women for wanting more of the company of men was the claim that men's work ensured that they led more interesting lives than they (that is women) did, and so were more interesting to be with. A 34-year-old woman schoolteacher commented, 'It's no wonder women's conversations are so boring when most of them have spent their whole lives looking after homes, children, and husbands. The nature of men's work makes them so much more interesting to listen to.

The inferior status of women's work and of women themselves is revealed in the practice of using a man's social standing to determine his wife's general social standing in the community. In turn, the general social standing of a man and his wife is largely determined by his occupational–

class position.[4] This is a common practice in Western societies, particularly in rural communities. Littlejohn reports that in his study of the Scottish community of Westrigg he found: 'When making class placements informants never separated husband and wife, but also in comments on the status of the family it was always attributes of the male head which were cited—his possessions, his education and so forth' (1963:120). In Smalltown, similar principles of status allocation are not negated, even where a woman holds a position in the work-force which should ensure that she has a higher social standing than her husband. So, for example, a woman who works as a bank clerk but is married to an unskilled labourer will still take her husband's status in activities other than those concerned directly with her employment.

The derivative nature of a woman's status is manifested when informants are being asked to provide some basic data on particular members of the community. In response to a question such as, 'Was Joan Smith born in Smalltown?' the informant will often reply, 'Now is that Mrs Bill Smith or Mrs Tom Smith?' Only once the identity of the woman's husband has been established will the informant be able to provide the information required. However, the reverse never occurs: that is, men are not identified by reference to their wives.

The further up the occupational status ladder one travels, the more likely it is that there will be exceptions to the rule that women take their status from their husbands. However, the extremely limited opportunities in this community for women to attain high occupational status ensure that there are few exceptions to the rule. The most notable are several women with professional jobs married to men with jobs of lower status than their own. These women rose to leadership positions in other areas of community life. None of them is married to a man playing a leadership role in a leading community organization.

Consequently, the husbands are not overshadowing these women, nor attempting to incorporate them in prestigious community activities. The social life of one wife is circumscribed because her husband lacks the occupational position and the personal skills to move in the circles his wife wishes to participate in and she needs a partner to ensure full participation. The other is married to a man with a middle-class job, and they do participate as a couple in informal social activities with people in a similar class position to themselves. For women generally, however, the fact remains that their inferior status is reflected in the practice of community members allocating them a position in the hierarchical structure which is largely determined by their husbands' position.[5]

The inferior status of women is also determined by a wife's greater dependence on her husband for a social life than his dependence on her. In order for women to exploit the opportunities that exist for them to socialize—especially in the evenings, when there are more social activities for men than there are for women—they need the co-operation of their husbands much more than their husbands need their co-operation. This is, in part, because it is women who have 24-hour-a-day responsibility for children and for home management (see Ch. 5). So while husbands are usually free to leave the care of the children to their wives while they engage in leisure activities, wives must either persuade their husbands to deputize for them or make arrangements for baby-sitting if they want to get out. This convention is supported by the belief in the legitimacy of men's leisure advantages, which, in turn, enunciates the superiority of men and the inferiority of women.

Women's dependency on men for a social life, and the inferior status this confers, is reinforced by other factors. One of these is the norm of respectability that wives should be accompanied by their husbands if they attend a mixed social function, whereas a husband can attend alone.

A second factor is the greater likelihood that a *husband's* organization will provide an opportunity to attend one of the town's social activities for men and women: many of the more desirable social activities take the form of special functions arranged by one of the men's organizations. Joining a women's organization creates the opportunity for interacting only with other women because, as a rule, these organizations are unable to attract the men to any of their activities. Eager for mixed company and a 'good night's entertainment', the wives of men belonging to a leading men's organization will apply pressure to husbands to suggest that their organization arrange a special social function that they can attend. Male members of such organizations exercise the option of interacting with men only most of the time. When they break the pattern and allow wives to attend, the wives come not as equals but as guests who are beholden to the men for allowing them to participate. The gift of entry confirms the superiority of the men.

Given the prevalence of the value discourses that I have delineated in this and the preceding sections it is not surprising that women plan their daily and weekly routine around their husband's lives and in so doing reflect the higher evaluation of men and their activities. They thereby facilitate the continuance of male dominance and female subordination in both the private and public domains.

Socialization for subordination and exploitation

Some recent writing on the family has stressed that the socialization experience of boys teaches them to expect women to wait on them and to see themselves in the future performing the superior role of bread-winner.[6] On the other hand, through performing tasks for brothers that are not reciprocated, observing their mothers, and taking part in family conversation, girls learn to view men's activities as superior, and their own as inferior. They learn to put their future spouse's interests before their own (Collins, 1985; Sharpe, 1976:Ch. 2; 1984; Griffin, 1985).[7] As Collins points out, one of the principal factors encouraging women to identify with traditional concepts of femininity and feminine roles is the internalization, from an early age, of key elements of an ideology of gender (1985). Those values internalized in earlier years are reinforced by exposure to key ideas of a feminine ideology in adulthood. In short, the cultural and symbolic boundaries between the sexes are drawn early and in such a way as to identify females with subordinate and inferior activities and males with privileged ones.

So effective are earlier socialization experiences that, even among Smalltown women who are dissatisfied with their husband's contribution to domestic life and who have grave doubts about the legitimacy of the prevailing division of domestic tasks, there are many who, nevertheless, feel it their duty to perform domestic tasks and provide 'all kinds of support' for their husbands. Similarly, engagement in full-time paid work does not usually lessen the strong internalized sense of responsibility for performing traditional domestic tasks and participating in a husband's leisure and work activities (see Ch. 5): 'I would feel I was failing if I did not look after him and the children and do the jobs around the place as well as my "own jobs"' (45-year-old Smalltown secretary). As Collins observes, 'Providing good service is proof that women are not neglecting their families by working outside the home' (1985:76).

One way of assessing the importance of adolescent socialization for the reproduction of the cultural, material and structural boundaries between males and females is to see if there is a gender-based difference in the division of domestic tasks among adolescents, and to examine the views that members of each sex express about performing tasks that traditionally have been performed by members of one sex rather than the other. The subjects of the enquiry should

Table 8.1 The participation of teenage boys and girls in household tasks in Smalltown*

Last time household task was done	Females			Males		
	Within a week	Week to month	Month +	Within a week	Week to month	Month +
Particular household task	%	%	%	%	%	%
1 Bed-making	93	3	4	60	8	32
2 Washing up	96	2	2	60	8	32
3 Vacuuming/sweeping	74	17	9	19	14	67
4 Cooking	77	14	9	25	9	66
5 Ironing	60	22	18	2	6	92
6 Washing clothes	55	19	26	6	9	85
7 Mowing lawns	5	16	79	28	38	34
8 Other/gardening	8	20	72	23	25	52
9 Looking after pets	65	11	24	71	3	26

*N = 159

be people who have yet to enter marriage or the paid workforce. If learning is unimportant—especially within the home—we would expect little gender difference in the division of labour among, say, adolescent boys and girls and in the attitudes displayed to performing specific tasks.

During the course of a survey we were making of Smalltown secondary-school pupils we did collect such data. More specifically, we asked the 159 participants in our survey who were aged between fifteen and eighteen years of age, and who were attending the community's two secondary schools, to provide us with information about how frequently they performed a number of specific household tasks (Table 8:1). At least 50 per cent of the girls sampled performed seven of the nine tasks we specifically enquired about, whereas boys reached this proportion on only three of the nine. The jobs that boys were most likely to carry out—the traditional male ones of mowing the lawn and gardening—were non-routine tasks (see Ch. 5 for a definition). They performed them less frequently than girls performed their tasks and the non-routine tasks were probably less onerous and less likely to place the boys in a servant role than the routine tasks that most girls performed. The girls were engaged in the tasks traditionally performed by mothers: vacuuming, cooking, ironing, and washing clothes.

There were some dramatic contrasts in the results we obtained. For example, approximately two-thirds of the boys compared to less than one-tenth of the girls rarely or never vacuumed or cooked. The two 'women's' tasks that the majority of the boys performed at least once a week were among the least demanding of such tasks: they were bed-making and washing up. Yet 30 per cent of the boys compared to less than 5 per cent of the girls rarely or never performed these jobs.

Some readers may wish to argue that it is not valid to draw the conclusions I have from the Smalltown data regarding the division of labour between boys and girls because the indices that are used are heavily biased in favour of traditional 'female' tasks. To answer that argument, the inclusion of these particular indices allowed us to establish how early the sex-stereotyping of work and gender-based roles occurred in this community. At the same time, the apparent gender-based imbalance in the list highlights the fact that the majority of domestic tasks—especially the more demanding ones—are jobs that women have traditionally performed and which are widely regarded as 'women's' work. For these reasons the so-called biased sample of tasks is inevitable.

Notwithstanding this inherent problem, we attempted in our enquiry to achieve as comprehensive and unbiased a picture as possible by asking open-ended questions aimed at establishing what additional domestic tasks were performed by members of both sexes in or around the home. Less than one-quarter of the boys (23 per cent) and less than one-sixth of the girls (13 per cent) nominated any additional tasks. On average, the boys nominated one-and-a-half and the girls two additional tasks. The task most frequently mentioned by boys was chopping wood. Although chopping wood is an apparently male task it was nevertheless cited by one-quarter of the girls answering the open-ended question compared to just over half the boys. Girls were most likely to mention cleaning windows, which was reported by 27 per cent of the girls and only 5 per cent of the boys.

In summary, these findings draw attention to the occurrence of a gender specific division of labour among adolescents. They confirm Sharpe's frequently cited claim that girls participate more in domestic work than boys (1976: 77–8); 1984: 189–96) and they corroborate the findings of Scraton's research among young women in Liverpool, England. The girls participating in her study were expected to help with housework and the care of younger siblings

(1987:165). The observation that the gendered boundaries are set in place early is corroborated by Sharpe's findings that boys were more likely to be paid by mothers to help with housework than girls and that mothers who tried to insist on boys helping were likely to be criticized by aunts and grandmothers for trying to treat boys as though they were girls.

As the age of this sample of girls and boys ranged from fifteen to eighteen years, it is clear that the inequitable division of labour in the domestic sphere described in Chapter 5 began long before members of the two sexes reached adulthood. It also needs to be stressed that this inequitable division of labour was one in which girls were not only doing more than boys, but what they were doing was likely to directly benefit boys, namely their brothers. Boys' domestic labour, by comparison, was less likely to directly benefit girls, namely their sisters. Unlike their fathers, these teenage boys were not bread-winners and therefore were not bringing in from outside a contribution which, some would argue, at least partially offsets their lesser domestic input.

If exploitation occurs when the labour of one party is used to enhance the resources or the recreational activities of another without appropriate reciprocity, then it is highly likely that Smalltown girls are often being exploited by their brothers and possibly their fathers. They are much more likely to be devoting more time to washing and ironing their brothers' clothes, washing their dirty dishes and vacuuming the floors they walked on than the boys are to be giving time to jobs that directly benefit the girls. In the light of the distinction introduced in Chapter 5 between routine and non-routine tasks and of information given on the quantitative and qualitative differences between routine and non-routine tasks, it would be difficult to argue that mowing lawns and possibly chopping wood benefit the girls nearly as much as washing, ironing, and cooking benefit the boys. Furthermore, it is worth stressing that, as much less is asked of boys at home, they are freer than their female age peers to spend time away from home.

In an attempt to establish the degree to which boys and girls were personally identifying with the tasks that were labelled by the culture of this community as the province of one sex more or less exclusively, we asked them to report on any resentment they felt over the performance of the tasks presented in Table 8:1. The proportion of boys who resented performing domestic tasks exceeded that of girls on seven of our nine indices. In particular, boys were more likely than girls to resent doing what is culturally described as 'women's work': cooking, washing up, etc. The only task which girls were more likely to report resenting than boys was the most 'male' task in the list: mowing lawns. These findings highlight the extent to which gender-specific identities had developed by this early stage in the life cycle.

The data were collected in the 1970s. We did not conduct a second study of adolescent socialization in the 1980s, but our observations during lengthy visits to several hundred Smalltown homes, and conversations with teenagers strongly suggested that little or nothing had changed since the early 1970s. The following extract from an interview made in 1990 with a Smalltown adolescent girl corroborates this claim. It focuses on the division of domestic labour between herself and her adolescent brother. She also reported that the experience of all her girlfriends is similar to her own. This is part of what she said:

Girl: If mum is not at home I am the one who has to take over.
Interviewer: Because you are the girl?
Girl: Yes, and my brother doesn't have to do anything. I'm the one who has to like get the tea, clean up afterwards, and so on.
Interviewer: Do you do it all?
Girl: Yes, it would be a real effort for him [that is the brother] to

help me do the dishes. It annoys me and I can't believe that because he's a male he does nothing.
Interviewer: Have you discussed this with your mother?
Girl: Yes, we argue about it a lot. She sees things from my point of view, and Dad says, 'Come on Tom, do something'.
Interviewer: Does Tom help out when asked like this?
Girl: Sometimes he does, but often he just goes out. Mum will tell him to make his bed but he won't always do it. Mum then asks me to make it.
Interviewer: How do you feel when that happens?
Girl: Sometimes it makes me mad. But other times it doesn't worry me because I know it is expected of me and so I just do it automatically. If mum's not there I do what she would do or no one gets any tea. It's like this for lots of my friends. One in particular whose mother works. When her mother leaves in the morning she leaves my friend a big list of things to do. She has to look after her brothers and sisters, get the tea, do the washing and ironing. She has older brothers but they go out for the day and don't have to lift a finger.

If this girl's experience is typical and if such socialization processes play the decisive role that many feminists believe they do in the perpetuation of an inequitable division of labour, then it is likely that the patterns I have described in Chapter 5 will be repeated.

Conclusion

The data we collected on adolescent socialization demonstrate that concepts of self are being formed that are congruent with the playing of traditional roles by members of both sexes. They also demonstrate that processes of female inferiorization are set in place at an early age. It appears that by adolescence, boys have learnt that they are entitled at some time in the future to have a wife who will free them from domestic jobs and child care for work and play. For their part, Smalltown girls graduate from their family home viewing males as worthy of their support and nurturing. They graduate skilled to care for them, not only because they have observed their mothers performing traditional women's tasks, but because they themselves have been, for several years, assisting their mothers in looking after their fathers and brothers. So there is a good chance that they will enter marriage committed to putting their husbands' interests and even their recreational activities before their own. If not emotionally committed, they will enter marriage knowing that this is what not only their husbands but their own family and most community members expect of them, and they will be aware of the kind of pressure to which they will be subjected to ensure they fulfil their expected role.

In Chapter 5 we saw that Smalltown wives use their domestic skills to facilitate both their husband's leisure activities and those of their mates and fellow club members. Marriage, we have seen, serves as a mechanism for incorporating women and their skills in the collective activities of men. The data presented here on the socialization of adolescent girls show how the way is prepared for these forms of incorporation and exploitation. We have seen that these socialization processes are, in effect, value discourses that help construct identities which are congruous with a hierarchical ordering of relationships between men and women. The socialization processes also prepare males and females for the gender discourses of later life. On the basis of experiences in the home, the latter discourses must seem to describe a natural order in which men and their activities are privileged and superior to women and their activities. The discourses of both adolescence and adulthood demonstrate that the inequalities women experience are mediated by their interpersonal relationships rather than being produced directly by their economic or physical oppression (Abrams and McCulloch, 1976). The next chapter shows that these discourses encourage females to take the view that it is *not* appropriate for them to aspire to the better-paying jobs occupied by males in this community.

CHAPTER 9

Occupational aspirations

In our research in Smalltown we wanted to push beyond an investigation of how primary socialization contributes to the development of gender roles in the domestic division of labour to an examination of its impact on the occupational aspirations of teenage girls and boys. We have already seen how the character of a man's town is established and maintained through men's dominance of most of the highly paid and prestigious positions in the community work-force. So, the major question was this: were males prepared for future dominance by their occupational socialization while girls were socialized to accept traditional feminized occupations in the paid work-force—occupations which receive inferior rewards? As Bott (1957), Bell (1968), and Bulmer (1975) have shown, the view an individual develops of the self is affected by experiences in their immediate social milieu, including peer group, school, and family. It was beyond our research resources to make a direct study of these socializing agencies. However, we were able to gain data from parents from which it was plausible to draw inferences about the familial socialization experienced by Smalltown teenagers. During the Community Survey we questioned parents with teenage children about the occupational aspirations they had for their sons and daughters. This enabled us to establish if parents had higher job aspirations for sons than daughters. We collected data on the occupational aspirations of teenage boys and girls participating in the School Survey 1 and compared them with those of the parent population. We argued that if women are going to challenge male dominance in the job market they must at least aspire to gaining some of the more coveted jobs. Whether they do aspire will depend to a considerable degree on whether their parents share their aspirations.

We were also interested in the relationship between job aspirations and outcomes. So, thirteen years after they were first surveyed, we located as many of the children as possible to find out what job they had, if any, the level of formal education they had acquired, whether they had married, and whether they had had any children. We established the whereabouts of 269 of the 314 children who participated in the original survey. Of the 269, 254 were or had recently been employed on a full-time or part-time basis. Fourteen females were not in the paid work-force but were married to males engaged in paid work, and one female was unemployed. In the next chapter I will report on their occupational achievements and relate these to the gender and family–class background of each child and the aspirations of the children and the parents. I will also examine how effective marriage proved to be as a vehicle of social mobility for the females in the sample. The major purposes of this chapter are to show what difference gender makes to a parent's aspirations for a child, and to the occupational ideals and realistic expectations of the children themselves, to draw some inferences about the significance of primary socialization for occupational aspirations by delineating any similarities between the aspirations of parents and children, and to describe what impact family–class background has, if any, on aspirations. The information presented in both chapters is based on the reduced sample of 269 participants.

Ideal jobs

In 1973 we asked students attending the two Smalltown secondary schools these questions:

> Suppose you were living in an ideal society and you had a completely free choice, what job would you choose?
>
> Now considering realistically your actual circumstances (for example such limitations as your family's financial position and your own ability), what job can you realistically expect to have?[1]

Parents who participated in the Community Survey and whose children were attending local secondary schools were asked similar questions in order to establish the aspirations and realistic job expectations they held for their children.[2]

A majority of girls and boys displayed the success orientation that other researchers have found among Australian teenagers (Connell, 1977:152, 181; Sinclair *et al.*, 1977). In this instance, this means they expressed a preference for middle-class (classes 1, 2, 3 or 4) as opposed to lower-middle- or working-class jobs. In conversations and interviews, most made it clear that they wanted to 'get on', and that they believed upward mobility was accessible to anyone with ambition and who was prepared to work. Neither young people, nor their parents, equated getting on with 'getting above oneself'.[3] Parents, daughters, and sons rejected snobbery as divisive and morally reprehensible behaviour and espoused the virtues of egalitarianism (see Dempsey, 1990a:34–5, Ch. 7). Yet, having said that, two-thirds of both girls and boys still reported that they would ideally like a middle-class job: that is, a job that fell into one of the four higher segments of the work-force (Table 9.1). Roughly three-quarters of parents expressed similar hopes for their daughters and sons.

There was some overlap in the specific jobs that children and parents of both sexes nominated as ideal, but boys proved to be more 'ambitious' than girls and parents more ambitious for sons than for daughters (see also Powell and Bloom, 1962; Douvan and Adelson, 1966; Clark, 1967; Sinclair *et al.*, 1977).[4] Boys were twice as likely as girls to nominate class 1 or class 2 positions as their ideal (Table 9.1). In other words they were much more likely than girls to dream about becoming a lawyer, doctor, engineer, accountant, or veterinary surgeon. Middle- and working-

Table 9.1 Ideal jobs

Occupation	Girls	Parents (for girls)	Boys	Parents (for boys)
Middle classes				
1 Higher-level professionals and administrators (e.g. doctors, lawyers)	17	13	31	33
2 Farmers	1	0	13	10
3 Business proprietors	0	0	0	0
4 Semi-professionals and administrators (e.g. nurses, teachers)	53	60	26	34
Lower middle class				
5 Ordinary white-collar workers and sales (e.g. typists, sales assistants)	8	16	2	9
Working classes				
6 Skilled manual workers and foremen (e.g. tradespeople)	0	3	20	13
7 Semi-skilled or unskilled manual workers (e.g. domestics, drivers)	21	8	8	1
Total				
%	100	100	100	100
N	142	77	138	88

class Smalltowners of all ages and both sexes view such occupations as 'top jobs'. Owning a prosperous town business, or holding a leading executive post such as town clerk, is also seen as highly desirable. The other top job is farming. Most of the boys who said they were dreaming about becoming farmers specified that they would ideally like to be 'big farmers'. In Smalltown the expression means a farmer with a big holding. This occupation commands a similar degree of respect to that of a doctor or lawyer and it requires property worth over $2 million.

While parents said they would ideally like to see daughters as well as sons obtain one of the more economically, socially, and psychologically rewarding positions in the work-force, they were more strongly attached to the notion of a son than a daughter obtaining one of the 'top jobs'. Parents were three times as likely to aspire to a son obtaining a class 1 or class 2 position than a daughter. Presumably this means they were more likely to be encouraging a son than a daughter to think about a career in a higher level occupation such as in medicine, law, accountancy, veterinary science, or farming. Indeed, we collected anecdotal evidence that suggested that some parents vigorously opposed any plans a daughter had to enter a traditional profession, no matter how tentative were those plans. For instance, one woman said during the course of the follow-up study that she abandoned her fantasy of becoming a doctor after her parents said she was aiming far too high. If she were really ambitious to get on, they said, she should think of becoming a nurse or a schoolteacher. Such jobs, they thought, were 'wonderful for a girl'. A second woman said she surrendered her dream of becoming a lawyer because she faced similar opposition from her parents.

In Smalltown, as in the wider society, higher professional jobs and farming are viewed as several 'cuts above' jobs in teaching and nursing (Broom and Jones, 1976). Girls did fantasize in large numbers about becoming nurses or teachers (Table 9.1), and they were supported in these aspirations by their parents (60 per cent said they would ideally like to see a daughter become a teacher or a nurse). Girls were twice as likely as boys to nominate teaching, or some other class 4 occupation, and half as likely as boys to nominate a job of the higher classes (that is, classes 1, 2 or 3). The jobs that girls and their parents perceived as ideal for them clustered in the middle of the class structure.

There were also striking contrasts between the proportion of girls and boys who said that they would ideally like to enter skilled manual work, and correspondingly in the proportion of parents who said they aspired to a son taking up a trade, as compared with a daughter doing so. No girl said she would ideally like to enter a skilled manual job (class 6) and only two parents expressed such a hope for a daughter.[5] However, one-fifth of the boys expressed such aspirations for themselves and one-seventh of the parents expressed them for their sons.

By contrast, girls were more than twice as likely as boys to say they would like to obtain unskilled work. Most of these girls nominated domestic work as their favoured occupation, but, as we will see later, this was more a protest about having to enter the paid work-force at all than an expression of a desire to work as a domestic servant. Notwithstanding this caveat, it is the case that in both the non-manual and manual sectors of the work-force, the jobs girls perceived as desirable and parents saw as desirable for daughters were usually less well paid and attracted less status than the jobs boys perceived as desirable or parents perceived as desirable for sons. The jobs girls perceived as ideal were principally of the nurturing or servicing kind.

The impact of family–class background on ideal jobs

Family–class position had little impact on the ideal job

aspirations of girls or of parents for daughters. Girls in all three major class categories (middle class, lower middle class, and working class) reported a similar pattern of job aspirations. Girls from middle-class (classes 1–4) homes were only slightly more likely than those from working-class homes to perceive higher professional jobs as ideal (Table 9.2).

Table 9.2 Girls' ideal jobs by family class

Family class	Class expectations							
	1	2,3	4	5	6	7	Total %	N
Middle classes 1–4	19	1	56	8	0	15	99	78
Lower middle class 5	0	0	50	10	0	40	100	10
Working classes 6, 7	16	0	49	8	0	27	100	49

Semi-professional jobs in teaching or nursing were the most preferred jobs for girls of all classes and for parents of all classes for their daughters (Tables 9.2 and 9.3). Middle-class girls were only slightly more likely than working-class girls to express a preference for semi-professional jobs.

Table 9.3 Parents' ideal jobs for girls by family class

Family class	Class expectations							
	1	2,3	4	5	6	7	Total %	N
Middle classes 1–4	20	0	60	13	2	4	99	45
Lower middle class 5	20	0	50	20	0	10	100	10
Working classes 6, 7	0	0	66	19	5	9	99	21

I will argue in this chapter that this inter-generational homogeneity in the jobs perceived as ideal is an important indicator of the greater influence of gender than of class on the jobs girls perceive as ideal and which they therefore prepare themselves to pursue. The factors that probably had the most significant bearing on the job aspirations of girls were their awareness of structural impediments to gaining particular jobs; their socialization experience, and the goals and self-identification these produced; and their awareness of community expectations of them as women coupled with their awareness of the social pressure applied to women to conform to these.

As Chapter 5 demonstrated, women in Smalltown are crowded into a narrow range of jobs, and adolescent girls are aware of this fact. In the early 1970s very few, if any, of these girls would have had any firsthand experience of women working as doctors, lawyers, or accountants, and they were aware that boys not girls usually inherit a farm or succeed their fathers as building contractors or major retailers. The previous chapter showed that by their early teenage years, girls were closely identifying with nurturing and caring roles, and had developed a sense of identity that was not easy to reconcile with entering occupations defined as men's jobs. Farming was one such job, and, to a lesser extent, so were medicine, law, accounting, and engineering. Our respondents knew, for instance, that a girl who farmed in her own right was likely to be perceived as a vicarious male rather than a suitable partner for marriage, or a suitable candidate for motherhood. Finally, the failure of most girls to aspire to the more rewarding male-dominated jobs was probably closely linked to the strong belief in Smalltown that marriage and motherhood were of overriding importance in a woman's life, and the girls' awareness of community opposition to women putting a career ahead of motherhood or support for a husband's career. Throughout the entire period of this study I can recall only a handful of respondents saying—either in the course of casual conversation or of a formal interview—that a girl should be able to pursue a career because she finds it intrinsically interesting. Rather, as I stressed in Chapter 7, a majority of respondents in the Gender Survey categorically rejected the suggestion that for a woman a career should serve as her major way of gaining personal fulfilment.

It seems likely that these gendered structural and cultural forces accounted for the findings that girls of each particular class were less likely than boys of the same class to perceive a higher professional job as ideal; and that the proportion of middle-class girls (classes 1–4) fantasizing about a higher professional job was less than the proportion of working-class boys doing so (19 per cent compared with 27 per cent) (Tables 9.2 and 9.4).

The ideal jobs: nursing or teaching

The factors that discouraged girls of all classes nominating a class 1, 2, or 3 job as ideal did not stand in the way of their aspiring to entering nursing or teaching. Why teaching or nursing in particular? Of the jobs available to Smalltown women in any numbers, these were (and remain) the most economically rewarding and the jobs with the highest prestige. Just as importantly, throughout this study they have been seen as appropriate for girls to pursue. Work in teaching and nursing is believed to interfere far less than higher professional jobs with a woman's responsibilities as a wife, home-maker and mother. A woman who is a teacher can be available to mother when school closes and during the school holidays, while a nurse can usually work suitable shifts or part time. At the same time these jobs are believed to provide an excellent opportunity for a woman to contribute economically to the family's well-being. Teaching and nursing are perceived as portable jobs, so, if a husband chooses to move in order to further his own career, a wife will be able to 'get work that always pays well and that fits in with looking after the kids in the family's new neighbourhood. On the negative side, qualifications for teaching and nursing cannot be obtained locally, which reduces the attractiveness of these jobs for some girls and for many more parents. But girls and parents alike are aware that a job as a typist or a clerk is the best that a girl who remains in Smalltown can hope to achieve, and that it is more likely she will end up working as a machinist or domestic, hence the appeal of teaching and nursing. The advantages inherent in teaching and nursing apply to women whatever their class background, and therefore probably help explain why girls and parents of all classes preferred semi-professional jobs (Tables 9.2 and 9.3).

The lack of appeal of secretarial and clerical work

We were surprised that so few girls perceived an ordinary white-collar job as desirable (less than 10 per cent) because, during the months before the survey, we were repeatedly told that a job as a typist or shop assistant was regarded as a 'real coup' for a girl who wished to remain in Smalltown. The reality then (as now) was that parents were much keener about the prospect of a daughter becoming a typist or secretary than the daughters themselves were (parents were twice as likely as the girls themselves to nominate typing or secretarial work as ideal). It was the attitudes of parents not their children that we had been eliciting before the School Survey. 'A job as a typist is a real plum job that any Smalltown parent would be delighted to see her daughter get' was the kind of comment frequently made to us during field-work, but it was more likely to be made by working-class or lower-middle-class than middle-class parents, possibly because their concern about funding a tertiary education affected their ability to fantasize about their daughter becoming a teacher or nurse (the favoured fantasy of parents of all classes). Some middle-class parents—including a number with a daughter sufficiently talented to acquire a tertiary educational qualification—expressed the same wish because, as they reported in interviews, they regard the city as a dangerous and undesirable place for a daughter to be, or because they did not want to lose her companionship (Dempsey, 1990a). The city is also too far away for daily or even weekly contact. Being prepared to settle for a lesser job for a daughter than she could actually obtain is not incongruous if parents believe, as they do, that marriage and motherhood are the pivotal roles in a daughter's life. Some of these parents approached local employers in the hope of gaining a white-collar job for a daughter. If they were successful this greatly increased the pressure on the daughter to stay.

Many daughters in our study took a more jaundiced view of ordinary white-collar jobs. First, they were often anxious to get away from parents who were too confining and a town which offered too little in the way of entertainment for young people and far too limited a choice of potential husbands. Second, there were those girls who wanted to leave because they held the view that a job as a typist was a poor reward for someone with considerable formal education. They were dreaming about a chance 'to forge a new life for themselves', and pursuing a semi-professional career in the city seemed far superior to 'settling for an office job in Smalltown'.

Parents of all classes, however, saw a job for a daughter as a typist or clerk as superior to a job as a machinist at the knitting mill, or as a domestic worker in one of the town's hotels or motels. Our most surprising finding was that the girls themselves were more likely to nominate a semi-skilled or unskilled job than an ordinary white-collar position as their ideal occupation. Almost 1 in 4 girls compared to 1 in 10 parents nominated domestic work as an ideal job. Why these contrasting results, given that in most instances the aspirations of parents and girls, or of parents and boys, mirrored each other? For their part, parents were unlikely to nominate a domestic job as ideal because they knew it was at the bottom of the system economically and socially. Many daughters nominated a domestic job as ideal to protest about having to enter the paid work-force at all rather than as a reflection of a genuine occupational choice. In conversations we had with some of these girls they reported that their selection of domestic work as an ideal job was their way of saying they wanted to realize as soon as possible their aspirations to be wives and mothers, so they chose the job that was closest to their perception of themselves as future home-makers. Perhaps surprisingly, approximately one-sixth of the middle-class girls in our sample nominated domestic work as their ideal occupation (Table 9.2). Possibly they were girls who were not achieving much educationally, but their choice, or rather the reasons advanced for it, reflect the profound impact of gendered socialization on self perception and the high priority these goals have for girls.

Chapter 8 demonstrated that, during the teenage years, girls were three times as likely as boys to be regularly performing domestic tasks traditionally identified as women's work, and by their early teenage years, girls were closely identifying with nurturing and caring roles. The great majority of the girls who participated in the 1974 School Survey nominated marriage and motherhood as their ultimate goals in life. They were growing up in a community whose residents shared with the members of many communities (urban as well as rural) the conviction that, while men's responsibilities were primarily in the system of paid work, women's were primarily domestic. So, the girls' 'choice' of domestic work as an ideal job reflected these gender-specific beliefs as well as their personal identification with wifehood and motherhood and the negative valence for them of entering the paid work-force. 'I only want to work until I get married' was a common remark. This interpretation was corroborated by the observations made by several teachers in the 1970s and 1980s. They reported that there were always a few girls in the secondary school who 'could not wait' to leave school and start a family. By Year 9 they had selected their future spouse from among the boys in the class. Most of these girls left as soon as they reached fifteen, the legal age to leave school.

Family–class position and girls' ideal jobs

Why did girls from different classes often nominate the same job as ideal? At one level of explanation, it is plausible to attribute the similarity in the ideal jobs of girls of all classes to the concentration of jobs of women in only a few sectors of the work-force. This concentration 'almost inevitably means that they will have quite similar chances of ending up there, whatever their social class origins' (Heath, 1981: 126). But this approach begs the question of why women are not found in other sectors. It fails to take account of job discrimination by men against women and of socialization processes which inhibit women from competing with men for certain jobs. On the first point, the similarity in job ideals of girls with different class backgrounds follows, in part, from the unwillingness of middle-class families to provide daughters with the capital—especially in the form of land—to replicate their families' advantaged position and, in part, from being socialized to identify with occupations traditionally performed by women. The class homogeneity, however, reflects girls' awareness that if they start competing with men for the jobs men dominate, or giving priority to a career over domestic and conjugal responsibilities, they will attract a good deal of criticism. Girls will only dream about what it is possible to achieve or what they will not be sanctioned too severely for attempting to achieve.

Family–class position and boys' ideal jobs

The job market for men was not nearly as contracted as it was for women. Whereas the job opportunities for girls were concentrated in two or three sectors of the occupational structure, whatever their family–class background, those for boys ranged over every sector. Accordingly, there was more opportunity for class background to have an impact on the job opportunities of boys and, insofar as their expressed job ideals reflected job opportunities, on those aspirations as well. For example, one-third of the boys from working-class homes compared to one-fifth of girls from middle-class homes said that they would ideally like to gain a higher level job.

There was also greater opportunity for class-linked diversity in job aspirations for males than females for these reasons. First, men, unlike women, were not excluded from many higher professional and executive positions. Second, as boys they had not been socialized to see the more valuable jobs in the work-force as inappropriate for them because of their gender, or to believe that marriage and fatherhood should take precedence over a career. On the contrary, they had been raised to believe their masculinity would hinge primarily on their occupational success, which in turn encouraged them to compete occupationally (Donaldson, 1991).

The considerable class-based diversity in the job aspirations of teenage boys and, in some instances, of parents for sons is illustrated by these findings:

Table 9.4 Boys' ideal jobs by family class

Family class	Class expectations							
	1	2, 3	4	5	6	7	Total %	N
Middle classes 1–4	31	18	24	3	16	9	101	80
Lower middle class 5	27	9	36	0	27	0	99	11
Working classes 6, 7	27	5	29	2	27	10	100	41

Table 9.5 Parents' ideal jobs for boys by family class

Family class	Class expectations							
	1	2,3	4	5	6	7	Total %	N
Middle classes 1–4	38	12	36	4	9	1	100	56
Lower middle class 5	13	3	25	13	38	0	102	8
Working classes 6, 7	28	0	33	22	17	0	100	18

1 Whereas there were only 4 percentage points difference between girls from middle-class families[6] and working-class families who would ideally like to gain a higher level job (class 1, 2, or 3), there were 17 percentage points difference between the boys from middle-class and working-class families who in an ideal world would like to gain a class 1, 2, or 3 job (Tables 9.2 and 9.4).
2 Working-class parents were less likely than middle-class parents to aspire to a son gaining a higher professional job, and the sons of working-class families themselves were marginally less optimistic than those of middle-class families about gaining a higher professional job (Tables 9.5 and 9.4).[7]
3 There was a considerable gap between the proportion of middle-class boys and working-class boys who would ideally like a class 2 job (farming) (Table 9.4)[8] and a similar gap between the wishes of middle- and working-class parents (Table 9.5). These results stood in marked contrast to those demonstrating the lack of impact of family–class background on the aspirations of girls and of parents for girls to take up farming: girls of all classes knew that farming was a man's occupation and they had been socialized to see farming as incompatible with their sense of femininity. However, no working-class boy had

been socialized to see farming as an inappropriate occupation for him. On the contrary, a working-class boy and his parents knew that if, by some miracle, he was able to make a career in farming, he would be viewed locally as a highly successful man, have far greater economic resources than his family, and probably experience greater personal satisfaction from farming than from any job he could realistically expect to enter.

There were no cultural impediments to working-class boys dreaming about farming, nor was there any evidence that the failure of parents to say that farming was an ideal job for their son was an example of working-class solidarity (Dempsey, 1990a). But there was a major structural impediment: working-class families could not provide sons with the necessary capital to farm, and this impediment affected their job aspirations. Consequently only 2 of the 41 working-class boys in our sample said that in an ideal world they would like to be farmers. Not one working-class parent acknowledged this aspiration for a son.

4 Working-class boys and their parents were more likely than middle-class boys and their parents to perceive a skilled manual job as an ideal occupation (Tables 9.4 and 9.5). Class did not have a similar impact on the aspirations of girls, or of parents for girls, because of the structural and cultural impediments to their entering the overwhelming majority of trade positions in Smalltown or the wider society (Tables 9.2 and 9.3). The class differences in the findings about boys, however, were fairly predictable. Boys from class 7 families (semi/unskilled families) were likely to aspire to a skilled job because it would constitute a significant upward movement in the Smalltown class structure, while for boys from class 6 (skilled families), who wished to remain in Smalltown, a trade position was the best they could hope to achieve.

5 A substantial proportion of boys from middle-class

families (16 per cent) said they would like to enter a trade (Table 9.4). Here a combination of factors was at work. Some of these boys were farmers' sons who knew they would not be entering farming or who did not wish to become farmers but wanted to remain in Smalltown. A trade position was the best they could hope for, and it might become the basis for a town business of some kind. Other respondents were the sons of businessmen who saw gaining a trade as the first step towards going into the family business, or eventually establishing a business for themselves. So, aspiring to enter a skilled position (and in some instances a semi-skilled position) was tantamount to aspiring to a job of equivalent standing to that of their fathers.

In summary, whereas a majority of girls aspired to jobs in the middle or at the bottom of the class structure, boys aspired to the most rewarding jobs economically, socially, and psychologically in the Smalltown work-force, especially farming and higher professional jobs. In Smalltown, higher professional jobs and farming were then, as now, viewed as several 'cuts above' the semi-professional jobs. Yet it was semi-professional jobs that parents reported as ideal for daughters and which the daughters themselves said they would ideally like to enter (Dempsey, 1990a: Ch. 7). In this instance the aspirations of children, and parents for children, were usually a mirror image of each other.[9]

Realistic job expectations

The chances of girls challenging male dominance of the more rewarding jobs in the paid work-force will be influenced by their realistic job expectations as well as by their job fantasies. If girls do not realistically expect to achieve a specific job, then there is even less chance that they will compete with boys for the position. What jobs then did girls realistically expect to achieve and what jobs did parents realistically expect their daughters to achieve? How did these expectations compare with those of the boys and of boys' parents for their sons? How were these expectations affected by the family–class background of girls and boys? What proportion of boys and girls expected to gain a middle-class job?

Table 9.6 Realistic expectations

Occupation	Girls %	Parents (for girls) %	Boys %	Parents (for boys) %
Middle classes				
1 Higher-level professionals and administrators (e.g. doctors, lawyers)	9	13	10	13
2 Farmers	1	0	23	18
3 Business proprietors	0	0	0	0
4 Semi-professionals and administrators (e.g. nurses, teachers)	44	46	26	21
Lower middle class				
5 Ordinary white-collar workers and sales (e.g. typists, sales assistants)	29	28	9	13
Working classes				
6 Skilled manual workers and foremen (e.g. employee plumbers, hairdressers)	1	1	22	30
7 Semi-skilled or unskilled manual workers (e.g. domestics, drivers)	16	13	9	6
Total				
%	100	101	99	101
N	140	80	134	87

When boys and girls were asked what job they could expect to obtain, given the limitations of ability and family finance, considerably fewer expected to gain a middle-class job than had previously perceived such a position as ideal for them (Tables 9.1 and 9.6). Nevertheless, more than half the girls and half the boys said it was realistic to expect to obtain a Class 1, 2, 3, or 4 job. Boys, however, displayed greater confidence of success than girls. For instance, 33 per cent of boys compared with only 10 per cent of girls said they realistically expected to gain a higher professional job or a career in farming. If girls expected to enter the middle class (as opposed to the lower middle class), it was principally by gaining jobs as teachers or nurses. They were four times as likely to expect to gain a job as a nurse or teacher (class 4 job) than to gain a class 1, 2, or 3 position. By contrast, boys were more likely to expect to gain a higher level job (class 1, 2, or 3) than to enter a class 4 position. Again, girls were three times as likely as boys to expect to have to settle for an ordinary white-collar position.

There was not much evidence in the data we collected from parents to indicate that they believed their daughters should or would successfully challenge men for the more rewarding jobs in the work-force, which they have traditionally monopolized. For example, the number of parents who realistically expected a daughter to achieve either a class 1 or class 2 position was less than half the number who expected a son to achieve one of these more desirable positions. It is plausible to argue that such convictions—especially when they are held by daughters as well as by parents—enhance the chances of the boys continuing to excel by removing half the competition.

Most parents did not see white-collar jobs as ideal, but they viewed them more favourably than their sons and daughters did, and many parents believed that they were the best jobs their children could realistically hope to gain. So, while only 16 per cent of parents perceived it as ideal for a daughter to become a typist or sales assistant, 28 per cent of them said they realistically expected a daughter to take up such a job (Tables 9.1 and 9.6). The proportion of parents realistically expecting a son to enter an ordinary white-collar occupation was less than half this size, reflecting the fact that there was a greater range of more desirable jobs available to sons than to daughters.

The influence of family–class background on realistic job expectations

Predictably, when we asked boys and girls what jobs they could realistically expect to gain in the future, children belonging to every class category proved less optimistic than when we asked them what jobs they would ideally like to obtain. Whereas 59 per cent of middle-class boys would have ideally liked a class 1, 2 or 3 job, only 49 per cent realistically expected to achieve a job at this level (Tables 9.4 and 9.9).[10]

Whereas 32 per cent of working-class boys had reported they would ideally like a high level job (class 1, 2, or 3) only 7 per cent said they realistically expected to achieve one (Tables 9.4 and 9.9). Only 4 per cent of working-class girls said they realistically expected to gain a higher level professional job whereas 16 per cent reported they fantasized

Table 9.7 Realistic class expectations of girls by family class

Family class	Class expectations							
	1	2, 3	4	5	6	7	Total %	N
Middle classes 1–4	12	3	44	26	1	14	100	81
Lower middle class 5	0	0	44	33	0	22	99	9
Working classes 6, 7	4	2	44	32	0	18	100	50

about taking up a professional occupation. This gap in expectations was not as great for girls from middle-class families: 19 per cent compared with 12 per cent (Tables 9.2 and 9.7).

These data show that the biggest decline in optimism was displayed by working-class children of both sexes.

We have seen that family–class background had a greater bearing on the reported ideal jobs of boys and of those made by parents for boys than of girls or of parents for girls. Similar results were achieved when we questioned parents and children about realistic jobs expectations (Tables 9.7, 9.8, 9.9 and 9.10).

Table 9.8 Realistic class expectations of parents for girls by family class

Family class	Class expectations							
	1	2, 3	4	5	6	7	Total %	N
Middle classes 1–4	18	0	49	22	2	9	100	45
Lower middle class 5	18	0	27	27	0	27	99	11
Working classes 6, 7	0	0	48	39	0	13	100	23

Table 9.9 Realistic class expectations of boys by family class

Family class	Class expectations							
	1	2, 3	4	5	6	7	Total %	N
Middle classes 1–4	14	35	25	8	13	6	101	80
Lower middle class 5	18	9	27	0	46	0	100	11
Working classes 6, 7	2	5	29	15	37	12	100	41

Table 9.10 Realistic class expectations of parents for boys by family class

Family class	Class expectations							
	1	2,3	4	5	6	7	Total %	N
Middle classes 1–4	13	27	22	8	23	7	100	60
Lower middle class 5	22	0	22	22	33	0	99	9
Working classes 6, 7	6	0	16	22	51	4	99	18

On the one hand, exactly the same proportion of girls of each of the three major class categories (middle class, lower middle class and working class) said they could realistically expect to obtain a job as either a teacher or nurse (44 per cent; Table 9.7). On the other hand, there was a great disparity between the proportion of middle-class and working-class boys realistically expecting to gain a job as a professional or farmer (49 per cent of middle-class boys compared with 7 per cent of working-class boys; Table 9.9).[11] There were only 3 percentage points difference between the proportion of middle-class and working-class girls expecting to do manual work compared with 30 percentage points between middle-class and working-class boys expecting to work as tradesmen or semi-skilled workers (Tables 9.7 and 9.9).[12]

The results in this section of the enquiry confirmed the earlier observation that gender rather than family–class position is the major determinant of the aspirations of girls and that there is much less opportunity for family–class position to influence either the fantasies or realistic expectations of girls than of boys.

Conclusion

The data that have been presented in this chapter show that girls of all classes did not usually aspire to the better positions in the work-force that men have traditionally dominated. It also shows that the job fantasies and realistic expectations parents held for daughters were very similar to those that daughters held for themselves and substantially different from those that parents held for sons. Parents were much more likely to aspire to sons than daughters gaining either a higher level non-manual or manual position.

I have argued that girls and their parents were aware of the structural impediments to females obtaining one of the more desirable jobs in the paid work-force and that this knowledge impeded them in even fantasizing about gaining such jobs let alone stating that they could realistically expect to do so. It is also possible that the aspirations of girls were affected by their knowledge of the pressure all females are subjected to throughout most of their lives to place marriage and motherhood before the pursuit of their own careers and to choose an occupation which actually facilitates them performing sucessfully as wives and mothers. If girls were responsive to these pressures it was because they had developed self-identities which were more compatible with putting husbands and families first than with competing against males for the jobs that men presently control in the Smalltown work-force and in the wider society.

The girls' own sense of femininity did not fit with entering farming or any of the trades on which Smalltown business enterprises are based. During the course of this investigation we collected a good deal of both anecdotal and systematic survey evidence that strongly suggested that most girls and their parents did not believe it was appropriate for females to compete with males for most of the valued positions males occupy. The reluctance of girls of all classes to aspire to the better jobs in the paid work-force, of course, facilitates the continuance of a system that produces the disadvantages that women suffer from and which, in turn, leads to their being socialized to accept as natural or at least as inevitable their subordination in domestic and community life, and perpetuates the inferiorization of females.

We have seen that the situation was somewhat different for the males in our sample. They knew that members of their sex were not concentrated in a limited number of job categories in the paid work-force. They were aware that, while women had to contend with men excluding them from most of the more desirable jobs, men did not have to contend with women excluding them from highly valued occupations. Furthermore, boys were not being socialized to see the more valuable jobs in the work-force as inappropriate for them, or to believe that marriage and fatherhood should take precedence over a career. Instead, boys of all classes were being educated, in the school as well as the home, to believe their manhood depended primarily on their occupational success, just as girls were encouraged to believe that their womanhood depended on their success as wives and mothers. Yet, whereas the gender of girls of all classes virtually ensured their exclusion from class 2 and 3 jobs and reduced considerably their chances of gaining a class 1 job, for boys, having the right class background opened up a special range of opportunities. This observation applied especially to boys from farming and town business families. Knowledge of these realities translated into great confidence about occupational success for many boys from middle-class families but, a widespread conviction among working-class boys, and their parents, that they had next to no chance of making a significant move up the local occupational ladder. Their best chance was to leave Smalltown and obtain qualifications that would enable them to pursue a professional, semi-professional, or administrative career.

In the next chapter we will see how things turned out both for the boys and girls who remained in Smalltown and for those who moved away.

CHAPTER 10

Occupational achievements

In 1986 we returned to Smalltown to find out about the working lives of the children we had surveyed thirteen years earlier. The visit revealed that most boys and girls had failed to realize their dreams and many had also failed to fulfil their realistic expectations. The gap between aspirations and realities occurred in part because social mobility, especially in an upwards direction, is inhibited in Smalltown by the presence of a fairly rigid class structure. The rigidity is due to several factors. First, most males and virtually all females do not have access to the major productive resource—farming land. Second, there are few middle-class jobs, such as professional and administrative positions, allocated on the basis of qualifications and experience. They are only half as plentiful in Smalltown as they are nationally.[1] Third, there are few skilled manual positions. They are a little more than half as plentiful in Smalltown as throughout Australia. Finally, the district has no tertiary educational institutions, which means that local young people do not have the opportunity to obtain the qualifications that would allow them to compete for the relatively few professional and administrative positions available. Together these factors make it difficult for working-class children, especially girls, to use a paid job to move into the middle classes. While the system guarantees the succession of a substantial minority of middle-class boys to their families' privileged position, it also promotes the downward mobility of most middle-class boys who remain in Smalltown, and virtually all middle-class girls who remain.

Parkin points out that the opportunities for social mobility are an expression of the balance of power in class relations and the lack of opportunities is the outcome of the practice of social closure by one class against another (1974). This chapter will show that patterns of mobility also demonstrate the superior power of men and the way they use the strategy of closure against women. In sum: social mobility is constrained by gender as well as by social class. However, there were girls and boys in our sample who were upwardly mobile despite their failure to inherit a privileged position and often despite coming from an economically deprived family. The paid work-force can be used for social mobility, but so can marriage. In the latter part of the chapter I will report on the extent to which women worsened or improved their social and economic position through marriage.

Fantasies, realistic expectations, and achievements

The previous chapter demonstrated that the great majority of the young people who participated in the 1973 survey were eager to gain one of the more rewarding positions in the job market. Roughly two-thirds of both the boys and the girls had fantasized about gaining a middle-class position (class positions 1 to 4; Tables 10.1 and 10.2). More than half of them had said that they realistically expected some kind of middle-class job. Their parents had made similar predictions: 59 per cent of parents with an adolescent daughter and 52 per cent of the parents with an adolescent son had said they were confident of their children gaining a middle-class job (Table 9.6). But things did not turn out nearly as well as either parents or children had hoped: only 40 per cent of girls and 37 per cent of boys gained some kind of middle-class job (Tables 10.1 and 10.2).

The proportion gaining a middle-class, or lower-middle-class job (classes 1 to 5) was boosted considerably by a substantial number of girls and boys gaining jobs as clerks, typists, and sales assistants. While these were not jobs that many respondents perceived as ideal (the proportion entering them exceeded the proportion desiring them by four to one for girls and nine to one for boys) they nevertheless resulted in 75 per cent of girls and 56 per cent of boys gaining a middle-class job of some kind.[2] Taken at face value, these results imply that girls did as well, or even better than boys. However, this only holds true if we ignore the relative economic and social value of various

Table 10.1 Girls' ideal jobs and achieved jobs

	Ideal %	Achieved %	Difference %
Middle classes			
1 Higher-level professionals and administrators	17	4	−13
2 Farmers	1	0	−1
3 Business proprietors	0	0	0
Sub-total 3 higher classes	18	4	−14
4 Semi-professionals and administrators	53	36	−17
Lower middle class			
5 Ordinary white-collar workers and sales	8	35	+27
Working classes			
6 Skilled manual workers and foremen	0	1	+1
7 Semi-skilled or unskilled manual workers	21	24	+3
Total			
%	100	100	
N	142	117	

positions in the middle, lower middle, and the working classes. So, if we disaggregate the middle-class category of job achievements a quite different picture emerges (Tables 10.1 and 10.2).[3]

In particular, the disaggregation shows that girls achieved jobs in only one of the top three strata of the middle class. Even in the stratum in which they were successful (class 1), they gained only one-third of the total number of positions that were achieved in that stratum by members of our sample. In the farming and petit-bourgeois business classes all positions were taken up by male members of the sample, and boys were roughly seven times as likely as girls to have

Table 10.2 Boys' ideal jobs and achieved jobs

	Ideal %	Achieved %	Difference %
Middle classes			
1 Higher-level professionals and administrators	31	8	−23
2 Farmers	13	10	−3
3 Business proprietors	0	11	+11
Sub-total 3 higher classes	44	29	−15
4 Semi-professionals and administrators	26	8	−18
Lower middle class			
5 Ordinary white-collar workers and sales	2	19	+17
Working classes			
6 Skilled manual workers and foremen	20	22	+2
7 Semi-skilled or unskilled manual workers	8	22	+14
Total			
%	100	100	
N	138	135	

achieved a class 1, 2, or 3 job. These jobs usually endow their incumbents with better incomes, fringe benefits, and higher social status than class 4 (semi-professional, middle management) positions. Girls occupied about 80 per cent of the positions gained by members of the sample in the lowest stratum of the middle-classes whereas boys occupied 90 per cent of the positions in the three higher strata. Girls gained a larger proportion of lower-middle-class jobs (ordinary white-collar positions) than boys, but for reasons I will elaborate upon, I believe that boys did as well as girls in the middle of the class structure. Although boys occupied a larger proportion of positions in the lowest class their jobs in that sector usually offered superior rewards to those gained by women employed in this sector.

It is customary for sociologists to place ordinary white-collar jobs on a higher level than trade jobs. In order to make my findings as comparative as possible I have followed this convention in this study (see Goldthorpe, 1980; Jones and Davis, 1986). However, where I am focusing on the relative opportunities of girls and boys to gain rewarding jobs, as in the present context, then I must stress that in Smalltown, ordinary white-collar jobs, especially those performed by females, are not economically or socially superior to skilled manual jobs. They offer inferior pay to skilled jobs and, in many instances, inferior status.[4] This is not compensated for by greater job security, nor usually by superannuation benefits, nor a career structure. Arguably most tradesmen have a more secure future economically because, traditionally, tradespeople have been and are in short supply in Australia, whereas traditional white-collar workers—the usual kind in Smalltown—are being replaced as a result of technological change. It is for such reasons that neither boys nor girls were keen to take up ordinary white-collar jobs; however, a much bigger proportion of girls than boys ended up in such positions. The only other realistic option for girls was a class 7 or semi-skilled or unskilled position because boys gained all but one of the skilled jobs that were filled by members of the sample in 1986. If trade positions are treated as the equivalent of ordinary white-collar jobs (and they are at least that), then it is clear that boys did as well as girls in the middle sector of the occupational structure (41 per cent of boys compared with 36 per cent of girls gained a class 5 or class 6 position; Tables 10.1 and 10.2). While the proportion of boys and girls in semi- or unskilled work was similar in Smalltown, the wages girls were receiving for this work were usually inferior to male wages (see Ch. 6).

Boys did much better than girls, principally because they had privileged access to better jobs. A 'closed shop' was (and still is) operating. Certain boys were told by their future employers (that is, their fathers) that they intended taking them into a family business or, alternatively, on to a family farm; understandably, this produced a closer correlation between job aspiration and outcome. In jobs to which entry is based on achievement factors, such as traditional professional and semi-professional jobs, the correlation was not as high. Being born into the right family did not work for the girls in our study because, as we have seen, their gender usually precluded them from succeeding a farming father or a father operating some kind of business based on a traditional male job.

All the members of our sample who, in 1986, were engaged in farming were farmers' sons; all but one had joined a father in farming a family property. While no female was engaged in business for herself, at the time of the restudy 11 per cent of the males were self-employed in a town business. There were opportunities for girls to establish businesses but they were not as numerous as the opportunities for boys. This was, in part, because most of these girls were married and raising young families (they were all in their mid-twenties). Even if their engagement in business had not been hampered by domestic tasks, they had fewer opportunities than males because most of the businesses were based on male occupations, especially traditional trades. Most of the boys who were in business were in fact in a family business: that is they had inherited rather than achieved on their own merit their privileged position in the occupational structure. Still other males were advantaged by the practice of earmarking most higher professional, executive, and trade positions as men's jobs, and often by the common practice of deliberately limiting women's entrance to such jobs.

More female than male members of the sample were married and raising children. As we saw in Chapter 4, these females were very likely to be impeded or prevented from taking paid work by their domestic work and child care.[5] Added to this was the fact that girls were hindered by their earlier socialization experience and community attitudes from competing for jobs that traditionally had been dominated by men.

Women's socialization experience, community opposition to their performing 'men's' jobs, and their domestic responsibilities produced gross inequities such as the total male dominance of the community's trade positions and the disproportionate number of higher professional and higher administrative positions achieved by members of the sample. These factors largely explain why, of the girls who failed to gain the teaching or nursing job they predicted for themselves, only 6 per cent achieved an alternative middle-class position, whereas 33 per cent of the boys who missed out on the farming or teaching jobs they confidently anticipated, nevertheless gained a higher professional or executive job, or were working in their own business. Jobs in teaching or nursing provided virtually the only chances of a middle-class job for these girls whereas it is apparent from the information above that there was a range of alternatives for boys.

Even in those instances in which girls appear to have

done as well as boys, the patriarchal character of the workforce will probably ensure that, over the long haul, they do not. For instance, the future for those women occupying ordinary white-collar positions is not as promising as that for men in equivalent jobs: a job as a typist leads nowhere, while a female clerk or a female bank teller is less likely to gain promotion than a male clerk or bank employee.[6] A variety of research studies has shown that while women usually languish in their jobs as typists, secretaries, bank tellers, sales assistants, or technicians, a substantial proportion of males who begin in ordinary white-collar jobs are eventually promoted to middle or high management positions. Those women who achieve management status are often confined to middle or marginal management jobs (Western, 1983, 149–63; Crompton, 1986; Walby, 1986; Williams, 1988:93–5).

A larger proportion of girls than boys had entered teaching (Tables 10.1 and 10.2), but it is highly likely that the males in our sample will be disproportionately over-represented and the females under-represented in senior teaching and administrative positions in the future. Even if they are not directly discriminated against, as Crompton points out, it is extremely difficult for women to fulfil the domestic responsibilities husbands delegate to them and, at the same time, successfully compete with men for executive positions. 'Qualified women who are unable to be geographically mobile, or who leave work in order to rear a family, will . . . find their promotion prospects curtailed' (Crompton, 1986:132).

The impact of geographical location on occupational mobility

Whether they remained in Smalltown or moved away, the girls in our sample did not do as well occupationally as the boys. This is because the structural and cultural impediments to women competing successfully with men for the scarce and valued positions in the work-force operate universally (Yeandle, 1984, Chs 1 and 2; Curthoys, 1986; Mann, 1986). However, girls who moved away had more opportunities to 'succeed' occupationally than the girls who remained. Girls who left were twice as likely as those who remained to gain a middle-class job (52 per cent compared with 23 per cent). By contrast, only 33 per cent of the boys who moved away compared with 46 per cent of those who stayed gained middle-class positions (Table 10.3).

Of the children who moved away, girls gained only four

Table 10.3 Occupational achievements of girls and boys by place of residence

	Girls		Boys	
	Local %	Non-local %	Local %	Non-local %
Middle classes				
1 Higher-level professionals and administrators	2	6	2	13
2 Farmers	0	0	24	1
3 Business proprietors	0	0	20	5
4 Semi-professionals and administrators	21	46	0	14
Lower middle class				
5 Ordinary white-collar workers and sales	40	32	6	29
Working classes				
6 Skilled manual workers and foremen	0	1	22	21
7 Semi-skilled or unskilled manual workers	38	15	27	18
Total				
%	101	100	101	101
N	48	69	55	80

of the nineteen positions in classes 1, 2, and 3, but of the children who remained, they gained an even smaller proportion of such positions (1 out of 27). Of the twenty-six middle-class positions achieved locally by boys, nineteen were either in a family farm or town business. These outcomes corroborate the view that entrance by ascription to the most numerous middle-class jobs in Smalltown exacerbates even further the inequities suffered by women. Even girls from petit-bourgeois families are usually as disadvantaged as children from families of all other classes, because of the common practice of favouring sons over daughters in the transmission of land and capital. There is no opportunity for girls from privileged families to compete. Insofar as there is competition, it is among the sons of families who cannot afford to take all their male offspring into the family business or to provide them with sufficient capital to establish a business of their own. I have not attempted to collect data on how families resolve such potentially distressing matters. I do know that some sons in our sample missed out, including sons who confidently predicted in 1974 that they would be working as farmers in the future. Almost 25 per cent of the farmers' sons realistically expected to farm when they 'grew up', but only 10 per cent were doing so in 1987. Over 33 per cent of the farmers' sons whose expectations were not realized only gained employment as manual workers.

Girls are discriminated against locally by entrepreneurial fathers practising social closure, so those who wish to gain a middle-class position must move from Smalltown to the city to study for tertiary qualifications. They may eventually gain professional jobs, but they are more likely to end up in semi-professional jobs with less pay and status than that gained as a birthright by a privileged minority of their male peers (often including their brothers) who remain behind.

Forty-six per cent of the girls who moved away did become nurses, teachers or social workers, all of which required a tertiary educational qualification. None of the farming or town business positions taken up by the boys who stayed in Smalltown required a comparable educational qualification and only one of the boys in such a position had obtained a tertiary qualification. A majority of the class 4 positions (semi-professional/middle management) gained by girls living in Smalltown at the time of the study also required a tertiary qualification. These women had left to gain professional qualifications and subsequently returned to Smalltown because they preferred to live where they had grown up.

Inter-generational mobility

In this section I will compare the occupational positions achieved by sons and daughters with those of their parents to try to establish the extent and direction of inter-generational mobility. Given that it is the sons, rather than the daughters of privileged Smalltown families who are favoured in decisions over succession, or the capitalizing of a business venture, it is reasonable to predict that sons will be more likely to reproduce their family's class position (or an equivalent position) through their own occupational activity than will daughters. However, as only a minority of sons of these families are taken into family concerns or established in businesses of their own, and the majority have to gain their own position in the occupational structure, then this hypothesis may be refuted as daughters outperform sons. The chances of this happening are reduced by the practice of designating many of the better jobs, which are, in theory, awarded on merit, as men's jobs. This practice applies to the better jobs in the manual as well as non-manual sector of the work-force for males. Accordingly, it is also plausible to predict that the sons of families located in the middle and lower classes in the structure will enjoy more upward social mobility than their sisters, despite the fact that—unlike petit-bourgeois families—these families are unable to transmit such positions to sons directly. There are several other factors operating in this social milieu that diminish the chances of either middle-class girls reproducing their families' class position or working-class girls improving theirs. These are their socialization to put motherhood and wifehood before the pursuit of a career; to be diffident about competing with men for jobs traditionally controlled by men; to view many of the better jobs in both the non-manual and manual sectors as

Table 10.4 Girls' inter-generational mobility

Family class	Daughter's class						
	1–3 %	4 %	5 %	6 %	7 %	Total %	N
Middle classes							
Classes 1–3							
Higher-level professionals and administrators, farmers, business proprietors	5	40	34	0	21	100	62
Class 4							
Semi-professionals and administrators	0	0	100	0	0	100	2
Lower middle class							
Class 5							
Ordinary white-collar workers and sales	0	38	0	0	63	101	8
Working classes							
Class 6							
Skilled manual workers and foremen	0	44	39	6	11	100	18
Class 7							
Semi-skilled or unskilled manual workers	7	22	41	0	30	100	27

incompatible with their own femininity; and their pursuit of such jobs as a threat to their social acceptance.

What then did we find when we compared the occupational class position of girls and boys with that of their families?

In Table 10.4 the italic figures on the diagonal moving from left to right indicate the percentage of girls who were in the same class position as their parents. The italic figures on the diagonal in Table 10.5 provide comparable information for boys. For the purposes of this exercise I am regarding classes 1, 2, and 3 as being on the same level, consequently they are bracketed together in these tables. If the classes (or class categories) were completely self-recruiting then all girls (Table 10.4) and boys (Table 10.5) would be in the same class position as their parents and the percentages in italics would stand at 100 (Abercrombie, *et al*., 1988:198). Clearly they do not: there has been a good deal of inter-generational mobility by boys and girls of all classes. A comparison of the findings presented in these two tables shows that girls experienced much more inter-generational mobility than boys: 89 per cent of girls compared with 56 per cent of boys were in a different class position from that of their parents.[7]

The remarkable degree of inter-generational mobility occurring among the girls in the sample is evident in Table 10.4, despite the fact that the three higher classes have been collapsed into one class category. It is even more evident if the seven classes are not aggregated (this table is not included in the text). The only class to recruit more than one-quarter of the girls born to its own members was the lowest class in the structure: class 7. No girl born into either a class 2, 3, 4, or 5 family managed to gain a job in the same class as her family and only one girl from a class 6 family did so.

Most of the mobility girls experienced was downwards. When classes 1, 2, and 3 are regarded as being on the same level, the rate of downward mobility is almost double the rate of upward mobility (58 per cent compared with 32 per cent; Table 10.4). Girls from higher-class families experienced a greater degree of downward mobility than boys from the same families. Only three of the sixty-four girls (5 per cent) compared with 34 of the 77 boys (44 per cent) born into privileged families successfully reproduced their families' privileged position or achieved a class position of similar standing (Tables 10.4 and 10.5).

These results highlight the dramatic difference that gender makes to an individual's opportunity to reproduce or

Table 10.5 Boys' inter-generational mobility

Family class	Son's class						
	1–3 %	4 %	5 %	6 %	7 %	Total %	N
Middle classes							
Classes 1–3							
Higher-level professionals and administrators, farmers, business proprietors	*44*	9	14	19	13	99	77
Class 4							
Semi-professionals and administrators	0	*40*	40	20	0	100	5
Lower middle class							
Class 5							
Ordinary white-collar workers and sales	9	9	*27*	27	27	99	11
Working classes							
Class 6							
Skilled manual workers and foremen	13	0	33	*40*	13	99	15
Class 7							
Semi-skilled or unskilled manual workers	11	4	19	15	*52*	101	27

achieve a valued position in the class structure, especially in a community where the majority of valued positions in the work-force are transmitted from father to son and most other higher positions are earmarked for men's occupancy.

Jobs as teachers or nurses offered Smalltown girls from middle-class families their best chance of gaining a position in the middle classes in their own right, yet only 40 per cent of girls from higher professional, farming, and business families achieved a semi-professional job. The gender-based impediments to girls obtaining a foothold in the middle-class sector of the work-force were illustrated by the fact that most of the girls from privileged families were employed either in ordinary white-collar jobs (class 5) or in semi-skilled, or unskilled manual work (class 7). Only 27 per cent of boys from these families drifted down into class 5 or class 7 jobs. A further 19 per cent of boys, but not one girl from a class 1, 2, or 3 family, were engaged in skilled trade jobs. This inequity in job opportunity matters a great deal because trade positions confer on their occupants a greater chance of ultimately entering the ranks of the petit-bourgeois class than jobs in class 5 or class 7, especially when the occupants come from families with the resources to facilitate a son's transition from employee tradesman to self-employed tradesman or business entrepreneur.

Working-class boys, who lacked the capital and the privileged access to petit-bourgeois positions, did not fare nearly as well as many of their middle-class male peers. Nevertheless, in the manual sector of the work-force, where closure is practised on the basis of gender, working-class boys did much better than working-class girls.[8] All the skilled positions gained by working-class boys were based on male jobs. The one girl who gained a trade position was employed as a hair-stylist.

There was one surprising finding which serves to emphasize the degree to which gender impedes the job success of females. Despite the advantaged position of males in virtually all sectors of the paid work-force, boys from working-class homes gained fewer middle-class jobs than their female peers. These women made their major gains in the sector of the job market least influenced by the practice of gender-based closure, though usually requiring tertiary educational qualifications; that is, the semi-professions. More specifically, fourteen working-class girls (31 per cent of all girls of classes 6 and 7) but only one working-class boy achieved a semi-professional job (class 4).

The greater occupational achievement of working-class girls was linked to better educational results. Working-class boys only gained a higher proportion of jobs in those sectors of the work-force where men are disadvantaged either because they are able to practise closure or because women's domestic responsibilities and earlier socialization experience discourage them from entering. More specifically, these are jobs in the higher professions and administration, petit-bourgeois enterprises based on male occupations, and trade positions. Five working-class boys compared with two working-class girls gained a class 1 (high professional or executive) or class 3 (petit-bourgeois) position. However, four of the five boys, compared with one of the two girls, lacked tertiary qualifications. These four boys were all engaged in petit-bourgeois employment.

Gender, education, and occupational success

The higher positions available to women in the work-force almost always demand a tertiary educational qualification. This holds as much for women from middle-class as from lower-middle- and working-class families. Four-fifths of the middle-class positions achieved by girls of all classes required a tertiary educational qualification. Conversely, just under two-thirds of the middle-class positions achieved by men of all classes did not require a tertiary qualification.

Those men who did gain a tertiary qualification were much more likely than the women to gain a class 1 job (50 per cent of the tertiary qualified men compared with 10 per cent of the tertiary-qualified women). Ninety per cent of the tertiary qualified women were employed as nurses or class-room teachers.

The critical difference that gender makes to occupational achievement among the tertiary-educated sector of our sample is highlighted if we restrict our comparisons to children from middle-class families. Of the thirteen boys from middle-class families with tertiary educational qualifications, seven (54 per cent) gained a higher professional position and one (8 per cent) entered farming. By contrast, only two of the twenty-three girls (9 per cent) with tertiary qualifications and from middle-class families gained a higher professional or administrative position.

Inter-generational mobility among children living in Smalltown

If we focus on the inter-generational mobility of those children who were residing in Smalltown in 1986, as opposed to those who had moved away, then the disparity between girls and boys in their opportunities to reproduce or improve on their family's class position are especially evident. Of the 20 per cent of girls residing in Smalltown who succeeded to their parents' class position, *all* were from families at the bottom of the class system. In other words they all reproduced a deprived position.

The situation among boys stood in striking contrast to that among girls. Almost two-thirds of the sons living in Smalltown at the time of the restudy succeeded to or reproduced their family's class position, and more importantly, almost two-thirds of those who did, reproduced a privileged position (that is a class 1, 2 or 3 position).

Girls were more than twice as likely as boys to be downwardly mobile in the Smalltown system (60 per cent compared with 25 per cent) and only slightly more likely than boys to be upwardly mobile (17 per cent compared with 13 per cent). If we exclude from the comparison children from the lowest class who are replicating their family's class position, then the calculation shows that 71 per cent of boys compared with only 17 per cent of girls maintained or improved on their family's class position. These are quite extraordinary results, particularly if they are compared with those obtained in other studies. For instance, in a study Heath made of the occupational mobility of a sample of British men and women, he found that 27 per cent of women moved upwards and 26 per cent moved downwards, whereas 32 per cent of the men moved up and 19 per cent moved down (1981:115–16). He also found that girls from the higher classes were not nearly as likely as boys 'to follow in their fathers' footsteps' and were downwardly mobile in large numbers. He observed: 'There appears to be a gross inequality of opportunity between men and women here' (1981:115). Similar trends were found in Smalltown, but the inequality in opportunities for upward mobility were even more marked than those Heath discerned.

The marital mobility of women

'Marital mobility' is used here to refer to any mobility detected when a woman's own occupational class position is compared with her husband's. I am making these comparisons because a woman's life chances and the status she enjoys are, as a rule, much more affected by her husband's occupation than his are by her occupation.[9] The convention in Western society is for a woman to marry a man whose occupation is more economically rewarding and confers more prestige than her own and then to share the benefits of his superior position, albeit often in a vicarious fashion (Finch, 1983:152). 'Marriage', says Finch, 'is the most economically viable option for most women, because a higher standard of living can be gained over a lifetime by being a wife than most women could achieve in their own right' (1983:151–2). Gittins observes:

> Marriage offers women their one main chance of social mobility. A woman who works as a secretary has almost no chance of improving her socio-economic position in her work career—as does a man in most white-collar jobs—but she does have (or is encouraged to think she has) the chances of social mobility by making an advantageous marriage with a man who is 'on the way up', if not the boss himself (1985:78).

Littlejohn (1963:125) found in the Scottish rural community of Westrigg that most upward movement was accomplished through marriage. After marriage, the sexual division of labour made any further movement for a woman through the mechanism of her own paid occupation highly unlikely.[10]

In Smalltown the quality of the house a wife occupies, the schools her children attend, the cost of the clothes she wears, the organizations she joins, the social functions she goes to and the social standing she has in the community are usually going to depend more on her husband's job than any job she has. Consequently, women remain dependent on a marriage as well as an occupational market (Gittins, 1985: 78).[11]

When the occupational positions of the married women in our sample were compared with those of their husbands, they show that just under three-quarters of the women experienced some form of marital mobility.[12] In more detail the main findings were:

1 Upward mobility was twice as common as downward mobility (49 per cent compared with 24 per cent). Girls were, in fact, far more likely to enter the higher classes (that is 1, 2, or 3) through marriage than through paid work. Only 1 per cent of the women in this sample achieved a class 1, 2, or 3 position through paid

employment whereas 42 per cent of them did so through marriage.

2 In many instances marriage served as a vehicle for long-range upward mobility. For example, just under half the women engaged in semi-skilled or unskilled work as machinists and domestics (class 7 jobs) married farmers or businessmen (class 2 or 3 jobs), while more than one-third of the women employed as typists, clerks and sales

Table 10.6 Husband's occupational class position by wife's occupational class position

Husband's class	Wife's class								
	1	2	3	4	5	6	7	N	Total %
Middle classes									
1 Higher-level professionals and administrators	*13*	0	0	63	25	0	0	8	101
2 Farmers	0	*0*	0	19	38	0	44	16	101
3 Business proprietors	0	0	*0*	17	50	0	33	6	100
4 Semi-professionals and administrators	0	0	0	*77*	23	0	0	13	100
Lower middle class									
5 Ordinary white-collar workers and sales	0	0	0	0	*67*	0	33	3	100
Working classes									
6 Skilled manual workers and foremen	0	0	0	18	64	*0*	18	11	100
7 Semi-skilled or unskilled manual workers	0	0	0	7	47	0	*47*	15	101

assistants (class 5 jobs) married men in class 1, 2, or 3 occupations.

3 There was also upward mobility within the middle-class sector because 41 per cent of the girls who had gained a foothold in this class through taking up semi-professional jobs (class 4) improved their class position by marrying men in class 1, 2, or 3 positions.

4 A girl's family–class background had little direct impact on her marital mobility. Girls in working-class jobs from working-class families were just as likely to marry a man with a middle-class job as girls from privileged families with working-class jobs (this usually meant they were working as domestics or machinists).

5 Similarly, having the right family background was no insurance against downward mobility. Thirty-eight per cent of the girls from class 1, 2, and 3 families married men engaged in some form of manual employment. There was, in fact, a larger proportion of middle-class than of working-class girls marrying men in manual jobs (38 per cent compared with 30 per cent).

6 The best insurance a girl from a middle-class family could have against downward marital mobility was a middle-class job of her own. Ninety-one per cent of the girls in the sample who had a middle-class job married a man with a middle-class job (class 1 to 4). However, only 41 per cent of the girls with a lower-middle-class job (class 5) or working-class job (class 7) made such an economically advantageous marriage.

7 Possessing a semi-professional job facilitated upward mobility through marriage for girls from working-class families.[13] These girls were 35 per cent more likely than girls from the same families who had only an ordinary white-collar or semi-skilled job to marry a man occupying a middle-class position in the work-force. When we controlled for a girl's own job, then girls from working-

class families were just as likely as girls from middle-class families to marry a man with a middle-class job.

What these findings suggest is that if the aim is to predict the class position of a girl's future husband, the single most important piece of information to have is knowledge of what the girl herself does for a living. This is more help than knowing her family–class background. As already stressed, she is much more likely to marry a man occupying a higher class position if she has a middle-class job than if she does not.

In the great majority of instances, to gain a middle-class job a girl needed a tertiary education. Consequently, knowing her educational level is almost as useful—for the purposes of predicting the nature of any marital mobility she experiences—as knowing what job she has achieved.

While a girl's family–class background does not, in itself, serve as a good predictor of the class position of her husband, it is reasonable to assume that it will have a big bearing on whether or not she receives a tertiary education and in that way on her chances of upward marital mobility. It is also reasonable to predict that privileged families (in this instance class 1, 2, and 3 families) are more likely than less privileged ones (classes 6 and 7) to help a daughter achieve a tertiary education. In the present instance, the daughters of privileged families proved no more likely than class 6 girls to achieve a tertiary education, and only marginally more likely than girls from class 7 families, the most underprivileged families in our sample (36 per cent of class 1, 2, and 3 families compared with 29 per cent of class 7 families). Furthermore, girls from underprivileged families were no less likely than girls from privileged families to translate their qualifications into a semi-professional job.[14]

While holding down a semi-professional job greatly enhanced a girl's chance of being upwardly mobile through marriage, nevertheless more than one-third of the girls who married a boy in a higher class position did not possess a professional job themselves. My subjective observations, and those of other researchers, suggested that these girls possessed other equally 'marketable' attributes in the pursuit of a marriage partner in Smalltown: physical attractiveness, charm, poise, and a willingness and ability to focus their attention and much of their activity on their partner or potential partner. Smalltown men searching for a marriage partner valued these skills and gifts more highly (and still do) than a woman's skill in the kitchen or the sewing room. It is with such attributes, rather than domestic skills, that a woman validates her femininity in a man's eyes. If this interpretation is accurate, it would help explain why girls from working-class families who themselves held down working-class jobs and who were regarded as attractive, were just as likely as girls holding down working-class jobs from middle-class families to experience long-range upward marital mobility.

The great likelihood of women—irrespective of their family–class background—improving their class position through marriage rather than through participation in the paid work-force was, of course, an inevitable outcome of men's dominance of the more rewarding jobs in the occupational structure. It was also another outcome of the ubiquitous cultural obstacles to women achieving equality with men in this sphere. These generalizations were supported in this instance by the fact that most of the Smalltown women who experienced long-range upward mobility through marriage did so by marrying men who had inherited their privileged position in the work-force, or who had used male monopolized trades to go into business for themselves. Just over half the daughters living in Smalltown who were from privileged families married men in a class 1, 2, or 3 job, but so did almost half the girls from working-class families who remained in Smalltown. Indeed if a girl from a middle-class family wanted to make a 'successful match', it seems, from our data, that she had a much better chance of doing it by remaining in Smalltown than by moving away: less than one quarter of those who were living outside the Smalltown district at the time of the re-study were married to a man with a class 1, 2, or 3 job compared with half of those who remained. Working-class girls who moved away were as likely as those who remained to marry well.

Marital mobility does have a vicarious quality to it and many readers will perceive it as qualitatively different and inferior to occupational-class mobility. It is true that while a woman who is married to, say, a farmer may be better off economically than one married to a mill worker, she is still—at the very least—partially economically dependent on her husband; her social standing is not as high as that of her husband; and it is also largely derivative. He enjoys at first hand rather than at second hand the status, the autonomy, and the measure of economic independence that usually flow from direct occupancy of a petit-bourgeois position in the Smalltown community.

However, as I have stressed previously, for the vast majority of women the only hope of gaining the most valued positions in the Smalltown economy is through vicarious access to them. As Finch (1983) and Burns (1986) have both argued, women are not stupid: they realistically assess the facts of the situation and see that marriage, and especially the 'right' marriage, offers them and their future offspring 'their best chance of a rewarding life' (Burns, 1986:222). That women who effect a 'good' marriage in Smalltown are envied by other women corroborates the arguments I have been reporting here.

The business of attempting to make a 'good' marriage and of being envied for 'pulling it off' remind us of the economic and social realities of life in a patriarchal community. In Smalltown the great majority of married women can only go as far as their husbands' class position allows them. Women may earn public esteem by their good works or their qualities as mothers, and they may help increase a family's status, but with few exceptions these gains will be made within the economic and social parameters set by a husband's class position. A woman is more likely to achieve the most economically through making her husband more successful at his job. She is also more likely to achieve significant public esteem through promoting her husband's causes than by seeking a reputation for good works independently of him (see Ch. 3).[15] If she wants to do more than enhance her family's public esteem and social standing within the class stratum to which they currently belong, she will have to help him move upwards in the class system. That demands a change in his economic circumstances, which usually means a change in his job, not just an increase in good works or conspicuous consumption on either her or his or their part (see James, 1981).

What the material presented in this and the previous chapters also shows is that few wives have any chance of achieving a privileged economic–class position through their own occupations. The valued jobs are not there for women to occupy and even if they did exist, the occupational position of a husband would almost certainly have a bigger bearing than her own on a wife's social standing and her access to some of the more exclusive social circles and activities in this community. Where a husband's job is one that brings high prestige, supporting him in his work 'offers her immeasurably greater opportunities for high status and prestige than she would otherwise obtain' (Finch, 1983:152). It also confirms her economic and social dependency.

CHAPTER 11

The chances of change

A man's town, in summary

The foregoing chapters show that men and women experience life differently in Smalltown. Their most intimate relationships—those with spouses, children and friends—are political and asymmetrical: males exercise a disproportionate control over the persons, activities, and resources, and often the ideas and values of the females in their circle. While it is overstating the case to view the females as helpless victims, the choices they do make are more restricted by the actions of men than vice-versa.

Michelle Barrett says that feminists have been right in viewing 'the family as a central site of women's oppression in contemporary society' (1980:214). The Smalltown data are consistent with her observation and I return to this issue later, but as Barrett recognizes, patriarchal relations are not confined to the family. In the community under study here they serve as indispensable organizing principles in most activities in the public as well as the private domain (Stacey, 1986). Men exclude women altogether, or, alternatively, incorporate them on their own terms in paid employment, sport, social drinking, most service-club activities, community decision-making and much informal social activity. We have seen that their power to effect closure and subordination in one institutional sphere or activity is a function of their ability to do it in other spheres as well.

Men's superordinate position in family life, and their ability to delegate responsibility for domestic work and child care to women, stems largely from their superior financial resources which, in turn, stem from their control of property and their dominant position in the job market.

These hierarchical arrangements are buttressed by men's ideological hegemony. The ideological processes which men use to dominate women have been described as value discourses (Bennett, 1985). These discourses render many of the socially constructed distinctions between men and women virtually unchallengeable by attributing them to biological differences (Willis, 1982, cited by Bryson, 1990). We have seen that these discourses have a dialectical character: by affirming the superiority of men and their activities they inferiorize women (Bryson, 1990).

Prominent among the ideas that are articulated in the value discourse occurring in Smalltown is the belief that men's role as providers entitles them to more 'say' in both domestic and public affairs, a bigger share of resources, and more autonomy than women to pursue their recreational interests. Smalltown women seem by and large to accept such beliefs.

For some women, however, acceptance of these beliefs is tempered by considerable ambivalence. After all, there are competing ideas circulating, including those that affirm that husbands should share responsibility for child care and domestic work, and that wives are just as entitled as husbands to have opportunities to find fulfilment through paid work or external leisure activities. Yet only a small minority of Smalltown wives have adopted them as their own and, as we have seen, those wives are often reluctant to act on them.

The economic superiority of men, their reluctance to participate in domestic labour and child care, and their belief in their entitlement to more leisure than their wives, facilitate their dominance of sporting and other leisure resources and activities. In turn, men's domination of the community's major decision-making bodies allows them to establish the recreational facilities they favour. So, although a woman edits the *Smalltown News*, it is owned and controlled by men—control based ultimately on men's economic dominance. This explains, in part, why men gain much greater media coverage of their sport and their charity activities than women do, but this superior coverage is also a product of the widely held conviction that men and their activities are superior to women and their activities. By promenading men's activities, the controllers of the local media reaffirm the inferiority of women's activities and thereby of women themselves.

Women are also inferiorized by being excluded from many men's service and sporting organizations and by male-dominated as well as exclusively male organizations displaying a paternalistic attitude. Often such organizations presume that men will take decisions in the way a father or husband does and that women will defer. For instance, a notice will be issued by a male-controlled sporting committee requesting women competitors to arrive before a tournament to cut sandwiches for lunch.

Women's subordination is mediated by their interpersonal relationships, and their marriage relationship is the principal mechanism for this subordination. It serves as a means of incorporating women in many of the community's recreational activities. For instance, we have seen that the vast majority of women who participate in auxiliaries, or in unofficial work groups supporting men's organizations, are the wives or future wives of members, or the widows of former members. In this manner, marriage slots women into pre-ordained roles (Finch, 1983:20) which facilitate their exploitation not only by their own husbands but by collectivities of husbands who comprise the majority, or the entire membership, of a service club, board of management of a charity or men's sporting club, or a local council.

Women's responsibilities in the home, particularly those of child bearing and home management, inhibit their participation in paid work and leisure activities. At times, husbands use their superior economic or physical power to prevent their wives participating in outside work and leisure, but they also constrain them by typifying them as inferior and, at times, their activities as inferior. Men's behaviour reduces the likelihood of women gaining access to occupational status, the friends that are often found at work, the income that may provide some autonomy, the time for leisure, and many specific leisure activities. While men substantially reduce women's participation in paid work, the minority who do work fails to challenge patriarchy either domestically or publicly: few wives work without their husband's consent. The fact that no husband needs a wife's permission to engage in paid work confirms the patriarchal quality of the relationship. After all, men's masculinity is defined primarily by their paid-work role, and, because of that role and its designation as a superior activity, most men stand in a relationship of superordination to their wives.

Several of the usual conditions surrounding a wife's entry to paid employment demonstrate the patriarchal character of marriage. A wife works when it is financially necessary for the family and not in order to establish some independence from her husband or to develop a career which interferes with her first priority—to be a good mother and wife (see Yeandle, 1984:140–8). A wife who engages in paid work does so under conditions dictated by her domestic responsibilities and often the explicit direction of her husband as to how much or little work she does. His permission may be withheld if he believes she will not be able to manage successfully either her regular domestic work and child care (if any) or the contribution she makes to his paid work. Her permission may be withdrawn if paid work interferes with any of these responsibilities. Her paid work is meant to supplement his income. He remains *the* provider even if she earns more than he does. She retains her dependent status.[1]

The entry of wives to the paid work-force in considerable numbers in the last couple of decades has failed to disturb patriarchal relations in the occupational structure because the gendered segregation of paid jobs is even stricter in Smalltown than in metropolitan centres. Wives have not been wresting jobs from men but, as we saw, engaging principally in jobs in the middle and lower end of the occupational structure and usually ones which are extensions of their domestic tasks or an expression of nurturing and caring skills.[2]

The stability of patriarchal relationships in the domestic and paid-work spheres has played a decisive part in ensuring that they continue to do so in leisure activities, voluntary organizations, and most community decision-making. The successful exercise of power, and more usually authority in several institutional spheres simultaneously, appears to have an exponential impact on the patriarchal quality of gender relationships. Men's dominance in all major activities is reinforced, and in all spheres it is premised on women's dependency and inferiority.

In Chapter 8 I argued that the persistence of patriarchal relations in all major institutional areas is facilitated by socialization processes that ensure the reproduction and implementation of the major tenets of the ideologies of masculinity and femininity and, equally importantly, the development of masculine and feminine identities that fit well with the existing hierarchical structure. Chapter 9 demonstrated how exposure to the key beliefs of these ideologies, coupled with firsthand knowledge of men's control of key jobs in the work-force, appeared to prevent both adolescent girls and their parents fantasizing about the girls achieving one of the more valued jobs in the work-force. The girls who moved to the city had more occupational success than those who remained, but that success was concentrated in the middle of the job structure. In Smalltown, men's dominance of privileged jobs was unassailed by the women who remained or who returned after a time in the city to make a living or to marry.

In summary, I have sought to demonstrate the pervasiveness of the patriarchal quality of gender relationships in Smalltown. Men's control of key positions and resources and their dominance of women reduces women's independence, their opportunities to gain economic equality with men, and their chances for leisure and self-fulfilment, and confirms their typification as men's inferiors and dependents. In the remainder of this chapter I will examine the likelihood of change in the patterns of superordination and subordination and in the structural arrangements and ideological processes supporting them.

General impediments to change

Parkin argues that for subordinates successfully to attempt to usurp the privileges of the superordinates they must make a collective effort rather than individual sorties. The likelihood of the disadvantaged making a collective effort depends, in turn, on their ability to mobilize socially (1974: 4–5; 1979:74). Parkin's argument makes sense because each woman's experience of deprivation and subordination is but one manifestation of a hierarchical and integrated system in which men collectively maintain and reproduce their several advantages over women. However, there are a number of impediments to women mobilizing themselves. First, women's responsibilities under the prevailing division of labour disperse them geographically over a great distance and inhibit their congregating and organizing. Second, certain socio-demographic features of the community discourage rebellion either individually or collectively because they facilitate sanctions against the rebellious. The critical factors are the community's small size, the stability of membership (three-quarters have lived in Smalltown for at least ten years), the prevalence of cross-cutting ties among members, and the residents' high degree of visibility. Where such features occur, news of any acts of 'deviance' is quickly transmitted through one or more of the community's numerous gossip chains.

Third, women's ability to mount a successful countervailing strategy is impeded by their subordinate position in the system: because they lack power it would be difficult to sanction those women who resist mobilization. As Parkin stresses, without the power to sanction the uncooperative, an attempt at social mobilization is unlikely to succeed, especially in a community where it is reasonably easy to sanction effectively those who try to mobilize to upset the status quo.

In addition to impediments to mobilization at the community level I must emphasize that the possibilities of change in Smalltown depend largely on external change. As Liebow said in an entirely different context, a local system is neither self-generating nor self-perpetuating; it is an integral part of the wider society; it is in close contact with that society; and it is greatly influenced by the structures, ideas and values of that society (Liebow, 1967). This is not the place to examine in detail the extent and nature of gender inequality in Australian society but in the light of the research that others have conducted one can mount a good case for describing Australia as a patriarchal or man's society (Western, 1983; Bryson, 1984; Burns, 1986; and Williams, 1988). Nor is it the place to examine the chances of a substantial reduction in gender inequality in Australian society, but it needs be borne in mind that its diminution in Smalltown is going to depend to a great degree on its diminution in the wider society. Nevertheless, local impediments are important and I will consider them as they work in various ways and with greater or lesser force in the institutional spheres I have focused upon in this book: paid work, unpaid work and child care, and leisure and status-enhancing activities.

The chances of reducing inequality in paid work

If the present inequity in the job market is to be reduced, women must wrest a substantial proportion of men's jobs from them because there are no prospects of a significant expansion in women's paid jobs. The number of jobs typified as women's jobs have been declining in recent years, and this applies to the best of them: jobs in nursing and teaching. However, the chances of women usurping some of men's jobs are meagre. There are fewer men's jobs than in the past: in the last two decades Smalltown has lost a substantial number of managerial, administrative and technical positions, as well as skilled and semi-skilled manual jobs. Farming is the most prevalent middle occupation and there has been a steady decline in the number of farmers. Virtually all of this job depletion is due to external structural developments over which local people have no control. Despite valiant and repeated attempts by local leaders to slow down, if not prevent, the external changes that are having such an adverse affect on Smalltown's employment opportunities, the trend will probably continue.

When the chances of employment for men are declining rapidly they are hardly going to hand over willingly to women positions in the work-force they have traditionally dominated. If women attempt in the future to usurp men's jobs they will face fiercer opposition than that experienced by those married women in the 1970s who were said to be taking the jobs of single women. The opposition would come from women as much as from men. If women enter jobs that have been traditionally the province of men, it reduces the pool of men able to serve as bread-winners for women who want to concentrate on the home and the family rather than a paid career. The great majority of Smalltown women do, in fact, wish to do this and they also believe it should be a woman's prerogative to make such a choice. Consequently, they would respond with hostility to women who attempted to compete for some of the better men's jobs.

There were no signs during our field-work that most Smalltown women were ready to mobilize to wrest some of men's occupational dominance from them. Even the minority of married women who wanted a career in the paid work-force were discouraged from challenging men for their jobs by the centrality of the goals of marriage and motherhood in their own lives. None of these women looked to become the family's principal bread-winner and each wanted a husband who could provide adequately for her and their children.

These women viewed child care as their first priority. Consequently few, if any, would be happy to hand over major responsibility for the care of young children to their husbands. They illustrated their commitment to motherhood by surrendering professional positions that it would be impossible to recover at a later date in order 'to stay at home with the children when they are young'. They could only realistically expect to gain the kind of job that would enable them to resume their earlier career by moving to a larger community. This would mean, of course, either leaving a husband or persuading him to move. Even though some of these wives were unhappy with their marriages, they said they were reluctant to precipitate a marital separation to gain a career for themselves because they believed 'the children need their father'.

Few of the husbands themselves would seriously consider leaving Smalltown. Many are farming properties they have inherited, some have invested substantially in other petit-bourgeois business ventures and would 'lose heavily if they sold up to move', while still others have settled for an arrested professional or managerial career because they enjoy such things as Smalltown's easy-going life-style and plethora of sporting activities, and they have a network of long-standing friendships.

Even Smalltown's more radical women are unlikely to offer a concerted challenge for men's jobs because they seem to take for granted men's monopoly of farming and most other middle-class occupations. If they are pressed on this matter they report that they have never thought about being, say, a farmer, or a self-employed carpenter, because they perceive these jobs as men's occupations. Many of the women we interviewed in the mid-1980s had participated in the School Survey in 1974; as adolescents none of these girls even fantasized about becoming farmers or business women and hardly any about achieving higher professional jobs. For most women the division of labour in the paid work-force is in tune with the personality and physiology of each sex. It is hard for them to reconcile taking up a man's job with their understanding of their own femininity. Even if it were possible they know it would be difficult to retain the public image and the level of social acceptance they desire.

Things are not likely to change because many rebellious wives are not that radical. Some, as we will see, are principally interested in achieving a more equitable division of domestic labour and a more companionable marriage rather than making a career of any kind in the paid work-force. Others do want a job or career that will provide personal fulfilment but not at the expense of marriage and motherhood. In many instances the socialization experience of females encourages them to view many jobs as a threat to their femininity (see Ch. 8 in this book and also Sharpe, 1976, 1984; Whitehead, 1981). If women were to engage in such jobs as farming, truck driving, or plumbing, it might jeopardize their positive stereotyping as 'lovely women' and highly desirable marriage partners and lead to them being negatively stereotyped as different and possibly as 'a butch'. Bradley says that:

> Women themselves seem not [to] have fought for specialist jobs, perhaps because in industrial societies farming and the outdoor life do not fit readily with what are now perceived as the desirable female characteristics: prettiness, sexiness, delicacy, refinement, domestic skills. It is all too easy for the land girl in her corduroy trousers to be portrayed as a bit of a joke (Bradley, 1989:92).

The following extract from an interview with a young woman who returned to Smalltown after several years in the city furthering her education illuminates the assumption that sex stereotyping of paid jobs is natural and gives some indication of the manner in which community members would respond if a woman took up a man's work.

Interviewer: How do you think Smalltown people would react if a woman was employed in a man's job, say as a plumber or carpenter?
Respondent: It wouldn't go down at all.
Interviewer: In what sense?
Respondent: People around here would think that there was something wrong with the woman. They wouldn't sort of ridicule her but they'd certainly talk about her and she'd probably get a bit of a ribbing.
Interviewer: Why do you think that would happen?
Respondent: Well because men have always done the job. There would be doubts that a woman would be up to doing the job, especially the manual bits.
Interviewer: Did you ever think of taking on a man's job. Say a job as a mechanic?
Respondent: No never!
Interviewer: Do you know of any girl at school with you who thought about it?
Respondent: None! The issue never came up for discussion—never. And I do not know of any girls who went on do such a job. Although some girls said they wanted to do the automobiles course at school. The boys didn't like the idea. But some of the

girls did it to spite the boys. It turned out they could do it as well as the boys and the boys came to accept that.
Interviewer: Did any of these go on to become a mechanic?
Respondent: No. None of the girls I went to school with went into a man's job. I can't explain it. It never came up for discussion. We just never thought of trying to do a man's job.
Interviewer: What about farming?
Respondent: Do you mean a woman doing it without her husband, like the manual work herself?
Interviewer: Yes. Doing the actual farming, being the farmer.
Respondent: One friend of mine tried it . . . not around here. But it didn't work out. She gave it up after a few months. I don't know of one woman around here who has done that.
Interviewer: How would it be viewed if a woman farmed?
Respondent: It would be seen as strange.
Interviewer: In what sense?
Respondent: Well farming has always been done by men; it is seen as a man's job. There would be doubts that women would be up to the tasks in the way a man would.
Interviewer: Do you think if a woman farmed it would raise questions about her femininity?
Respondent: Yes it would. There'd be a good bit of talk.

As Curthoys points out, 'once a job . . . [is] firmly entrenched as male or female, only people of the sex seen as appropriate for that job . . . [are] trained to do it. This restricted supply further reinforce[s] perception of the job as male or female' (1986:338).

The chances of reducing domestic inequality

The domestic division of labour and child care together comprised the second major area of gender inequality that we examined in this book. The likelihood of women achieving more equity in these spheres is directly related to their slender prospects of gaining a substantial share of men's jobs. Without a marked increase in paid work they will not be able to rival husbands as economic providers. Consequently, in most instances husbands, as *the* providers, have the power and authority to continue delegating to their wives as much of the domestic labour and child care as they choose.

The chances of change in this sphere are also remote because the structural boundary between men and women based on men's superior economic resources is complemented by a cultural boundary. Women are accomplices in the maintenance of reproduction of the cultural boundary. Members of both sexes view the jobs that women perform at home as less important, less challenging, and generally inferior to men's jobs, and often to men's leisure interests. These attitudes stand in the way of women developing a collective sense of injustice that might serve as a basis for women's mobilization against domestic inequality.

We did not question our respondents in great detail about their attitudes to performing domestic work, however, the impressions we gained during hundreds of interviews and conversations conducted in the homes of Smalltown is that most have a positive view of child care, and for probably most of them the good features of domestic work exceed the bad features. More than 80 per cent of the wives participating in the Gender Survey said that they were generally happy with the present division of responsibilities between themselves and their husbands, and about the same number indicated they were not looking for any substantial changes. Rather than complain about their responsibilities some were ready to focus on the drawbacks of their husbands' jobs and say that they as wives had the 'best of the bargain'. Women engaged in full-time paid work were almost as likely as those who were not to say they accepted a division of labour which patently disadvantaged them.

Only a small minority of women would accept the judgement made in this book that the division of domestic labour exploits members of their sex. Most wives displayed a strong ego involvement in their domestic work and in their child care. Many took considerable pride in their cooking and in the presentation of their homes. Smalltown women value domestic work in part because it enables them to exercise some control in the domestic sphere (Ferree, 1987). So, for example, when, during an interview, one of our researchers commented to a wife that she appeared to be doing virtually all of the housework, it was highly likely that she would say, 'The only way to make sure that the job is done properly is to do it yourself', or something of that kind (see also McRae, 1986, and Ferree, 1987, for similar findings).

It appeared that surrendering control in the domestic sphere was tantamount to surrendering a portion of a woman's identity as a wife and mother. As Game and Pringle point out in commenting on the reluctance of women engaged in paid work to give up control of some of their domain to men: 'The home is supposedly women's world—their space to manage and control' (1983:137).

The immense contribution that performing well as a housewife can make to a woman's self-esteem and social esteem helps explain why, as Sharpe found, some of the Smalltown women who engaged in paid work attempted to organize their domestic work as if they were not engaged in paid work (1984:188). This was, in part, because they were trying not to disrupt family life, to compensate for their absence at times when they would previously have been available, and to win approval for doing both jobs well. However, it was also because they were eager to retain the personal satisfaction they experience from performing various domestic tasks. This is not surprising because, as Green and her colleagues observe, 'Being a good wife and mother is one of the few avenues available to [women] . . . for securing respect and approval' (1987a:90).

Some researchers would be sceptical about the claim that Smalltown's women view their traditional roles positively. Davidoff argues that domestic tasks are so inherently tedious and burdensome that no one would perform them out of choice (1976). The women participating in Oakley's British study reported that housework lacked any positive features (1974). The findings of a number of other researchers, however, are similar to our findings; they show that women can view housework as rewarding as well as tedious and difficult (Ferree, 1987:338).

Many Smalltown women did mention that housework had significant drawbacks. Some wives complained that their domestic duties restricted their ability to leave the home, while a number said that such tasks as cleaning, ironing, and washing were boring and repetitive. For many Smalltown wives the positive and negative features that characterized domestic duties were so finely balanced that they produced a chronic sense of ambivalence. Some of our survey findings reflect this ambivalence. For example, a majority of the female respondents in the Gender Survey said that wives should be able to find a substantial degree of personal fulfilment through their home and family, whereas a similar proportion also said that in order to feel fulfilled women needed something more than home and child care. Only a small minority of female respondents went as far as to say that wives may need a full-blown career in the paid work-force in order to find personal fulfilment, but a majority did say that wives needed a break of some kind from the home. In their comments many of these respondents volunteered that housework and child care were often demanding and tiring and for these reasons women needed 'outside interests'.

Women were far more likely to concede that there were negative aspects of domestic life than husbands were to acknowledge that such work had drawbacks for their wives: 'Women need the chance to spend time with friends or play some sport; you could go dotty stuck at home with just the kids to talk to every day' (35-year-old farmer's wife). This kind of statement, which was fairly common, takes some of its significance from the fact that child care is more highly valued by Smalltown women than cooking, cleaning and picking up after everyone (see also Oakley, 1974). Yet, as a rule, the statements that indicated that there were negative aspects to domestic work and child care were made in the context of an overall acceptance of traditional roles.

The constraining effect on women of their acceptance of the validity and naturalness of the existing division of labour was borne out by the sanguine experience of some of the women. One businessman's wife said:

> I learnt early in the piece to keep my mouth shut because if I complained about my husband's failure to help much with the children I drew looks or words of rebuke from other women. Nobody spoke up in my support because they spend their lives running after their husbands.

Just how effective this informal control of women can be was revealed in an account offered by one of the younger women of an incident in which she was rebuked for criticizing her husband for not sharing sufficiently in the raising of their children. The woman made her complaint in the presence of several other women who belonged to the same organization as she. She linked her husband's failure to help sufficiently with the children to what she perceived as his unnecessary preoccupation with his business. She reported that her complaint drew a sharp rebuke from one of the older women and that, when the rebuke was made, no other woman defended her. The older woman said:

> If that's how you feel about things you should never have married a businessman. It's a hard job for them to make a good living in this town. They need and deserve to get all the support they can get and to have a chance to get away from all the worry of their jobs and enjoy themselves.

The woman who was reprimanded said during the interview that because she was making her life in Smalltown it was important to be liked and accepted. She continued, 'The last thing I need is a reputation for being an ungrateful wife and bitch.' She said that after this awful incident she never 'opened her mouth again' to complain about 'things at home' and she never would in the future. Prescribing identities and roles for women that entail home-based, round-the-clock commitment, and assessing their ultimate worth on their performance in such roles, are powerful mechanisms of control which severely restrict women's engagement in paid work, political decision-making and leisure activity (Green, *et al.*, 1987a:90).

Finally, I should stress that there are no indications that men want a radical redistribution of tasks. Why would they? While they make light of what women do, they are fully conscious of the intrusion on their 'freedom to come and go as they please' that would be entailed if they took over child care and provided meals two or three times a day for other family members. When they ridicule women's domestic work they focus on tasks over which women have most control: the washing and ironing, say, rather than on those that keep women house-bound or tied up in other ways, such as constantly caring for younger children and helping husbands with their farms, businesses, or professional work. Men know that if roles were reversed it would curtail their ability to spend time engaged in activities with their mates, especially those that stretch over several successive days, such as a fishing trip.

Men have little to gain by varying the division of labour significantly and much to lose in a community with high visibility and numerous overlapping social ties. As well as threatening their masculine self identities it would put at risk their public identities as 'real men'. Many, and probably most, fear replacing a reputation for being a man's man with one for being a hen-pecked husband.[3] If the domestic division of labour were reorganized as a result of wives gaining (or moving towards) equality with men as breadwinners, the prestige and authority men enjoy because they are the major or only source of money would be eroded.[4] From men's point of view there is a high price to be paid for any role reversal.

Failing to challenge men's recreational superiority

The third sphere of gender inequality I have concentrated on in this book is men's exclusion of women from their leisure activities coupled with their practice of exploiting women to further those activities. Our survey findings, as well as our direct observations, indicate that the great majority of Smalltown women are no more concerned about men incorporating them either individually or collectively in their leisure activities or using their domestic skills to facilitate these activities than they are about men excluding them from most of the better paid jobs. Furthermore, they are even less concerned about men using them to facilitate their leisure activity than they are about men delegating total or near total responsibility for domestic work.

There are women who are dissatisfied with present leisure arrangements but the chances of the dissidents mobilizing most women to challenge the superordination of men are slim. Many women accept their designation as an inferior group, they believe in the legitimacy of most male leisure advantages, and they are morally committed to roles which facilitate the leisure of their husbands and often of many other men as well. Only a very small minority perceive as exploitative the relationships their incorporation in men's leisure produces. They also take the tasks they perform in connection with men's leisure for granted. When we questioned them about their incorporation, most made one or more of the following types of comments:

I never thought about it until you raised it.

It's really no trouble at all to get the afternoon tea; doing it yourself is the only way of guaranteeing it's done properly.

Many also stressed that the men played their part by doing such things as erecting trestles for a street stall or putting out the chairs for afternoon tea.

There is some structural potential for women mobilizing to reduce men's leisure advantages in the plethora of voluntary organizations. More than 50 per cent of Smalltown women participate in voluntary organizations, however the potential for most of these organizations to bring together a cross-section of women is seriously impeded by their class and age homogeneity. For example, the middle class are over-represented and the working class under-represented in eight out of nine well-known voluntary women's organizations. In five of these nine organizations working-class women comprise only 12 per cent or less of the total membership. Many of Smalltown's women's organizations are also religiously homogeneous in the sense that members are drawn disproportionately from either the Roman Catholic or one of the Protestant churches.

The chances of these groups serving as a base for an assault on men's recreational privileges are especially limited by the fact that a majority of them exist principally to facilitate the leisure activities of a superordinate men's organization. Most of the remaining organizations are composed of women who are strongly committed to maintaining the traditional sexual division of labour: they include such groups as local chapters of the Red Cross and the CWA (Country Women's Association).

As Cohen emphasizes, shared activity, including ritualistic behaviour, can strengthen social identity and a sense of social location (1985:50–1), but because the collective activity of most women's groups is directed at facilitating the success and enhancing the status of men's organizations the social location confirmed is *not* one of autonomous, or potentially autonomous, women, but of men's supporters and dependents. When the executive of a women's auxiliary hands over a cheque to the executive of a men's organization the ritual reaffirms women's collective identity as men's subordinates. The ritual is an excellent example of the dialectical nature of the ideological processes operating in this community. It contains a dual message: men and their activities are sufficiently worthwhile to warrant women devoting their time and resources to furthering the men's activities and in so doing they signal their own inferiority (Bryson, 1990:173). Similarly, when wives attend the change-over dinner of the executive of their husbands' service club, the rituals associated with the occasion enhance the experience of community for the men, reinforce the boundary between them and the women, and inferiorize the women. The content of the evening, its pace and mood are set by the men. The women are there to witness and applaud. Insofar as the sense of community experienced on the occasion extends to the wives it is of a community in which the wives occupy for a short period of time a marginal and inferior position.

Potential rebels

There are Smalltown women who have more potential than most to provide the nucleus for some form of collective rebellion against Smalltown husbands and their privileged position in community recreational life and decision-making as well as against their perceived failure to do their share of work in the home. These women are—as a rule—under forty years of age, and married to men in middle-class occupations. Their husbands work long and often irregular hours and their work and frequently their leisure activities take precedence over any share they accept of child care or any contribution to domestic work. These women usually possess professional qualifications but most of them are prevented by their family responsibilities, and, to a lesser extent, their incorporation in their husbands' work, from pursuing their own careers, or at best are only able to pursue them in a 'stop start' fashion. Many of these women are critical of the community's limited leisure facilities and the local preoccupation with organized sport.

Typically they would like far greater opportunities to engage in paid work, especially interesting and personally fulfilling work, but what they are most troubled by is the gap between what they would ideally like from marriage and the realities of their particular unions. Without exception these women want their husbands to participate far more in child care, and they want a companionable marriage. They are intensely disappointed and dissatisfied with husbands who prefer work or time with their mates or fellow club members to time with them. The wives say they spend too much time alone or with only young children for company. Some of these women are disappointed that husbands take the more important decisions which bear directly on their well-being and that of their children.[5] A small minority also say they resent their incorporation in their husbands' leisure activities, such as the expectation that they will attend functions that do not interest them or send along a plate of food to a social occasion to which they are not invited.

But while these women express their dissatisfaction and disappointment to their husbands, they do not attempt to mobilize socially to bring about change. There are several reasons for the inertia. The women know that any attempt they make to usurp men's monopolies would be viewed as an attack on the status quo and would be vigorously opposed (Parkin, 1974:9–11). Smalltowners believe that it is a wife's job to 'look after and support her husband' in everything that he does, which is similar to the commitment expected of diplomats' wives, whose highly institutionalized role is based on the premise that they are dedicated to assisting their husbands with their work and promoting their careers (Callan, 1975). Consequently, the failure of a Smalltown wife to respond to a husband's need for support with his leisure activities—including his club's activities—

is viewed by many community members as a serious breach of a woman's duty to be a good wife. I pointed out in Chapter 8 that, as well as attracting sanctions from the husband, this attracts criticisms from community members generally and strains her relationships with acquaintances, neighbours and friends. These younger women are well aware of the expectations held of them and report that if they rebel they risk being labelled a 'bitch' and possibly being ostracized by members of their own community.

Younger women are also reluctant to rebel because they claim their spouses, and possibly their children, would be sanctioned as well as themselves. Their fears are real ones: we have witnessed the public criticism and ostracism of individual women who have done such things as repeatedly trespass on men's territory, or forgotten that it is their place to play a supportive rather than a leadership role in activities in which men as well as women are participating. Two of the women that we witnessed being ostracized were relatively recent arrivals in the community and married to men in professional positions. The first woman offended by regularly going without her husband to drink in the public bar of one of the town's hotels. She said during an interview that when she served at the school tuck-shop other women left her out of their casual conversation. I witnessed the woman and her husband being ignored at several public functions. They left the community prematurely because they told me the ostracism was 'too painful to live with'.

The second woman offended principally by trying to change things in the organizations she joined. The proposed innovations implied criticism of existing practices, which is never well received in Smalltown, especially when offered by a 'newcomer'. Within days of her arrival in Smalltown she was being 'bad-mouthed' in casual conversations. Those who had initial dealings with her were warning others 'to steer well clear of her'. Her subsequent attempts to join certain voluntary organizations eager for new members were rejected. She was chastized by the leaders of organizations she did manage to join for trying to take over, and her offers of assistance with various existing programmes within these organizations were refused. She reported during an interview feeling lonely, rejected, and mystified by her treatment. As she saw it she was only trying to help in ways she had helped in other rural communities in which she had lived.

The process of marginalization and ostracism reached its culmination during a business meeting of one of the organizations she belonged to and in which her husband held a leadership position. After she offered some criticisms of existing programmes and suggestions for improvements a leading member of the organization rose to his feet and attacked her for driving people away from the organization and placing its future in jeopardy. Her husband was present at the meeting. He said nothing, but he told me the next day that he was appalled over the treatment of his wife and that he intended to ask his employer for a transfer to another town. They left several months later.

The two women whose stories I have just referred to were newcomers to Smalltown and married to men engaged in itinerant occupations. They never developed a sense of attachment to the community, nor did they form any close friendships. When living in Smalltown became intolerable, their husbands were able to respond to their dilemma by arranging new appointments in distant settlements. Few of the wives we have studied are as fortunate. The vast majority of them are married to men who are tied economically, socially, and emotionally to Smalltown. Such realities discourage these women from rebelling, especially publicly. They have witnessed the price paid by women subjected to criticism for failing to support a husband in his public activities. They have a strong sense of belonging to Smalltown and well-established friendship networks they do not want to risk losing. During an interview, one of the most discontented of the younger women described the dilemma she and other women who share her point of view experience. She explained that she had chosen to make her life in Smalltown and that it was imperative to make it as comfortable and pleasant as possible for herself and her family: 'I have to live here and get on with people. I can't afford to be seen as a stirrer, a trouble maker.'

The potentially rebellious women are committed to being good mothers. The well-being of their children takes precedence over any career they might be pursuing or any hankering they have for 'bright city lights'. They want to stay in Smalltown in part because it offers a healthy physical and social environment in which to raise children. Consequently, even if they privately resent it, they are careful to fulfil the widely held expectations that they will be solicitous of the needs of their husbands' friends or fellow committee members, tolerant of the intrusions the latter make on their time and space, and enthusiastic about their husbands' individual and club leisure activities.

It is apparent from the arguments advanced here that there are pragmatic as well as emotive and idealistic reasons for women not rebelling. As I pointed out in Chapter 7, Finch (1983) has argued convincingly that once a woman has chosen marriage it makes good sense materially and socially for her to work at making a success of a husband's career rather than branching out on one of her own. If these observations are apposite for city-based women, they certainly hold for women in Smalltown where there are far fewer job opportunities. In the present instance they also make good sense socially for, in Smalltown, social activities and public standing are more dependent on marriage than they are in metropolitan settlements. A majority of Smalltown's potentially rebellious women have acknowledged these realities during interviews.[6]

As Finch (1983) has shown, wives are not merely passive

victims of the structural and cultural forces that impose limits on their choices. As far as possible they work around or exploit these forces in the pursuit of their own goals. So, while it would clearly be in the interests of Smalltown's 'wife-mothers' to have more equitable relationships with husbands and with men generally, and to enjoy more autonomy, it is not at all surprising that they do not engage collectively or individually in open rebellion over their social or economic deprivations. Nor is it surprising that they are careful 'not to push things too far' in the private sphere with husbands who are unsympathetic to their attempts to gain more autonomy for themselves by incorporating their partners more fully in child care or domestic tasks. The material, social, and emotional costs of rebellion are just too high, and they know it: 'It's in a wife's interests to keep in her husband's good books!' A number of younger wives volunteered such a comment.

It seems that the observations Stacey made about the subordinate and dependent position of women in the English town of Banbury thirty years ago are still applicable in Smalltown today: 'A wife cannot resign from her work without breaking from her husband and children, nor can she leave her husband without losing her job' (1960:136). In Smalltown losing her job means losing the particular social standing it bestows in the community, many of the specific social relationships built on the marriage, and most of all of her economic resources. If rebellion ends in divorce, in the interests of making a living the wife often has little choice but to leave a community to which she has a strong sense of belonging.

Consequently, rarely, if ever, does the collective response of these women go beyond discussing with several friends over coffee such things as their dissatisfaction with the division of tasks in the home, the segregated life-style imposed by their husbands' participation in exclusively male organizations or regular visits to the pub, and the loss of autonomy these practices bring, especially while the children are young.

As a number of participants in such 'grizzle' sessions have told me, rather than posing a potential threat to the prevailing order, or even to the advantages of their particular husbands, such sessions tend to preserve the status quo. The women say, 'Because we have the chance to let off steam in these ways it makes it possible to go on putting up with the situation at home.' Usually such 'get-togethers' occur at times that do not interfere with their obligations as wives and mothers, nor with their husbands' leisure activities. Such practices affirm the power and authority of the husbands, and the community endorsement of that power and authority, rather than constitute any challenge.

Occasionally, some of the younger middle-class women organize for their husbands to mind the children while they go away as a group for a weekend's recreation. Behaviour of this kind is cited in conversations as evidence that men's subordination of women is declining. However, as far as I can establish, only 1 or 2 per cent of Smalltown women participate in what are locally called 'weekend flings'.

The most serious attempt by younger women to organize themselves to usurp some of the advantages enjoyed by men occurred in the first half of the 1970s. At that time a number of women who had recently arrived in the community and who were married to professionals or businessmen formed a group for two purposes. The first was to reduce their isolation by having a social 'get-together' for one afternoon a week, and the second was to try to find practical solutions to the problems of isolation, loneliness, and boredom likely to be experienced by young mothers who had recently arrived in Smalltown. They called themselves the Women's Action Group, and conducted a survey aimed at ascertaining if there was sufficient support to establish a child-minding centre. This, and their name, sparked off a lot of criticism and public denunciation from some of the older women leaders of organizations dedicated to affirming women's traditional home-making roles and skills. The younger women were accused of wanting the child-minding centre so that they could escape from their responsibilities as wives and mothers by joining the work-force. This criticism caused a number of members to leave the organization; still more left when a play group was established some months later. The remaining members shrank from any further action that would lead to their being stigmatized as deviants and trouble-makers, and the group evolved into a social club.

As Woodward and Green point out, the understandable retreat of women from conflict, 'Serves to reinforce the status quo and to protect male leisure [and other privileges] usually at the expense of women's free time, autonomy, and release from domestic labour and child care' (1988:135).

Conclusion

Men's domination and exploitation of women in virtually every sphere of Smalltown life is, in large measure, the result of wider structural and cultural forces. Especially significant is a social order which assigns to men the major role as bread-winner and to women the subordinate and unpaid roles of wife and mother. These roles ensure the financial and social dependence of women on men and encourage their emotional dependence as well. Such an interpretation seemingly exonerates Smalltown men from responsibility for the injustices experienced by the women, but they cannot be excused so easily. They too invoke the local traditions and implement the practices that so markedly disadvantage women and typify them as inferior. Smalltown men have the power to create a more equitable if not totally equitable situation for women, and to reduce significantly and even end their dependency. Men have failed to change things for the better in the past. What are the chances of them changing things in the future?

I have already argued that men are unlikely to surrender their considerable advantages willingly because they ensure so much freedom from routine domestic activity and allow men to pursue their own interests in the company of other men. The chances of their entering into more equitable and companionable relationships are reduced even further by their failure to acknowledge that things should be any different. Repeatedly men have shown during the course of interviews in which their wives participated that they cannot comprehend what their wives are complaining about: 'Women have a much better deal than we do. Staying home and spending time drinking coffee with friends is a 'piece of cake'—being a good provider is a much tougher job.'

The chances of men changing are also reduced because many of them fail to share women's need for more companionable relationships with members of the opposite sex, including their own partners.[7] Here is a brief excerpt from an interview with a wealthy farmer which illuminates many men's values on this matter. Similar comments were made in interviews and conversations with businessmen, teachers, and tradesmen, etc.

Interviewer: Do you think Smalltown men prefer the company of other men to that of women, or is that going too far?
Farmer: It all depends; if you want to discuss farming you're not going to do it with a woman. I mean what would they know about it? If you go to the races you don't want to go with the women, if you go to the pub it is to drink beer with a bunch of the boys, or if you go to the football match you don't want to be, you know, tied down to the women. There is a time and place for everything [pause] I mean isn't there?

These attitudes serve as 'symbolic devices' (Cohen, 1985:50) for expressing and reproducing the boundaries that define the community of men. Their affirmation of women's inferiority increases men's 'awareness of and sensitivity to their community' (Cohen, 1985:50). No matter how hard they try women will not become full members of this community until the symbols and the values they reflect change. It is hard to see that change coming from inside. The best chance for change lies in the possibility—however remote—of cultural as well as structural developments in the wider society. Unfortunately, change from outside appears a long way off because, despite the pervasiveness of feminist ideas and the vigorous efforts by many women to achieve political, economic and social equity, men have not only maintained their dominance of the structures and institutions of Australian society but also their cultural hegemony.

APPENDIX 1

Research method

I have spent more than fifteen months in Smalltown conducting field research, most of which was carried out between 1973 and 1977, and 1982 and 1987. The longest field trip was of five weeks' duration and most were only of two or three weeks because they had to be slotted into my full-time teaching—conducted some 250 kilometres from the study site—and into the programmes of those people assisting with the study. Bruce Bickerdike, David Hamilton, John Lawrence and Helen Oliver each accompanied me on at least six field trips in the 1970s, and Rae Ball participated in most of the field-work in the 1980s. During these trips men and women have been observed in a wide range of public and private situations including many sporting activities, in a variety of voluntary organizations, church groups, private parties, barbecues, and informal drinking in hotels. I and several research assistants have lived with thirty families for a total period of ninety weeks.

As well as observing the community we have surveyed it extensively, and conducted more than 2000 interviews, of which approximately 1500 have dealt with the relationships between women and men. I have personally conducted more than 800 interviews and done most of the coding and computer analysis of the data produced by the interviews and the administration of 750 questionnaires. The interviews have combined a structured and semi-structured approach. In order to exploit as fully as possible the data gained from 'open-ended' interviewing I have quantified as much of it as possible. Many of the percentages concerning attitudes, beliefs and activities of various kinds are the result of time-consuming quantification of qualitative data. Adopting this procedure is very revealing. One so often finds that the impressions of what most people think or believe, gained during conversations and interviews, are, at best, only partly right. On returning from field-work, a careful quantitative analysis frequently shows that what one reported verbally to colleagues as a major trend turns out to be a minor one. For me it has called into question the validity of those traditional observational studies which rely mainly on casual conversation and unquantified subjective impressions gleaned during interviews.

The following major surveys were used in this study.

1 1973 A random sample survey of approximately one-third of all households in the community in which information was collected on demographic and occupational characteristics; voluntary organizational membership and kinship ties of household members; intra-generational and inter-generational occupational mobility; the perceptions of class and of its significance in the community; attitudes to differences in wealth and income; degree of satisfaction with work and earnings; occupational aspirations for children; religious and political beliefs and behaviour; feelings of identity with the community and attitudes to the city (N = 443) (Community Survey).

2 1973 A survey of the town's secondary-school pupils covered similar topics to those covered in the Community Survey (N = 350) (1973 School Survey).

3 1974 A survey of all Year 9, 10, 11, and 12 pupils collected information on adolescent leisure activities, participation in domestic labour, and relationships with parents (N = 159) (1974 School Survey).

4 1974 A survey of regular church attenders provided information on religious beliefs and practices and the attitudes of Catholics and Protestants to each other (N = 230) (Religious Survey).

5 1974 A study of a purposive sample of families, most of whom had participated in the initial Community Survey. Respondents provided information on kin, friendship, and neighbouring activities, the division of labour within the family, child care and leisure activity (N = 110) (Family Survey).

6 1974 Lengthy interviews with a purposive sample of working- and middle-class men and women aimed at gaining an understanding of their conceptualizations—if any—of the class structure and its significance in the life of the community (N = 35) (Class Survey).

7 1975 A random sample survey of the quality of life and social integration of elderly people. This produced data on household composition, kinship, friendship, and neighbourhood relations, organizational participation, leisure activity, the division of labour, and morale (N = 182) (Elderly Survey I).

8 1976 A restudy of a sub-sample of the elderly sample focused on the experience of retirement, changes with increasing age in contact with kin, friends, neighbours and participation in community activity, and in relations with younger people (N = 145) (Elderly Survey II).

9 1982 A study of church leaders, ministers, and ministers' wives concerned the place of clergy, their wives, and the church in the town (N = 25) (Church Survey).

10 1983–85 Semi-structured interviews gathered data from a purposive sample of community members on the topics of class and status, community leadership and authority, the social standing of various local occupations and voluntary organizations, and of the churches and the social acceptance of 'newcomers' (N = 179) (Status Survey).

11 1983–85 A study of friendship using data provided by a purposive sample of 175 community members concerning several of their friendships (N = 485) (Friendship Survey).

12 1984–86 Semi-structured interviews conducted with a purposive sample of women and men to gain data on gender relationships and beliefs about the identities, roles and appropriate relationships of men and women. Topics investigated included domestic and marriage relationships, leisure, work and voluntary organizational activity and perceptions of community expectations of men and women (N = 112) (Gender Survey).

13 1986–87 A follow-up study of the educational achievements and social mobility of adolescents. The subjects were first surveyed in 1973 and questioned about their educational and occupational aspirations. In the mid-1980s data were collected on their occupational and educational achievements (N = 252) (Mobility Survey).

14 1986–87 A study of the social characteristics of members and leaders of 40 of the town's 130 voluntary organizations and committees (N = 2500) (Organizational Survey).

APPENDIX 2

Smalltown's class structure

Among sociologists there is no universally acceptable definition of class or method of measuring class but, as Jones and Davis (1986:1) observe, most approaches fall into two broad categories. First, there are those—such as Marx—who view classes as key elements in the course of human history: real groups effecting social change on a national or international level. Second, there are those—such as Weber—who view classes as 'broad aggregations of people rather than actual groups' (Weber, 1968:926–8). Each aggregate is distinguished by its economic interests, or what Weber calls its 'market power'. Market power refers to the ability of members of one class aggregate to compete successfully for valued goods and services with other class aggregates in the market-place.

The approach I am using here is similar to Weber's. In developing the model of class in Smalltown I have drawn on the work of the British sociologists Lockwood (1958) and Goldthorpe (1980), who have taken Weber's model, refined it, and developed ways of using it to allocate members of society to one of several class categories. To do this they make use of Weber's notion of market situation and of the notion of work situation. Market situation means, says Lockwood, 'the economic position narrowly conceived consisting of source and size of income, degree of job security and opportunity for upward occupational mobility' (1958:115). Lockwood views power in the market place as the product of a bundle of factors including occupational income, career prospects, job security, material fringe benefits such as superannuation and so on. The notion of work situation refers to job autonomy and employment status, that is, whether or not the workers are self-employed, employers or employees. The crucial issue concerning the work situation is the degree of autonomy a person experiences in her or his work. It can be expressed in the following questions: Is the worker receiving or giving orders? Is she or he controlling her or his hours of work? Is she or he taking decisions over what is done and when it is done?

In summary, classes are defined here as aggregates of people sharing similar market and work situations as indexed by occupation, degree of work autonomy and employment status. As Marsh (1986:139) points out, a major problem with this approach is that, 'Since the majority of people at any one point of time have no job, to whose occupational group should they be assigned?' There is never an entirely satisfactory answer to this question. Where class position is based on occupation it is not, in a strict sense, possible to assign a class position to any person not engaged in paid employment (Marsh, 1986:139–40). This generalization applies to children, most of the elderly, and most wives in the Smalltown community. The problem of allocating a class position to the elderly is usually resolved by assigning a class position based on the major occupational activity of the respondent (or, in many circumstances, the respondent's spouse) during the course of his or her working life. This procedure is adopted here for the Smalltown elderly who are no longer engaged in paid employment or who are married to somebody no longer engaged in paid employment. About 90 per cent of Smalltown's elderly belong to this category.

Children are given a derivative class position which is

determined by the occupation of the major bread-winner in the child's household, usually the father. The difficulties associated with assigning a class position to women are so complex that they require an extended comment.

The class position of women

The class position of women is one of the most controversial issues in contemporary sociological research and writing (see Cass, 1978; Garnsey, 1978; Britten and Heath, 1983; Goldthorpe, 1983; Stanworth, 1983; Dale *et al.*, 1985; and Baxter, 1988). It is almost two decades since Parkin said, 'inequalities associated with sex differences are not usually thought of as components of stratification' (1971:14), and Giddens claimed that 'given that women still have to wait their liberation from the family it remains the case in capitalist societies that female workers are largely peripheral to the class system' (cited by Heath, 1981:107–8). These statements sound quite anachronistic now but they are not without their supporters today (see, for example, Lockwood, 1986).

Britten and Heath state: 'The treatment of women in classifications of social class has become something of a scandal' (1983:46). From their point of view, women, especially married women, have been unjustifiably excluded from class analysis. Feminists have been particularly critical of what is called the conventional approach to class analysis. This approach has been vigorously defended by Goldthorpe (1983, 1984). Goldthorpe argues that it is the family, not the individual, that is the participating unit in contemporary systems of class stratification. Accordingly, class position should be based on the position held in the labour market by the household head, who will usually be the male. Women are viewed as more peripheral to the labour market than men: in part, because they are more likely to spend considerable periods of time out of the market and, in part, because they are less committed to participating in the labour market than men.

This approach has been contested for the following reasons. First, it fails to take account of the contribution a woman in paid work is making to the family budget; second, it ignores the growing number of women who are not participating in a family or are heading single-parent households; and third, it presumes equality within a relationship but, in reality, the economic position of the dependent wife does not equal that of her husband (see Cass, 1978; Stanworth, 1983).

Problems for analysis are also produced when the class positions of individuals within the family are not homogeneous and marriages break down. For example, does a working-class woman married to a middle-class man and, therefore under the conventional approach, viewed as middle class, lose that position if she is divorced or widowed (Stanworth, 1983; Leiulfsrud and Woodward, 1987)?

There are other theoretical problems in treating the family as the unit of analysis in the study of social stratification. Garnsey points out that 'in a system of individual waged labour families are not engaged as units in the occupational division of labour. It is as individuals that household members are engaged in roles in the system of economic production' (1978:226).

It is possible to show that all of these observations have empirical validity in Smalltown. First, women for example, are often in a subordinate economic position within the family. Second, a sizeable minority of women are making crucial contributions to the household income, even if that contribution is usually less than the husband's. Third, a small minority are heads of single-parent households. Fourth, while divorce is fairly uncommon, widowhood is very common in an ageing population. The market situation of, say, the widowed farmer's wife is often very different from that of the farmer's wife. Similarly, the economic and social realities of a woman married to, say, a man with a higher professional job are very different from those of the man himself. The same generalizations would also apply to a woman who derives her class position from a man in a working-class position. The man will almost certainly be exercising greater control—perhaps the ultimate control—of the money and any capital associated with his work. It is he rather than she who has the opportunities for upward career mobility and it is he rather than she who is effectively freed from domestic labour and child care and enjoys any authority and autonomy associated with the work.

Baxter observes that we need to develop class theories and indices of class position which consider both class and gender processes. She continues: 'women's position in the class structure is determined by both class exploitation and gender domination, and class theory needs to take account of both rather than subsuming one under the other' (1988:121). Unfortunately, there is no satisfactory model for doing so. None of the schemas that have been proposed for including women in class analysis offer solutions to these problems, which are empirically more viable than those offered by the conventional approach.

In the present context, if the decision is taken to use an individual's position in the labour market as the unit of analysis, it creates more problems than it solves, especially if we fail to find a way of indicating the class position of women engaged in unpaid labour. If the analysis is restricted to only those people engaged in the paid work-force, then we would exclude 44 per cent of the members of this community and, in particular, roughly two-thirds of all women aged fifteen years and over. Clearly, in a study of this nature in which so many facets of the lives of community members are examined, such large proportions cannot be excluded. As far as married women are concerned, it is probably less misleading to categorize a woman not engaged in paid work herself as belonging to her husband's class than to place all non-waged wives in a homogeneous class. The latter practice masks important economic and life-style differences between, for example, a woman married to a man in a middle-class occupation and one married to a blue-collar worker.

Until class theory is rethought so that it can accommodate 'women's dual experience as both unpaid housewives and members of the labour force' (Baxter, 1988:121) so that they can be included in class analysis, then there is no alternative to giving such people a derivative class position based on the position of the working father or husband.

Leiulfsrud and Woodward are right when they say, 'in class analysis . . . the unit of analysis should be chosen to illuminate the issue under study' (1987:395). Unfortunately, neither the conventional method, which uses the family as the unit of analysis, nor a method using the individual as a unit of analysis can satisfactorily illuminate all the issues under investigation here. What is needed, observe Crompton and Mann, is a completely revised occupational scheme that accommodates gender-based differences and experience (1986:7). In the absence of such a scheme the solution has to be a compromise imposed both by conceptual limitations and the empirical realities facing this particular research context. Accordingly, the following procedures were adopted for the classification of women's class position.

1 Wives or widows who had not been engaged in paid employment for most of their working lives or who were currently not engaged in paid employment, whatever their age, took the class position of their husbands or former husbands. Among the drawbacks of this approach is the fact that it obscures 'the presence or absence of economic independence' (Britten and Heath, 1983:46). Yet Britten and Heath, as well as other scholars who have used a cross-class analysis (Leiulfsrud and

Woodward, 1987; Baxter, 1988) have been forced to adopt the same procedure.

2 Where both a husband and wife are engaged in stable paid employment, they both take the class position of the one who has the highest position in the occupational structure. In Smalltown, with only a handful of exceptions, husbands and wives have the same position, or the husband has the superior position.

This approach fails to meet the major criticisms that feminists have levelled at the conventional study of class: that is, it fails to take account of the real differences in the economic situation of men and women within the same family or to give any weighting to the economic contribution of the partner whose class position is derived from the other, who, of course, is usually the woman. However, it is the best option available in the present circumstances.[1]

A description of Smalltown's seven classes

Class 1: the higher level professional and executive class

Members of this class have in common higher incomes, economic security, and the prospect of economic improvement or a career advancement. Furthermore, incumbents usually exercise authority and a considerable degree of autonomy at work. This is always a small class numerically: two or three doctors, three or four lawyers, a couple of engineers, two or three local-government executives, and a handful of other people in managerial positions.

Class 2: the farmer class

This consists of farmers, both those with large and small holdings, and farm employees. This is a prosperous farm industry and some of the farmers enjoy a standard of living comparable to that of members of class 1. These farmers possess superior economic assets. Probably no more than a dozen of Smalltown's three hundred farmers have full-time employees. Farmers rely heavily on family labour. On about 50 per cent of the district's two hundred farms there are at least two male members of the immediate family 'farming the property'. It is because the vast majority of people who list themselves as farm employees are, in fact, members of the farmer's family who will eventually inherit the property or become part-owners of it, that I have adopted Jones's and Davis's practice of bracketing farm employees with farmers to create a farmer class. The reasons that Jones and Davis (1986:275) advance for following this practice are valid in Smalltown: farm employees are rapidly declining in numbers because, as Nalson notes, farming families 'put off non-family labour in an attempt to reduce costs' (1977:305).

Bracketing farm employees with farmers slightly distorts the class system of Smalltown but a far greater degree of distortion is introduced if farm labourers are grouped with town labourers because almost all the farm labourers will, sooner or later, become farm proprietors, whereas almost all of the town labourers will remain just that.

Class 3: the business class

This is made up of proprietors of small and medium-sized enterprises. By national standards, all are small businesses. The class includes shopkeepers, farm-machinery agents, livestock and insurance agents, transport contractors, building and earthmoving contractors, a handful of small-scale manufacturers, and a variety of self-employed skilled workers. Together they form Smalltown's second petit-bourgeois class, the first being the farming class. Most of the members of the business class rely exclusively on their own labour or that of their immediate family, especially wives and sons. As is so often the case with petit-bourgeois enterprise, without their wife's labour, many of these businessmen would have to close their doors (Finch, 1983:9). In general, members of this class possess much less capital than members of the farming class, but they have more job security and work autonomy than many white-collar workers or employees who are skilled workers. The standard of living of most business families appears to be somewhat below that of the more prosperous farmers, and as the work of business families is often more labour intensive, they usually enjoy less freedom 'to take time out when it suits them' than do farmers. According to businessmen, their labour input and that of their wives is inequitably rewarded: 'We're not even working for wages given the 60 to 70 hours a week we put in, and that is leaving out the wife's labour. You feel much of the time you are working for virtually nothing.'

Class 4: the semi-professional and executive class

This is comprised of semi-professionals or lower level professionals: principally teachers and nurses, salaried managers, higher technicians, and police. Members of this class enjoy similar benefits to members of class 1, but to a lesser degree. These benefits include economic security, relatively high salaries, and considerable autonomy at work. However, unlike members of class 1, members of this class are, at the same time, subject to more control from those higher in the organization than themselves, and they have less job autonomy and less economic security in the form of capital than members of class 2 and often of class 3. The majority of members of this class will, in the interests of advancing their careers, leave Smalltown.

Class 5: the lower middle class

This class is often referred to as the ordinary white-collar class, and consists of clerks, typists, secretaries, and sales personnel. Members of this class have fewer marketable qualifications and are almost always poorer career prospects than members of classes 1 or 4. They certainly have less capital and usually inferior incomes than members of classes 2 or 3. They have less job autonomy and are much less likely to be exercising authority than members of any of the higher classes. There are, however, important gender differences in the career prospects of this class. Males have superior career opportunities and usually better incomes than either female members of this class or employee manual workers of either gender (see Ch. 6). Sometimes, but not always, white-collar workers enjoy greater job security than manual workers. Again, there is an important gender difference because more than 90 per cent of shop assistants in Smalltown are females and they have no security of tenure, whereas most male white-collar workers are employed by local government bodies, government departments, or banking corporations. Even the males engaged in sales generally have better incomes than females working in sales. Most of the males are working for stock and station agencies, insurance companies, and car and machinery dealers.[2]

Class 6: the working class

This class is comprised of skilled employee manual workers and includes plumbers, carpenters, mechanics, electricians and hair-stylists. It also includes heavy-equipment operators, foremen, and other supervisory workers. Although members of this class often have more job autonomy than members of the ordinary white-collar class, they are subject to closer control at work. In this community the incomes of employee skilled workers are often not superior to those of semi-skilled or unskilled workers but their skills ensure that they can always obtain work. A small minority of the members of this class will eventually use their occupation as the basis for establishing a business and, providing they are successful, in this way elevate themselves to membership of the petit-bourgeois class. Chapter 6 shows that men monopolize the skilled trade positions in the local class structure.

Class 7: the lower working class

This consists of semi-skilled and unskilled employee manual workers including labourers, railway workers, drivers, domestics, and machinists. Members of this class usually have less job security than members of all other classes. Many of them work on a casual basis, and about half the female members of this class are employed part-time. As a rule, members of this class have poorer incomes than members of other classes (see Ch. 6). They exercise no authority at work and they do not usually experience any autonomy.

Notes

1 Introduction

1 This is the second book on this community. In the first book—entitled *Smalltown*—I examine inequalities of class, age and gender. I try to understand why individuals experience a strong sense of belonging to this community, and why the community itself remains highly cohesive despite the pervasive social inequalities (Dempsey 1990a).

2 See, for example, Lynd and Lynd, 1929; Dollard, 1957; Dennis, Henriques and Slaughter, 1969; Vidich and Bensman, 1960; Stacey, 1960; Littlejohn, 1963; Bryson and Thompson, 1972; Wild, 1974; Oxley, 1978; Dempsey, 1990a; Gray 1991.

3 The back-cover blurb of Gretchen Poiner's 1990 book *The Good Old Rule* contains the most recent expression of this often-repeated complaint. 'Studies of rural communities in Australia have been few in number. Moreover, these studies have been undertaken by men, who have focused on male participation in such communities and on areas of traditional interest to men; women have remained mostly invisible.'

4 Stacey, 1960; Dennis, Henriques and Slaughter, 1969; Bryson and Thompson, 1972; Williams, 1981.

5 Littlejohn 1963; James, 1979, 1981; Poiner, 1990; Gray 1991.

6 Rew, 1978; James, 1979, 1981; Poiner, 1990; Gray, 1991.

7 Deem, 1986; Green, Hebron and Woodward, 1987b; Wimbush and Talbot, 1988.

8 Dixey and Talbot, 1982; Deem, 1982, 1986; Wimbush, 1986; Green *et al.*, 1987b.

9 See for similar findings, Whitehead, 1976; James, 1981; Imray and Middleton, 1983.

10 For example, Zaretsky, 1976, Ch. 1; Whitehead, 1976:170; and Curthoys, 1986. The failure to find satisfactory answers reflects, in part, the underdeveloped nature of theory. As Connell stresses; 'the

social theory of gender is not a tightly-knit logical system. It is, rather, a network of insights and arguments about connections' (1986:343). Among the issues Connell says gender theory currently links are several that are focused upon in this study, 'the social subordination of women, and the cultural practices that sustain it; . . . the sexual division of labour; [and] the formation of character and motive, so far as they are organized as femininity and masculinity' (1986:343).

11 See Davidoff, 1976; Barrett, 1980; Hartmann, 1979; Connell *et al.*, 1982; Bryson 1984; and Connell, 1986.

12 Paid work is to be a priority for men 'not simply in terms of time and organisation, but also in terms of identity' (Finch, 1983:144).

13 To illustrate the process of inferiorization I will borrow and adapt an example from Bryson (1990). When Smalltown football supporters denigrate a player whose performance is disappointing them by calling out, 'You're playing like a woman', they are inferiorizing women generally.

14 See Dempsey (1991) for an account of the significance of organized religion for Smalltowners.

15 More than two-thirds of the population have at least one close kin, other than a member of their own household, living in the community.

16 That is in settlements where individuals relate to one set of actors in their paid employment, another in the street where they live, still another at their tennis club, and so forth, and where there are few if any social ties between these various groups or quasi groups.

17 Here is one example of the way in which field-work can provide unexpected insights on decision-making processes. Before making a visit to Smalltown I would arrange interviews by phoning the household of the potential interviewee. The purpose was to arrange interviews with both husbands and wives. I learnt that it was essential to speak to a husband directly because few wives would agree to an interview for themselves without first discussing the matter with their husband, and none would commit a husband to an interview. However, I found that, more often than not, a husband would say yes to an interview on behalf of his wife when he was only being asked to agree to one for himself. If I said something of this nature, 'I would like to speak to your wife to see if she is agreeable to doing an interview', a common reply was, 'No need to ask her. She'll do it. You just let us know when you're coming and we'll be here.'

2 Place and people

1 When we began research in Smalltown the flour mill employed approximately 150 people; today its successor, The Stock Feed Company, employs fewer than fifty people.

2 The complex relationships of farmers and businessmen and their wives are discussed in Chapter 7.
3 In 1991 the average price of a dwelling in Smalltown was $50 000–$60 000, whereas the average price of a Melbourne house was between $120 000 and $140 000.
4 It is impossible to provide precise figures on the number of women currently working in Smalltown who have followed this career path, but it is certainly fewer than one dozen.
5 Employees are included with owners because the great majority of them are sons of farmers who will eventually inherit the farming property or become part owners (see Appendix 2).
6 The supervisory personnel are foremen.
7 In the Community Survey, references to these factors accounted for 53 per cent of all responses to an open-ended question aimed at establishing what Smalltowners like best about living in their own town.
8 As Simmel observed, the degree of amity existing within a group is, in large measure, due to the perceptions of enmity arising outside the group (1955:96–105).
9 See Kendig, 1986:85–109), for similar findings.
10 Women were twice as likely as men to experience loneliness. Widowed women were more likely than widowed men to experience loneliness and social isolation because they were much more likely to be living alone (83 per cent compared with 57 per cent).

The link between living alone and social isolation is supported by some of our findings. The majority of those who live alone reported they watched television alone and ate alone (80 per cent of those living alone ate at least nineteen meals a week alone, whereas 90 per cent of those living with someone ate fewer then two meals a week alone). Even those with children living locally ate most of their meals alone. The elderly who lived alone were more likely than those elderly who lived with someone else to report that they had not spoken to a neighbour for more than three days (70 per cent compared with 54 per cent). They were twice as likely to report that they experienced loneliness than those living with someone else (68 per cent compared with 33 per cent).
11 See Dempsey, 1990a, Chapter 4 and Dempsey, 1990b for a fuller discussion of the segregation and marginalization of the elderly.
12 'No-hopers' are not peculiar to Smalltown. They form a distinctive stratum in each of the six New South Wales and Victorian towns in which I have either lived or conducted research. Wild reports their presence in Bradstow where the middle class speak despairingly of them (1974:56).

3 A man's town

1 This issue is discussed at length in Chapter 4.

2 'The seats of power are everywhere a "male preserve"', Imray and Middleton (1983:18). In their paper they demonstrate that this generalization holds for such widely diverse groups as the British House of Commons, the trade unions of Western societies, and the pre-literate Askwe-Shavante of Brazil and the Iatmul of New Guinea.

3 'Until the old House of Commons was burned down in 1834, women in Britain were allowed to hear the activities going on in the Chamber from the roof space where they were concealed. After the fire, the building was redesigned but it was still basically a Men's House with no provision for women *inside* the Chamber' (Imray and Middleton, 1983: 18–19).

4 During the Status Survey these three organizations received more than four-fifths of all the nominations when respondents were requested to nominate the organizations with the highest social standing in the community.

5 It will also be seen that they are much more committed to this cultural value than their womenfolk are.

6 This information was communicated to me by a member of the state executive of the Jaycees.

7 This was a sensitive matter, and so I did not attempt to establish what proportion of members adopted this view. Certainly most did not volunteer the view and in casual conversation at least two said that they were glad women had been admitted to the club. I was told by one member that four men had left in protest; another respondent said six had left. Several others confirmed that a number had left because women had been admitted.

8 What was also relevant were these facts: the woman was a transient without any kin or close friends living locally, whereas the two men were members of families that had been resident in the district for many years; and the men and their wives had ties of friendship with several other members of the club, or the spouses of those members.

9 The parish priest has since retired. I have not approached the new priest as his appointment was taken up after I had completed this section of the research programme.

10 The next most common responses were those which made reference to men who were keen to find secure employment, or who had a friendly disposition and mixed in well with other people. Answers of this nature accounted for more than one-third of the responses.

When we asked respondents to describe the kind of women who would feel at home in Smalltown more than half the respondents said that it was women who loved a home or family-centred life or both. We were told repeatedly that women who liked sophisticated entertainment would feel 'out of things' in Smalltown (see Ch. 8).

11 These norms date back to Victorian times when, as Gittins points out, 'Middle-class Victorian morality earmarked drink as one important area for defining respectability—drunkenness, particularly for women, was condemned' (1985:125).

12 The average age of these pupils was fifteen.

13 Bryson reports that in Australia: 'the more costly sports are almost invariably those where males predominate' (1987:353).

14 The observation that men control major sporting facilities should not be interpreted as necessarily meaning that women are without influence. For instance, in 1991 the treasurer and secretary of the tennis club were both women. Women's influence on the administration of this sport was greater than that on any of the other sporting activities cited in Table 3.1. Nevertheless, in 1991 a man was president of the club and a man had been president for as long as anyone could recall.

15 There are signs of change occurring in bowling in the 1990s. A mixed pairs club championship was recently established.

16 Bussey points out that in Australian society males are more strongly sex typed than females and males are probably at greater risk than females of losing status and power by engaging in cross-sex behaviour (1986:102).

17 Women participants in the Marriage Survey were twice as likely as men to say they were *not* spending enough time with their spouse.

Men are more entitled than women to resist participating in a partner's leisure. The understanding—sometimes only implicit but often made explicit—is that men's superior contribution to the partnership through serving as *the* provider places a wife in his debt. He is bestowing a gift upon her for which she should respond with a display of deference (Bell and Newby, 1976a). A husband's superior position in the relationship excuses him from joining in recreational activities that do not interest him. On the other hand, participating in a husband's leisure activities is an integral part of being a good wife. It does not usually place a husband in a wife's debt.

18 The remaining members of the sample either said they spoke to both sexes equally or that who they spoke to depended on the nature of the social event.

19 Only 2 per cent of the men said they preferred the company of women to that of men, but two-thirds said they preferred men's company. The remainder made qualified statements such as: 'It depends on the circumstances' or, 'It depends on the person'. Among women only one-quarter said they preferred the company of women, whereas more than one-third said they preferred men's company.

4 Married to the game

1 Griffin, 1985; Deem, 1982, 1986; Woodward and Green, 1988.

2 Chapter 5 is given over to showing that women perform most domestic work and take most responsibility for child care in Smalltown. Some readers may wish to familiarize themselves with the quantitative evidence produced in that chapter before proceeding with Chapter 4.

3 Edgell, 1980; Deem, 1982, 1986; Dixey and Talbot, 1982; Hochschild, 1988.

4 See Bryson (1984) for a review of the part Australian husbands play in child care, and Edgell (1980), for a similar review for Britain. The participation of Smalltown husbands is discussed at some length in Chapter 5 of this volume.

5 Our surveying showed that community members generally support the position adopted by most of the husbands we interviewed. Only a minority of Smalltown people subscribe to the view that children are as much a husband's as a wife's responsibility. Almost all of those who think this way are younger women with tertiary educational qualifications. Very few of these women are married to men who share their view. Here is what one of these women had to say on the subject:

> In this community if a kid is in trouble or just has untidy clothes the mother is always blamed. 'It's her fault.'
> That's my husband's attitude too. He won't take responsibility for Bill [their 18-month-old child]. He says, 'The kid's her worry, not mine!'

6 In his study of a sample of British middle-class couples Edgell found that the lack of any physical or temporal boundary between work and non-work seemed to result in the wives 'working' longer hours and, compared with their husbands, having fewer leisure interests and activities that were quite unconnected with their primary role responsibilities (1980:78).

7 The wife of the mayor always prepares the supper served to councillors following a council meeting. One councillor estimated that the mayoress assisted with her husband's local government activities on forty to fifty occasions each year. The mayor's position is an honorary one.

8 Griffin, in her study of a sample of younger British women, demonstrates that the one-sided character of friendship relationships begins well before adulthood. Stable friendships among girls, in her study, frequently ended once a girl started going steady, often at the insistence of the boyfriend. However, male friendships survived the formation of heterosexual friendships. '"The lads" continued to see their friends in local pubs and at football matches' (1985:61–2).

9 In Smalltown almost three-quarters of the middle class compared with one-half of the working class belong to at least one voluntary organization.
10 These auxiliaries are usually comprised of wives, girlfriends, mothers, and widows of the men who form or formed the superordinate group.
11 The evening is not catered for by the husbands but by some of the women members of the golf club.
12 Although men bring food, as a rule their wives, mothers or sisters prepare it.
13 Meetings are now held in a clubroom at the new football pavilion (1992).
14 This is, of course, men's territory also.
15 There is a constant demand for catering by women's organizations because there are no professional caterers but numerous functions to cater for. Consequently, a number of women's voluntary organizations raise money by providing three-course meals for weddings, etc.
16 The merits of women being admitted to full membership were being widely debated in the mid-1980s. The local male members, with whom I discussed the issue, took the view that if women wanted full membership they should not only pay the same fees as men but play off the men's tees. Until women were prepared, or able, to do that, they should be denied membership. This was a transparent example of men justifying their elite status in the club by alluding to their physical superiority. Women's tees are usually placed many metres in front of men's to compensate for many women being unable to hit the ball as far as most men. Golf clubs have been reluctantly accepting women as full members because of the threat of prosecution under equal-opportunity legislation.
17 The recent admission of women, many of whom are wives of male members, to the golf club is at most a partial exception to this generalization. Men it seems are effectively resisting their full participation.
18 An observation Abrams made about the failure to recognize the worth of unpaid labour is valid in this context. He says, in a system in which 'a person's capacity to work is bought and sold in exchange for a wage, labour, which is performed on the basis of personal relations rather than on the basis of monetary exchange, is not recognised as labour' (1978:160).
19 See Deem, 1986:68 and Woodward and Green, 1988:132 for similar findings.
20 See, for example, Barrett (1980), Deem (1982, 1986), Griffin *et al.* (1982), Woodward and Green (1988).
21 The research of Deem (1982) and Green *et al.* (1987a: 85–6) has

shown that men at times threaten to and sometimes do use their superior physical power to impede the leisure activities of wives or facilitate their own.

5 Dividing the jobs: unpaid work

1 In a previous article one of the authors said that within the home 'the old distinctions between men's and women's jobs [those still made] become increasingly blurred' (Wilmott, 1969:294–5 cited by Edgell, 1980:54).

2 Edgell, 1980: Ch. 4; Williams, 1981:146–52; Russell, 1983; Schooler *et al.*, 1984; Collins, 1985:70–2); Harper and Richards, 1986:Ch. 10; McRae, 1986:Ch.7; Hochschild, 1988:271-3; Bittman, 1991.

3 The focus of our research on these tasks is apposite because Bittman's less recent study of time use in Sydney showed that cooking, cleaning, and laundry accounted for 58 per cent of all the time women devoted to unpaid domestic labour (1991:33).

4 Oakley, 1974; Harper and Richards, 1986; Bryson, 1985; Collins, 1985; McRae, 1986.

5 Sharpe, 1984; Yeandle, 1984; Berk, 1985; Bryson, 1985; Collins, 1985; McRae, 1986; Michelson, 1985; Ross, 1987; Bittman, 1991.

6 The proportions were approximately the same for both the full-time and part-time samples.

7 Twelve months later his wife reported that his input had declined considerably. He blamed his increased work load; she, his increasing boredom with domestic routine and a preference for the company of his mates.

8 Thomas and Zmroczek (1985) observe that: 'the most remarkable feature of husbands' domestic work time is how little it changes . . . in response to changes in wives' working patterns' (1985:115). So, in Smalltown, 'in moving into the work force, women may well be adding another dimension of patriarchal control to their lives' (Bryson, 1985:97).

9 One woman expressed the attitude of a number of women in the following way: 'You can't expect a man to start washing clothes and cleaning once he is retired, it's a bit much when he has worked hard all his life. Anyhow, men are a bit like children! They just don't know how to look after themselves.'

10 We did not collect data on the actual time each partner to a marriage contributed to domestic labour. However, a number of studies have demonstrated that if women enter the paid work-force, the total hours they spend working (at home and in paid employment) increase at a faster rate than those that husbands spend working (Pleck, 1985; Sharpe, 1984; Bittman, 1991).

11 The gender ideology refers to the beliefs that it is natural and appropriate for women to centre their lives on the roles of wife and mother while men, as 'the providers', focus their lives on their paid work.

6 Dividing the jobs: paid work

1 Of those participating in the work-force one in three of the women was employed on a part-time basis compared with only one in fourteen of the men.

2 In 1871 women comprised only 11 per cent of the town's work-force; in 1933, 18 per cent; and in 1961, 20 per cent. In 1976 the proportion rose to 26 per cent.

Unfortunately, it is impossible to give a precise indication of the real size of the increase of women in the work-force in the 1960s and 1970s. This is due, in part, to a 'redefinition of workforce status which led to the inclusion of many part-time workers' (Broom *et al.*, 1976:37–8) who had not been regarded as members of the work-force in earlier censuses. It is also due in part to an increase in the practice of income splitting by male farmers. This resulted in many women who previously stated their occupation as 'home duties' stating it as farmer. This practice was adopted to minimize the family taxation bill. It did not mean that either the work or economic relation of the wife to the farm had changed. Our field-work strongly suggests that it did not mean that these wives actually received the income shown against their name on either census or taxation schedules. Nor did it mean that they were usually as free as the men to dispose of the property and in that way gain a measure of financial independence. On the basis of information gained through random sample surveying in this district as well as first-hand knowledge of local farming practices, I would estimate that more than 97 per cent of the 149 women who in 1981 declared themselves to be in farm jobs were, in fact, women who had married into farming families rather than women who had inherited farming land in their own right. On the basis of the estimates made by leaders in this industry of just how many women are farmers 'in their own right' I have placed their number at 1 per cent for this analysis. This is not a satisfactory solution because it appears to ignore the substantial contribution farmers' wives make to the economic success of a farm. I do, however, deal explicitly with this contribution in the next chapter. But to include women farmers in the large numbers in which they appear in the census data would be even more misleading given the realities of farm management, control of farm capital and income, and its transmission from father to son (see Ch. 7 and also see Baxter *et al.*, 1988).

3 OECD Report, *Women and Employment*, 1980:44–6.

4 While this is generally true, it is also true that in the context under study here we are able to delineate several processes which contribute in a significant way to the reproduction and maintenance of aspects of this system.

5 This information has been gleaned from the 1871 census for the State of Victoria and the community's published history.

6 Unfortunately, there are no census data available on Smalltown's occupational structure for most of the twentieth century. Australian Bureau of Statistics data are available on the breakdown of the work-force according to industry, also occupational data from the 1981 census organized into the class categories used in this study, and data we ourselves collected on the occupational history of respondents and from direct observation.

7 This is the most recent year for which I have occupational data in sufficient detail to allow these gendered comparisons.

8 This family business passed into receivership in the first half of 1991.

9 In this study classes are defined as aggregates of people (not social formations) with a similar market and work situation. Occupation and employment status (e.g. employee, self-employed) are used as the major criteria for determining an individual's class position.

10 The tertiary sector of the work-force includes white-collar jobs in education, finance, the police force, sales, local government, etc.

11 The lower average income of women is probably also due, in part, to discrimination by employers. Chapman and Miller (1983) found that in the Australian work-force men with identical qualifications to women received higher remuneration even when they did very similar jobs (see Ch. 7).

12 She stresses that they also need to be armed with 'more specific ideas concerning . . . equality for women' (Wearing, 1984:104).

13 It needs to be borne in mind that there are a large number of studies which show that wives in full-time paid employment retain a disproportionate share of responsibility for domestic labour and child care, and devote much more time to such tasks than their partners (McRae, 1986; Deem, 1986: Bittman, 1991). The data we do have on the domestic division of labour in Smalltown households where wives are engaged in full-time paid work also fail to corroborate Bryson's and Wearing's hope that possessing greater economic resources will produce greater equity in marriages.

Detailed studies of domestic expenditure show that the superordinate position of husbands is usually not eroded through a working wife's economic activities. More specifically they demonstrate that, in relative terms, working wives contribute a larger proportion of their income to the household than their husbands do. They also show that husbands hold back more money both absolutely and relatively for their personal use (Pahl, 1990). I did not make a detailed study of domestic expenditure in Smalltown households, however I did establish that husbands are more likely to spend a greater proportion of money on their leisure activity than are wives engaged in paid work.

14 It has not been possible to gain a breakdown of weekly hours of employment for married women for 1986. However, if the ratios of part-time to full-time employment are similar to those that applied in 1981 (and our first-hand knowledge of the community does not suggest otherwise) then between 15 per cent and 20 per cent of the married women were working full-time in 1986. In 1981, 42 per cent of married women were employed in the Australian labour-force.

15 The mill was owned by a national corporation and housed in a building rented to it by the local council. Managed by a man, it provided full-time employment for more than seventy female machinists, fifty-five of whom were living in the Smalltown community.

16 Reported in the *Smalltown News* published on that day.

17 Growth is less in rural than in urban Australia but the rural growth that is occurring is restricted to a limited number of geographical locations which are usually those with a concentration of government, business, and industrial services (Baxter *et al.*, 1988:23).

18 Sixty-one per cent of married women had an income of $4000 or less. About one-quarter of the married women with an income in this category were receiving the old-age pension. This meant they were at least partially dependent on the State for their income. It does not follow, of course, that they had total control of the disposal of their pension. At least a minority of husbands controlled their wives' pensions.

19 The findings for this segment of the population are not shown in any table.

20 For example, married men between the ages of twenty and sixty-four are more than twice as likely as married women of a comparable age to have an income in excess of $10 000.

21 The Elderly Survey II showed that no widows were working and less than 10 per cent of widowers had a paying job.

22 Twenty-two per cent hedged their bets by saying something of this nature: 'Some women are dependent and some are not.'

7 Excluding women from paid work

1 This account is, of course, not exhaustive. There are other factors responsible for the lower rate of participation by women in paid work. One of these, which is dealt with elsewhere in this study, is

indirect discrimination resulting from socialization processes which encourage women to put caring ahead of personal career (Sharpe, 1976, Ch. 2; Whitehead, 1981:103–5) and which lead to the development of a sense of femininity which does not square with aspiring for many of the better jobs men hold (see Ch. 8).

Excellent examinations of the factors responsible for the lower degree of participation of women in paid work in an Australian context are given by Power (1975b) and Curthoys (1986).

2 This estimation was made in the mid-1980s by local leaders in the farming industry.

3 The status of a farmer who has gained access to land through marriage is always dubious. A man's role as provider is being at least partially usurped when he marries a woman who has inherited a farm. A 'real' man will not rely on a woman in this way. A man who has become a farmer through marrying a woman with land is sometimes referred to derogatively as a 'suitcase farmer', implying that he has moved in with nothing more than a suitcase.

4 I have placed the word *explanation* in quotation marks because, for the reasons advanced earlier, job stereotyping is viewed here as only a correlate, and not an explanation of women's absence from certain sections of the work-force.

5 We did not question the daughters to see whether they would feel uncomfortable in pursuing such jobs, or feared ostracism if they did so. The occasional conversation suggested that they did not think of entering them because they perceived them as men's jobs. However, a study conducted by Lucas of 43 South Australian women who had taken up jobs traditionally regarded as men's jobs, showed that about four-fifths of them experienced harassment or discrimination from fellow male workers in the work-place (cited by Williams, 1988:93–4).

6 In the 1970s one woman was self-employed as a tailor.

7 It was shown in Chapter 5 that the division of domestic tasks in Smalltown was similar to that reported in numerous studies conducted in Australia and overseas (Edgell, 1980; Deem, 1982; Bryson, 1984; McRae, 1986; Bittman, 1991).

8 The situation varies according to her stage in the life-cycle, the age of children, and the nature of the employment of her husband. But the generalizations being offered here are more rather than less true. A woman may have greater opportunity to participate in paid work when her 'children are off her hands' but, by then, the chances of pursuing a well-rewarded career, as opposed to taking a job, are likely to be slender, or non-existent.

9 Ferree and others show that the practice of regarding a wife as a supplemental worker rather than a co-provider, even if, in reality, she is making a similar or greater financial contribution than her

husband, is related to the custom of linking masculinity to the provider role (Haas, 1986 cited by Ferree, 1990).

10 Ninety-six per cent of mothers expressed the same viewpoint. When a wife holds such a belief it makes it easy for a husband to deter his wife from working by manipulating her sense of guilt.

11 The practice of girls emigrating to obtain work was also opposed by some because it was believed to put the girl at risk physically and morally. It was highly likely that she would have to move to Melbourne to obtain employment. Major cities are feared as centres of physical violence, corruption and moral decadence (Dempsey, 1990a).

12 The results were published in the *Smalltown News* but they failed to stimulate any correspondence or any comment that reached me.

13 The man had enjoyed a secure job for most of his working life. The notion of a working-class man being *the* provider and his wife *the* home-maker is not a new ideal, but one that reaches back at least to the nineteenth century and a time when the occurrence of secure employment for skilled workers led to the emergence of a blue-collar 'labour aristocracy'. As Ferree observes, the ideal may survive the reality (Hareven, 1982 cited by Ferree, 1990:872). In Smalltown the wives of some of the working-class men who most strenuously advocated this position were engaged in full-time employment.

14 An eminent American historian of women and the family notes that in contemporary American society:

> Women are still the primary child rearers, even when they work, and the purpose of their work in the main is to support and advance the family, *not* to realize themselves as individuals (Degler, 1980:452–3 cited by Kessler-Harris, 1987:521).

15 Because they were 'non-locals' holding radical views they were unlikely to exercise much influence.

16 It seems it is difficult to reconcile any role reversal, or serious modification of traditional roles, with the preference for a husband who is economically successful. Such success confers economic security, a superior life-style, and higher social esteem on a wife. It is also difficult to reconcile role reversal with the superior earning capacity of most husbands.

17 Finch offers an excellent creative synthesis of what is a diverse and fragmentary literature on the participation of wives in their husband's paid work in her book *Married to the Job*. To those familiar with her work its influence on this account will be apparent.

18 These terms are taken from Finch's *Married to the Job* (1983).

19 It was beyond our research resources to enquire in a systematic manner about the attitudes of wives to their incorporation, but it should be reported that hardly any volunteered any criticism. It

appears they took their participation for granted: a natural expression of their marriage partnership.

20 The limited participation occurs, notwithstanding the steady decline over the last thirty years in the size of the hired rural labour-force. The likelihood of a wife serving as an 'additional worker' depends a good deal on the type of farming. Wheat and sheep predominate in Smalltown. Technology has transformed these industries so that, given the size of local holdings, the need for regular labour other than that of the farmer himself is usually slight. By contrast it is the exceptional wife who escapes with the milking on a dairy farm.

21 These expectations are much more likely to exist if a husband is farming on his own rather than in partnership with his father or brother.

22 Such action by middle-class wives draws mixed comment. On the one hand, the wife is admired for helping her husband in a way few wives could or would help; on the other hand, it is not perceived as 'quite the right thing' for a wife to do. Trucking belongs to the world of men: it is dirty, rough and 'macho', often associated with drinking, swearing, and the swapping of dirty stories. A woman who engages in it is crossing the boundary and she may raise doubts about her respectability. Men may be excited about this but other women are likely to condemn it.

23 Similar comments were also volunteered by a number of the wives of husbands in other professional jobs, and by some of the wives of farmers and businessmen. In addition, many of these wives pointed out that they saw it as their responsibility to provide 'a worker-husband with a comfortable environment in which he can relax' (Finch, 1983:85).

24 The survey of wives and paid work was conducted among a subsample of forty-eight participants in the Gender Survey.

8 Ideology and oppression

1 It is common practice to emphasize male power in accounts of gender inequality. See, for example, Power, 1975a and 1975b; Mann, 1986; Gillespie, 1972; Edgell, 1980.

2 This issue of the paper did also present a wife as her husband's partner in a farming enterprise. The story detailed the bookkeeping and record-keeping activities of the wife and their importance to the business, but the account of the husband's innovative farming techniques occupied most of the space. The report left no doubt as to who was the 'hands-on' farmer—the husband, who was assisted by his two sons. Woodward and Green make the interesting suggestion that representation of gender-appropriate roles in the popular media stimulates hostility towards those who fail to conform to

the stereotypes. This is a plausible proposition, but unfortunately I have no data to confirm or refute it (1988:131).

3 The gender imbalance in the *Smalltown News* is, of course, not peculiar to this paper. It is commonplace in national dailies and is indicative of the subordinate and marginalized position of women in this society generally. Newspaper management and editorial staff know their readership and they are giving them what they want. Men are better placed to make news and their news is, of course, more interesting by definition, and the contents of newspapers reflect these realities.

4 General social standing, as understood here, is similar to what Plowman *et al.* describe as total status: the status which is based on firsthand knowledge of an individual, of the positions they hold and the performances they give (1962). In Smalltown a man's occupation and employment status are the major determinants of his own and his wife's total status (see Dempsey 1990a, especially Ch. 7).

The derivative character of a woman's social standing is hardly surprising because it has been shown repeatedly in this book that marriage, not employment, mediates a woman's relationship to this community. Consistent with this principle, a husband's status is far less dependent on his wife's occupation (if she has any) than vice versa.

Many Smalltown women's organizations are class homogeneous (Dempsey, 1990a, 1990b) and participation in these organizations is more dependent on the class position derived from a husband's occupation than on the personal esteem of a woman.

5 This is a most crucial form of dependency which enhances men's power and which helps explain women's deference in various areas of public and private life.

6 If learning of this nature is occurring it will play an important part in the maintenance of the patriarchal system. As well as facilitating the acquisition of skills and social identities that are compatible with relationships of superordination and subordination it helps ensure the reproduction of an ideology of gender (paternalistic ideology) which legitimates men's dominance and privileges.

7 The socialization experience is not confined to the home. It occurs for each sex with members of their network of friends and in the classroom and school playground.

9 Occupational aspirations

1 I am indebted to Dr Don Edgar, Director of the Australian Institute of Family Studies, for providing these questions.

2 Parents provided information on 159 of the children in the School Survey.

3 See also Pearson, 1980 for similar findings concerning the New Zealand community of Johnsonville.

4 What was especially interesting was how often the proportion of boys aspiring to a job, and the proportion of parents aspiring to it for a son, mirrored each other, while contrasted with the proportion of girls aspiring to the same job, and of parents aspiring to it for girls. The aspirations of girls, and of parents for girls, were also quite similar (Tables 9.1 and 9.2). Clearly we were tapping the one culture, which contained two sub-cultures—a male and a female.

5 These parents said they wanted their daughters to become hair-stylists, not carpenters or plumbers.

6 This category excludes lower-middle-class families.

7 Working-class parents did perceive higher professional jobs as very desirable. For example, during the course of the Status Survey a majority of working-class respondents said higher professional jobs were the most prestigious or among the most prestigious jobs in the community.

8 I have collapsed classes 2 and 3 for the purposes of this table but all of the expressions of ideal jobs focused on jobs as farmers.

9 Parents did not want their daughters to be employed in domestic work but, otherwise, their wishes for their daughters matched those of the daughters themselves (Table 9.1). The evaluations of Small-towners of the respective worth of 'men's jobs' and 'women's jobs' were similar to those prevailing throughout Australia (Broom *et al.*, 1976).

10 This comparison excludes boys from lower-middle-class families.

11 There were only 9 percentage points between the proportion of middle-class girls and of working-class girls realistically expecting to enter class 1, 2, or 3 jobs.

12 The pattern of choices our questions about realistic expectations produced from girls and from their parents is probably a function of similar factors to those which I believe produced homogeneous job fantasies among girls from different classes and among parents of these girls. These are: awareness of the practice of closure against women in local petit-bourgeois enterprises and in traditional trades; the typification of many jobs as male-only positions; self-identities which encourage girls to see it as more natural for them to work in 'feminine' rather than 'masculine' type jobs, and to avoid jobs that might interfere seriously with their roles as wives and mothers; and the awareness of girls that in adulthood they would be subjected to constant pressure to put motherhood and a husband's career before their own activities, including their paid work.

10 Occupational achievements

1 Jobs of this kind comprise 11 per cent of the local work-force compared with 22 per cent of the Australian work-force.

2 The proportions are based either on the job the respondent had at the time, or if they were not currently working—as was the case for about one-third of the women—they were based on the last job they had before leaving the work-force.

3 Disaggregating the middle class is necessary when comparing occupational achievements because doctors, accountants, lawyers, and senior administrators are more highly rewarded economically, have a more secure future, experience more job autonomy, and enjoy higher status than, say, teachers, nurses, and social workers. Girls predominate in the latter jobs and boys in the former. It is also necessary to disaggregate when comparing the job achievements of boys and girls because employment as a farmer or a business entrepreneur (male jobs) is usually economically superior and psychologically and socially more rewarding than work as a teacher or a nurse, and certainly superior to work as a typist or sales assistant (female jobs in the lower-middle-class sector).

4 Twenty-nine per cent of the girls belonging to the ordinary white-collar class were, in fact, employed as shop assistants. These women had a very low income, no job security, and as low a social standing in Smalltown as any sector of the work-force, including unskilled manual labourers.

5 At the time of the restudy, 70 per cent of the females were married and 72 per cent had one or more children. By comparison only 52 per cent of the males had married and 50 per cent had fathered one or more children. All of the married men were working, but approximately one-third of the married women were *not* engaged in paid work in early 1987.

6 Game and Pringle point out that women now have formal equality of opportunity with men in banking but that women have to push for promotion and few of them achieve managerial status (1983: 46–9).

7 These figures can only be regarded as a rough guide to the amount of mobility occurring because they make no allowance for the effects of changes in the structure of the work-force and the economy on children's ability to match their parents' class position.

8 Ten working-class boys (24 per cent of all boys of classes 6 and 7) but only one working-class girl (2 per cent) gained a trade position.

9 The expression 'marital mobility' is—as Heath stresses—perhaps unfortunate because it implies that wives are merely the passive beneficiaries of their husbands' economic and social activities rather than contributors to their husbands' well-being (1981:111). It has been pointed out that in Smalltown wives are married to their husbands' jobs and husbands gain considerable economic, emotional and social benefits from this 'marriage'. It is also the case that about one-third of Smalltown wives participate in the paid work-force, at least on a part-time basis. Working wives improve the income and

sometimes the asset base of their families. Through their activities in the paid work-force these wives bring to their husbands a greater degree of economic security than they would otherwise experience.

While, as Gittins (1985) points out, a man's mobility depends much less on his marriage than it does on his own occupational activities, it is plausible to argue that the marital mobility of men should be examined. As I lack data on both the occupation of the wives of the males in my sample and the occupation of fathers-in-law, this is not possible.

10 Smalltown women assume major responsibility for housework and child care, and they support their husbands in their paid work and in their leisure activities (see Chs 4 and 5). These commitments leave time at most for a routine job rather than for the degree of dedication a woman has to display if she is going to be upwardly mobile in her paid work, presuming that there is a career stucture available to her in the paid work-force. Hardly any woman who remains in Smalltown has such an opportunity. Whatever her own occupational achievements, her husband's will remain the major determinant of her status.

11 While it is common knowledge in Smalltown that most girls are eager to be upwardly mobile through marriage, it is impossible to argue that the benefits flowing from a husband's job to a wife are commensurate with those enjoyed by the husband himself. The delivery of many of its potential benefits requires the cooperation of a husband. For instance, there is nothing to guarantee that a husband will pass on to his wife an equitable share of his economic gains. There is no way he can transmit to her as much prestige as he himself enjoys if he occupies a high position in the work-force, even if he wished to. If the marriage ends, a wife may lose all access to a husband's income, the economic benefits of any future promotions and his superannuation. She will at least have her access curtailed substantially.

Notwithstanding these caveats, 'the right' marriage offers many Smalltown women their only opportunity of access—even if of a secondary and derivative nature—to the economic and social rewards attached to the better jobs in the paid workforce.

12 The data presented in this section are based on a reduced sample of seventy-two married women. Ninety-eight of the women in our sample married but fifteen of these had not worked, and we lacked information on the occupations of the husbands of a further eleven.

13 Seven of the eight girls from working-class families with semi-professional jobs, compared with only ten of the twenty without, married a man with a middle-class job.

14 Roughly four-fifths of both educated working-class and middle-class girls gained a middle-class job.

15 Littlejohn found in his study of the Scottish parish of Westrigg that a husband's reputation was a much bigger issue than his wife's (1963).

11 The chances of change

1 This account sounds as though men are all powerful and women powerless, but other researchers have found similar patterns of husbands regulating the entry of wives to the paid work-force and of wives indicating that they defer to husbands in this way (Collins, 1985; Sharpe, 1984: Yeandle, 1984). Yeandle reports that as far as the issue of wives' paid employment was concerned, husbands held the balance of power: 'in general wives sought husbands' permission, or at least approval, in taking a job' (1984:148).

Having acknowledged the superiority of male power, I must also stress that in some instances wives' compliance with a husband's demands may reflect a consciousness of the structural constraints on their choice rather than a belief in the legitimacy of his dominance. In other words they comply because they believe that they have no choice or because they perceive that they have more to gain than to lose by doing so.

2 These are typified here and elsewhere as key feminine traits.

3 Even wives are troubled by this possibility. Some have said in the course of casual conversation that they want a husband who is a man's man. Because a wife wants her husband to maintain his 'man's man' status, she will agree to him going off to the pub with his mates rather than staying home and keeping her company.

4 The provision of an indispensable and highly valued resource bestows authority on the provider. It will be recalled that Bryson emphasized that much of men's power derived from their ability to get their work defined as economic and women's as non-economic (1984:114–15).

5 In Smalltown families the important decisions are either taken unilaterally by the husband or by the husband and wife 'jointly'. Important decisions mean those entailing large expenditures such as the purchase of a new car or combine harvester or additional farming land, or whether to have a child educated at a private school. The Gender Survey showed that this pattern is broken in only 5 per cent of partnerships. In these cases it seems the wife has the final say in decisions entailing large expenditure. By contrast, in 45 per cent of cases the husband has the final or only say. In about 50 per cent of cases respondents claimed that major decisions were taken jointly or together. In my view this figure exaggerates the proportion of wives exercising the same power as husbands in important family decisions. A joint decision is not necessarily one in which both partners exercise equal influence. It may only mean that one partner is consulted by

the other but that the first ultimately takes the decision after considering what the other partner has to say. It was apparent in many instances, either from comments made during the course of the interview or in casual conversation before or after the interview, that a so-called joint decision was ultimately a husband's decision. 'John would never buy a new tractor without talking it over with me first', and 'Dave wouldn't move to another town if he knew I was against it [this woman indicated that if Dave had his heart set on such a change she would be very reluctant to veto his plans]—these were the kinds of comments that support this observation.

6 They have reported that single women have inferior social status to married women, fewer opportunities to participate in cross-sex social activity, and probably an inferior standard of living to that which they would enjoy in the city.

7 In the Gender Survey 40 per cent of wives compared with only 15 per cent of husbands stated they would like to spend more time with their spouse.

Appendix 2

1 I have made no attempt to introduce a cross-class schema of the kind used by either Britten and Heath (1983) or Baxter (1988) because there are an insufficient number of cross-class marriages in the Smalltown samples.

2 One could make out a very good case for moving sales assistants, especially women, into the lower working class. Certainly, people in Smalltown regard them as being at the bottom of any occupational status structure. However, I have placed them in the lower middle class in order to make this model as comparative as possible with those of Goldthorpe; and Jones and Davis.

Bibliography

Abercrombie, N., Warde, A., Soothill, K., Urry, J., and Walby, S. (1988), *Contemporary British Society*, Polity Press, Cambridge.

Abrams, P. (1978), *Work, Urbanism and Inequality: U.K. Society Today*, Weidenfeld & Nicolson, London.

______ and McCulloch, A. (1976), *Communes, Sociology and Society*, Cambridge University Press, Cambridge.

Baker Miller, J. (1976), *Towards a Psychology of Women*, Penguin, Harmondsworth.

Barbalet, J. (1982), 'Social Closure in Class Analysis: A Critique of Parkin', *Sociology*, **16**, 484–97.

Barnes, J. (1954), 'Class and Committees in a Norwegian Island Parish', *Human Relations*, **7**, 1.

Barrett, M. (1980), *Women's Oppression Today: Problems in Marxist Feminist Analysis*, Verso, London.

______ and Mackintosh, M. (1982), *The Anti-Social Family*, Verso, London.

Baxter, J. (1988), 'Gender and Class Analysis: The Position of Women in the Class Structure', *Australian and New Zealand Journal of Sociology*, **24**, 1, 106–23.

______, Gibson, D., Kingston, C., and Western, J. (1988), *The Lives of Rural Women: Problems and Prospects of Employment*, Department of Anthropology and Sociology, University of Queensland, St Lucia.

Bell, C. (1968), *Middle Class Families*, Routledge & Kegan Paul, London.

______ and Newby, H. (1976a), 'Husbands and Wives: The Dynamics of the Deferential Dialectic', in D. Barker and S. Allen, *Dependence and Exploitation in Work and Marriage*, Longman, London.

______ (1976b), 'Community, Communion, Class and Community Action: The Social Sources of the New Urban Politics', in D. Herbert and R. Johston (eds), *Spatial Perspectives on Problems and Policies*, vol. II, Wiley, London.

Bennett, T. (1985), 'Really Useless "Knowledge": A Political Critique of Aesthetics', *Thesis Eleven*, **12**, 28–52.

Berk, S. (1985), *The Gender Factory: The Apportionment of Work in American Households*, Plenum, New York.
Bittman, M. (1991), *Juggling Time*, The Office of the Status of Women, Department of the Prime Minister and Cabinet, Canberra.
Blood, R. and Wolfe, M. (1960), *Husbands and Wives*, The Free Press, New York.
Bott, E. (1957), *Family and Social Network*, Tavistock, London.
Bourdieu, P. (1984), *Distinction*, Routledge & Kegan Paul, London.
Bradley, H. (1989), *Men's Work, Women's Work*, Polity Press, Cambridge.
Britten, N. and Heath, A. (1983), 'Women, Men and Social Class', in E. Gamarnikow, D. Morgan, J. Purvis, and D. Taylorson (eds), *Gender, Class and Work*, Heinemann, London.
Broom, L. and Jones, F. L. (1976), *Opportunity and Attainment in Australia*, Australian National University Press, Canberra.
Bryson, L. (1983), 'Sport and the Oppression of Women', *Australian and New Zealand Journal of Sociology*, **19**, 413–26.
______ (1984), 'The Australian Patriarchal Family', in S. Encel *et al.* (eds), *Australian Society: Introductory Essays*, Longman Cheshire, Melbourne, 113–69.
______ (1985), 'Sexual Divisions and Power Relationships in the Australian Family', in P. Close and R. Collins (eds), *Family and Economy in Modern Society*, London, Macmillan.
______ (1987), 'Sport and the Maintenance of Masculine Hegemony', *Women's Studies International Forum*, **10**, 4, 349–60.
______ (1990), 'Challenges to Male Hegemony in Sport', in M. Messner *et al.*, *Critical Perspectives on Sport, Patriarchy and Men*, Human Kinetics Publishers, Illinois.
______ and Thompson, F. (1972), *An Australian Newtown*, Penguin, Melbourne.
______ and Wearing, B. (1985), 'Australian Community Studies—A Feminist Critique', *Australian and New Zealand Journal of Sociology*, **21**, 349–66.
Bulmer, M. (ed.) (1975), *Working Class Images of Society*, Routledge & Kegan Paul, London.
Burns, A. (1986), 'Why Do Women Continue to Marry?', in N. Grieve and A. Burns (eds), *Australian Women: New Feminist Perspectives*, Oxford University Press, Melbourne, 211–33.
Burton, C. (1986), 'Equal Employment Opportunity Programmes: Issues in Implementation', in N. Grieve and A. Burns (eds), *Australian Women: New Feminist Perspectives*, Oxford University Press, Melbourne, 292–304.
Bussey, K. (1986), 'The First Socialization', in N. Grieve and A. Burns (eds), *Australian Women: New Feminist Perspectives*, Oxford University Press, Melbourne, 90–104.
Callan, H. (1975), 'The Premise of Dedication: Notes Towards an

Ethnography of Diplomats' Wives', in S. Ardner (ed.), *Perceiving Women*, Routledge & Kegan Paul, London.

Cass, B. (1978), 'Women's Place in the Class Structure', in E. L. Wheelwright and K. Buckley (eds), *Essays in the Political Economy of Australian Capitalism III*, ANZ Book Company, Sydney.

Chapman, B. and Miller, P. (1983), 'Determination of Earnings in Australia: An Analysis of the 1976 Census', in K. Hancock *et al.*, *Japanese and Australian Labour Markets: A Comparative Study*, Australia–Japan Research Centre, Canberra.

Clark, E. T. (1967), 'Influence of Sex and Social Class on Occupational Preference and Perception', *Personnel and Guidance Journal*, **45**, 440–4.

Cohen, A. (1985), *The Symbolic Construction of Community*, Tavistock Publications, London.

Collins, R. (1985), '"Horses for Courses" Ideology and the Division of Domestic Labour', in P. Close and R. Collins (eds), *Family and Economy in Modern Society*, Macmillan, London.

Connell, R. (1977), *Ruling Class, Ruling Culture*, Cambridge University Press, Sydney.

______ (1985), 'Theorizing Gender', *Sociology*, **19**, 2, 260–72.

______ (1986), 'Theorizing Gender', in N. Grieve and A. Burns, *Australian Women: New Feminist Perspectives*, Oxford University Press, Melbourne.

______, Ashenden, D., Kessler, S., and Dowsett, G. (1982), *Making the Difference*, Allen & Unwin, Sydney.

Crompton, R. (1986), 'Women and the "Service Class"', in R. Crompton and M. Mann, (eds), *Gender and Stratification*, Polity Press, Cambridge.

Curthoys, A. (1986), 'The Sexual Division of Labour: Theoretical Arguments', in N. Grieve and A. Burns (eds), *Australian Women: New Feminist Perspectives*, Oxford University Press, Melbourne, 319–41.

Dale, A., Gilbert, G., and Arber, S. (1985), 'Integrating Women into Class Theory', *Sociology*, **19**, 3, 384–408.

Daniels, A. (1983), *Power, Privilege and Prestige*, Longman Cheshire, Melbourne.

Davidoff, L. (1976), 'The Rationalisation of Housework', in D. Barker and S. Allen (eds), *Dependence and Exploitation in Work and Marriage*, Longman, London.

Deem, R. (1982), 'Women, Leisure and Inequality', *Leisure Studies*, **1**, 1, 29–46.

______ (1986), *All Work and No Play?*, The Open University Press, Milton Keynes.

______ (1987a), Putting Leisure in Women's Lives—Towards Better Policy and Provision, paper presented to the First International Conference on the Future of Adult Life, The Netherlands, Leeuwenhorst.

______ (1987b), 'Unleisured Lives: Sport in the Context of Women's Leisure', *Women's Studies International Forum*, **10**, 4, 423–32.

Delamont, M. (1980), *The Sociology of Women*, Allen & Unwin, London.

Delphy, C. (1976), 'Continuities and Discontinuities in Marriage and Divorce', in D. Barker and S. Allen (eds), *Sexual Divisions and Society: Process and Change*, Tavistock, London.

______ (1984), *Close to Home: A Materialist Analysis of Women's Oppression*, Hutchinson, London.

______ and Leonard, D. (1986), 'Class Analysis, Gender Analysis and the Family', in R. Crompton and M. Mann (eds), *Gender and Stratification*, Polity Press, Cambridge.

Dempsey, K. (1986), *The Fate of Minister's Wives*, La Trobe University Sociology Papers **15**, Melbourne.

______ (1989a), 'Gender Inequality in the Domestic Division of Labour Among the Elderly', *Australian Journal on Ageing*, **8**, 3, 3–10.

______ (1989b), 'Is Organised Religion Still Relevant in the Private Sphere? An Australian Case Study', *Sociological Analysis*, **50**, 3, 247–64.

______ (1990a), *Smalltown: A Study of Social Inequality, Cohesion and Belonging*, Oxford University Press, Melbourne.

______ (1990b), 'The Elderly: Integrated or Segregated?', *Australian Journal of Ageing*, **9**, 2, 37–43.

______ (1991), 'Inequality, Belonging and Religion in a Rural Community', in A. Black (ed.), *Religion in Australia: Sociological Perspectives*, Allen & Unwin, Sydney, 63–77.

Dennis, N., Henriques, F., and Slaughter, C. (1969), *Coal Is Our Life*, 2nd edn, Tavistock, London.

Dixey, R. and Talbot, M. (1982), *Women, Leisure and Bingo*, Trinity and All Saints College, Leeds.

Dollard, J. (1957), *Caste and Class in a Southern Town*, 3rd edn, Doubleday, New York.

Donaldson, M. (1991), *Time of Our Lives*, Allen & Unwin, Sydney.

Douvan, E. and Adelson, J. (1966), *The Adolescent Experience*, Wiley, New York.

Edgell, S. (1980), *Middle-Class Couples*, Allen & Unwin, London.

Edwards, M. (1984), 'The Distribution of Income within Households', in D. Broom (ed.), *Unfinished Business: Social Justice for Women in Australia*, Allen & Unwin, Sydney.

Eliot, F. (1986), *The Family: Change or Continuity?*, Macmillan, London.

Encel, S. (1970), *Equality and Authority*, Cheshire, Melbourne.

Ferree, M. (1987), 'The Struggles of Superwoman', in C. Bose, R. Feldberg, and N. Sokoloff (eds), *Hidden Aspects of Women's Work*, Praeger, New York.

______ (1990), 'Beyond Separate Spheres', *Journal of Marriage and the Family*, **52**, 864–84.

Finch, J. (1983), *Married to the Job: Wives' Incorporation in Men's Work*, Allen & Unwin, London.

Frankenberg, R. (1966), *Communities in Britain*, Penguin, Harmondsworth.

——— (1976), 'In the Production of their Lives, Men (?) . . . Sex and Gender in British Community Studies', in D. Leonard Barker and S. Allen (eds), *Sexual Divisions and Society: Process and Change*, Tavistock, London.

Game, A. and Pringle, R. (1983), *Gender at Work*, Allen & Unwin, Sydney.

Garnsey, E. (1978), 'Women's Work and Theories of Class Stratification', *Sociology*, **12**, 2, 224–43.

Gillespie, D. (1972), 'Who Has the Power? The Marital Struggle', *Recent Sociology*, **4**, Macmillan, London.

Gittins, D. (1985), *The Family in Question*, Macmillan, London.

Goldthorpe, J. H. (1980), *Social Mobility and Class Structure in Modern Britain*, Clarendon Press, Oxford.

——— (1983), 'Women and Class Analysis: In Defence of the Conventional View', *Sociology*, **17**, 4, 465–86.

——— (1984), 'Women and Class Analysis: A Reply to the Replies', *Sociology*, **18**, 4, 491–9.

Gray, I. (1991), *Politics in Place*, Cambridge University Press, Sydney.

Green, E., Hebron, S., and Woodward, D. (1987a), 'Women, Leisure and Social Control', in J. Hanmer and M. Maynard (eds), *Women, Violence and Social Control*, Macmillan, London.

——— (1987b), *Gender and Leisure: A Study of Women's Leisure in Sheffield*, The Sports Council, London.

Griffin, C. (1985), *Typical Girls*, Routledge & Kegan Paul, London.

———, Hobson, D., MacIntosh, S., and McCabe, T. (1982), 'Women and Leisure', in J. Hargreaves (ed.), *Sport, Culture and Ideology*, Routledge & Kegan Paul, London.

Harper, J. and Richards, L. (1986), *Mothers and Working Mothers*, revised edn, Penguin, Melbourne.

Hartmann, H. (1979), 'Capitalism, Patriarchy, and Job Segregation', in Z. Eisenstein, *Capitalist Patriarchy and the Case for Socialist Feminism*, Monthly Review Press, New York.

Heath, A. (1981), *Social Mobility*, Collins, London.

Heer, D. (1958), 'Dominance and the Working Wife', *Social Forces*, **36**, 4, 341–7.

Hey, V. (1986), *Patriarchy and Pub Culture*, Tavistock, London.

Hiller, D. (1980), Determinants of Household and Childcare Task-sharing, presented at the American Sociological Association meetings, New York.

Hochschild, A. (1988), *The Second Shift*, Viking, New York.

Imray, L. and Middleton, A. (1983), 'Public and Private: Marking the

Boundaries', in E. Gamarnikow *et al.* (eds), *The Public and the Private*, Heinemann, London.

James, K. (1979), 'The Home: A Private or Public Place? Class, Status and the Actions of Women', *Australian and New Zealand Journal of Sociology*, **15**, 1, 36–42.

______ (1981), 'Public or Private: Participation by Women in a Country Town', in M. Bowman (ed.), *Beyond the City*, Longman Cheshire, Melbourne.

Jones, F. (1983), 'Sources of Gender Inequality in Income: What the Australian Census Says', *Social Forces*, **62**, 134–52.

______ (1984), 'Income Inequality', in D. Broom (ed.), *Unfinished Business: Social Justice for Women in Australia*, Allen & Unwin, Sydney.

______ and Davis, P. (1986), *Models of Society*, Croom Helm, London.

Kendig, H. (1986), 'Intergenerational Exchange', in H. Kendig, *Ageing and Families*, Allen & Unwin, Sydney, 85–109.

Kessler-Harris, A. (1987), 'The Debate over Equality for Women in the Workplace: Recognizing Differences', in N. Gerstel and H. Gross (eds), *Families and Work*, Temple University, Philadelphia.

Leiulfsrud, H. and Woodward, A. (1987), 'Women at Class Crossroads: Repudiating Conventional Theories of Family Class', *Sociology*, **21**, 3, 393–412.

Liebow, E. (1967), *Tally's Corner*, Little, Brown, Boston.

Littlejohn, J. (1963), *Westrigg*, Routledge & Kegan Paul, London.

Lockwood, D. (1958), *The Blackcoated Worker*, Unwin University Books, London.

______ (1986), 'Class, Status and Gender', in R. Crompton and M. Mann (eds), *Gender and Stratification*, Polity Press, Cambridge.

Lown, J. (1983), 'Not So Much a Factory, More a Form of Patriarchy: Gender and Class During Industrialisation', in E. Gamarnikow, J. Purvis and D. Taylorson, *Gender, Class and Work*, Heinemann, London.

Lynd, R. and Lynd, H. (1929), *Middletown*, Harcourt, Brace & World, New York.

Macpherson, C. B. (1973), *Democratic Theory*, Oxford University Press, London.

McRae, S. (1986), *Cross Class Marriages*, Clarendon Press, Oxford.

McRobbie, A. (1978), 'Working Class Girls and the Culture of Femininity', in Women's Studies Group, Centre for Contemporary Cultural Studies, University of Birmingham (eds), *Women Take Issue*, Hutchinson, London.

Mann, M. (1986), 'A Crisis in Stratification Theory', in R. Crompton and M. Mann (eds), *Gender and Stratification*, Polity Press, Cambridge.

Marsh, C. (1986), 'Social Class and Occupation', in R. G. Burgess (ed.), *Key Variables in Social Investigation*, Routledge & Kegan Paul, London.

Mason, J. (1988), 'No Peace for the Wicked: Older Married Women and Leisure', in E. Wimbush and M. Talbot (eds), *Relative Freedoms*, The Open University Press, Milton Keynes.

Michelson, W. (1985), *From Sun to Sun: Daily Obligations and Community Structure in the Lives of Employed Women and Their Families*, Rowman & Allenheld, Totowa, NJ.

Moir, H. (1984), 'Comment on Women in the Australian Labour Force', in D. Broom (ed.), *Unfinished Business: Social Justice for Women in Australia*, Allen & Unwin, Sydney.

Murgatroyd, L. (1982), 'Gender and Occupational Stratification', *Sociological Review*, **30**, 4.

Nalson, J. (1977), 'Rural Australia', in A. Davies, S. Encel, and M. Berry (eds), *Australian Society: A Sociological Introduction*, 3rd edn, Longman Cheshire, Melbourne.

Oakley, A. (1974), *The Sociology of Housework*, Martin Robertson, Oxford.

O'Connor, K. (1981), The Emergence of Regional Centres in Employment Change in Non-metropolitan Australia 1971–1976, paper presented to the Australian Institute of Agricultural Science Symposium on Country Communities, Glenormiston.

Ossowski, S. (1963), *Class Structure in the Social Consciousness*, Routledge & Kegan Paul, London.

Oxley, H. G. (1974), *Mateship in Local Organization*, University of Queensland Press, St Lucia.

_____ (1978), *Mateship in Local Organization*, 2nd edn, University of Queensland Press, St Lucia.

Pahl, J. (1990), 'Household Spending, Personal Spending and the Control of Money in Marriage', *Sociology*, **24**, 1, 119–38.

Parkin, F. (1974), 'Strategies of Social Closure in Class Formation', in F. Parkin (ed.), *The Social Analysis of Class Structure*, Tavistock, London.

_____ (1979), *Marxism and Class Theory*, Tavistock, London.

Pearson, D. (1980), *Johnsonville*, Allen & Unwin, Sydney.

_____ and Thorns, D. (1983), *Eclipse of Equality*, Allen & Unwin, Sydney.

Playford, J. (1972), 'Who Rules Australia?', in J. Playford and D. Kirsner (eds), *Australian Capitalism*, Penguin, Melbourne.

Pleck, J. H. (1985), *Working Wives/Working Husbands*, Sage, Beverley Hills.

Plowman, D., Minchinton, W., and Stacey, M. (1962), 'Local Social Status in England and Wales', *Sociological Review*, **10**, 2, 161–202.

Poiner, G. (1990), *The Good Old Rule*, Sydney University Press, Melbourne.

Powell, M. and Bloom, V. (1962), 'Development of and Reasons for Vocational Choices of Adolescents through the High-school Years', *Journal of Educational Research*, **56**, 126–33.

Powell, R. and Jensen, R. (1981), The Structure and Dynamics of Rural

Communities, paper presented to the Australian Institute of Agricultural Science Symposium on Country Communities, Glenormiston.

Power, M. (1975a), 'Women's Work is Never Done—By Men: A Socio-Economic Model of Sex-Typing in Occupations', *The Journal of Industrial Relations*, **17**, 225–39.

——— (1975b), 'The Making of a Woman's Occupation', *Hecate*, **1**, 25–34.

Rew, N. (1978), 'Preface', in H. G. Oxley, *Mateship in Local Organization*, 2nd edn, University of Queensland Press, St Lucia.

Ross, C. (1987), 'The Division of Labor at Home', *Social Forces*, **65**, 3, 816–33.

Rowbotham, S. (1972), 'Women's Liberation and The New Politics', in Wandor, M. (ed.), *The Body Politic*, Stage One, London.

Russell, G. (1983), *The Changing Role of Fathers?*, University of Queensland Press, St Lucia.

Schooler, C., Miller, J., Miller, K., and Richtand, C. (1984), 'Work for the Household: Its Nature and Consequences for Husbands and Wives', *American Journal of Sociology*, **90**, 1, 97–124.

Scraton, S. (1987), 'Boys Muscle In where Angels Fear to Tread: The Relationship between Physical Education and Young Women's Subcultures', in D. Jary, J. Horne, and A. Tomlinson (eds), *Sport, Leisure and Social Relations*, Sociological Review Monograph, **33**, Routledge & Kegan Paul, London and Keele.

Sharpe, S. (1976), *Just Like a Girl*, Penguin, London.

——— (1984), *Double Identity: The Lives of Working Mothers*, Penguin, London.

Siltanen, J. (1986), 'Domestic Responsibilities and the Structuring of Employment', in R. Crompton and M. Mann (eds), *Gender and Stratification*, Polity Press, Cambridge.

Simmel, G. (1955), *Conflict and the Web of Group-Affiliations*, The Free Press, New York.

Sinclair, K., Crouch, B., and Miller, J. (1977), 'Occupational Choices of Sydney Teenagers: Relationships with Sex, Social Class, Grade Level and Parent Expectations', *The Australian Journal of Education*, **21**, 1, 41–54.

Spender, D. (1980), *Man-Made Language*, Routledge & Kegan Paul, London.

Stacey, M. (1960), *Tradition and Change*, Oxford University Press, London.

——— (1986), 'Gender and Stratification: One Central Issue or Two?', in R. Crompton and M. Mann (eds), *Gender and Stratification*, Polity Press, Cambridge.

Stanworth, M. (1983), 'Women and Class Analysis: A Reply to John Goldthorpe', *Sociology*, **18**, 2, 159–70.

Thomas, G. and Zmroczek, C. (1985), 'Household Technology: The "Liberation" of Women from the Home?', in P. Close and R. Collins (eds), *Family and Economy in Modern Society*, Macmillan, London.
Tulloch, P. (1984), 'Gender and Dependency', in D. Broom (ed.), *Unfinished Business: Social Justice for Women in Australia*, Allen & Unwin, Sydney.
Vidich, A. and Bensman, J. (1960), *Small Town in Mass Society*, Doubleday, New York.
Walby, S. (1986), *Patriarchy at Work*, Polity Press, Cambridge.
Wearing, B. (1984), *The Ideology of Motherhood*, Allen & Unwin, Sydney.
Weber, M. (1968), *Economy and Society*, **1** and **2**, G. Roth and G. Wittich (eds), Bedminster Press, New York.
Western, J. (1983), *Social Inequality in Australian Society*, Macmillan, Melbourne.
Whitehead, A. (1976), 'Sexual Antagonism in Herefordshire', in D. Barker and S. Allen (eds), *Dependence and Exploitation in Work and Marriage*, Longmans, London.
——— (1981), '"I'm Hungry, Mum": The Politics of Domestic Budgeting', in K. Young, C. Wolkowitz and R. McCullagh, *Of Marriage and the Market*, C.S.E. Books, London.
Wild, R. (1974), *Bradstow*, Allen & Unwin, Sydney.
Williams, C. (1981), *Open Cut*, Allen & Unwin, Sydney.
——— (1988), 'Patriarchy and Gender: Theory and Methods', in J. Najman and J. Western, *A Sociology of Australian Society*, Macmillan, Melbourne.
Wimbush, E. (1986), Transitions in Work, Leisure and Health Experiences in Early Motherhood, paper given to the 1986 British Sociological Conference, University of Loughborough, March.
——— and Talbot, M. (1988), *Relative Freedoms*, The Open University Press, Milton Keynes.
Woodward, D. and Green, E. (1988), '"Not Tonight, Dear!": The Social Control of Women's Leisure', in E. Wimbush and M. Talbot, *Relative Freedoms*, The Open University Press, Milton Keynes.
Yeandle, S. (1984), *Women's Working Lives*, Tavistock Publications, London.
Young, M. and Wilmott, P. (1973), *The Symmetrical Family*, Penguin, Harmondsworth.
Zaretsky, E. (1976), *Capitalism, the Family and Personal Life*, Pluto Press, London.

Index